D1433597

THE OFFICIAL HISTORY OF
THE FOOTBALL
ASSOCIATION

Previous page: 'How odd it is that, in any noisy disorganised crowd of small boys, there may be one, apparently just like the others, who has some extraordinary talent in him, some name that may soon be familiar all over the world, though it is still only an undistinguished collection of syllables – like Stan Matthews.'

Maurice Edelston and Terence Delaney, *Masters of Soccer*, 1960.

Opposite: 'This is Wembley ... a vast curving elliptical basin, its sweeping banks tight packed, the rim of it far up there cutting the sky. It is alive with people, though from a distance they do not resemble people. Their faces are blurred. What do they resemble? Flowers? No. More like a hill of pink gravel. The Colosseum of ancient Rome must have been like this.' Geoffrey Green in *Soccer: the World Game*.

Wembley with its best bib and tucker on for the 99th FA Cup final, West Ham 1, Arsenal 0, 10 May 1980.

THE OFFICIAL HISTORY OF
THE FOOTBALL ASSOCIATION

BRYON BUTLER

Queen Anne Press

ACKNOWLEDGEMENTS

Warm gratitude is owed to many for their encouragement and expertise. The Football Association (David Barber in particular) deftly supervised the game-plan. Queen Anne Press editor Ian Marshall let play run smoothly without recourse to the whistle. Graham Smith, Gordon Wallis and Paul Macnamara hospitably provided the key to their admirable collections. Sincere thanks are also due to Audrey Adams (for morale and an eagle eye), Jane Baxter, Duncan Bond, Tina (for angelic patience) and Mark Butler, Keith Butler, Raymond Gill, Mike Ingham, Harriet Joll (Christies), Peter Robinson, Bob Thomas and Peter Stewart.

A QUEEN ANNE PRESS BOOK

© The Football Association 1991

First published in Great Britain in 1991 by
Queen Anne Press, a division of
Lennard Associates
Mackerye End, Harpenden
Herts AL5 5DR

Revised edition 1993

Cover design: Roger Abraham at the Creative Space
Design: Peter Champion and Roger Abraham

A CIP catalogue record for this book is available from the British Library

ISBN 1-85291-538-2

Typeset by Tradespools Ltd, Frome
Printed and bound in Great Britain by
Butler and Tanner Ltd, Frome and London

CONTENTS

HRH The Duke of Kent presents the FA Cup to Bryan Robson, captain of Manchester United, after their 1985 final victory over Everton.

York House
St. James's Palace
London S.W. 1

In the closing years of the twentieth century, Football has become the most popular game of all. It is played with fervour and watched with excitement almost the world over.

Although the game has many origins, it was the formation of the Football Association in 1863 which gave it the order and shape in which it is now recognised everywhere. I am proud that in this sense, England has some claim to be the birthplace of the modern game.

As the guardian of fair play, the Football Association has needed to keep in step with growing interest in the game and to evolve in order to reflect changing public attitudes. This it has done with success for almost 130 years. Now as always, there are important milestones ahead, and I am confident the Association will continue to protect the best interests of all involved and that football will continue to develop successfully into the next Century.

H.R.H. The Duke of Kent
President

INTRODUCTION
BY BOBBY CHARLTON CBE

Football has taken me all over the globe and, no matter what the length and direction of the journey, one thing has always seemed clear to me: the Football Association has a special place in the heart of the world game.

The absorbing history of football is part of its present. The drama and detail of the past give extra meaning to the here and now, and I have often been surprised by the knowledge people in other countries have of the Association's role in the birth and development of the game. Football carries a tag wherever it is played: 'Made in England'.

The FA, however, is much more than simply a pioneer. I was always aware of the Association when I was a player, especially when I was wearing the three lions of England on my shirt and when FA Cup time came around to give a lift to every season, but it was not until my time as a member of the FA Council that I discovered how much hard work is required to keep a firm and fair hand on the game at all its levels.

FA headquarters at Lancaster Gate is always full of people beavering away on some committee or project, and the dedication involved is something you cannot put a price on. Their only concern is the good of football and the only reward for most is the knowledge that they are helping a game they love. It is my privilege to still be involved in the game after a playing career in which I was lucky enough to achieve everything I set my heart on – apart from winning the World Cup overseas – something which Bobby Robson and his players came so splendidly near to managing in Italy in 1990.

Football has changed since I played my first game for Manchester United in 1956. Pitches and facilities have improved and the ball and other equipment is lighter. The number of competitions has increased and the season is tighter and longer. Travel has become easier and faster and the glare of publicity is harsher. The players themselves are stronger athletes and infinitely better paid for their labours. The game is quicker and there is a tremendous intensity about everything. I often hear people say that 'the game is not what it was' – inferring that modern football is a poorer thing. I prefer to say that it is just different.

Yet some things have remained constant to give this marvellous obsession of ours a degree of stability. The Laws of the game have stood up to the test of time and so, too, has the authority, honesty and diligence of the Football Association.

Bobby Charlton

Bobby Charlton – member of the England side which won the World Cup in 1966. Won 106 caps (1958–70) and is England's leading scorer with 49 goals. Helped Manchester United win the European Cup, three League championships and the FA Cup. Voted Footballer of the Year and European Player of the Year in 1966. Director of Manchester United and Honorary Member of the FA.

Bobby Charlton receives a plaque from FA chairman Sir Andrew Stephen to mark his 100th cap for England, against Northern Ireland at Wembley, 21 April 1970.

THE 'FATHER' OF FOOTBALL

EC MORLEY
(1831–1924)

The Football Association is properly regarded as the 'father' of organised football; but on the laden shelves of the game's literature there is no more than passing reference to the man who was the 'father' of the Association. Ebenezer Cobb Morley deserves better.

Morley's initiative led to the meeting at which, on his proposal, the FA was formed; he was the FA's first secretary (1863–6) and its second president (1867–74); he drafted the FA's first set of playing laws at his Thames-side home at 26, The Terrace, Barnes, Surrey; he scored the first goal in the first representative match (London v Sheffield, 31 March 1866); and he was a principal guest at the FA's Golden Jubilee dinner in 1913. He died in 1924 – a year after the opening of Wembley – at the age of 93.

Morley was born in Hull but lived in Barnes from 1858 and, after playing football on The Green, formed the Barnes club (1862) which was based at the Limes Field at Mortlake. Morley, according to one reference, was 'not a public school man', but old boys from several public schools joined the Barnes club and there were feverish disputes about the way the game should be played. Morley, the Barnes captain and a natural and willing organiser, wrote to *Bell's Life* suggesting that football should have a set of rules in the way MCC had for cricket. There were other letters to newspapers on the same subject, but it was Morley's which led to the first historic meeting at the Freemason's Tavern, Great Queen Street, at which the FA was formed.

It was also Morley who, after two meetings, drafted the first set of laws for the FA – 14 in all, one forbidding tripping and hacking. Morley, according to the first minutes, told his fellow committee members: 'I confess I think that the "hacking" is more dreadful in name and on paper than in reality; but I object to it because I think that its being disallowed will promote the game of football ... If we have hacking, no-one who has arrived at the years of discretion will play at football, and it will be entirely relinquished to schoolboys.'

Morley, as a player, was described as 'a pretty and most effective dribbler', and, after a game between Barnes and the Forest club in March 1863, *Bell's Life* recorded: 'We cannot abstain from saying that the play of Mr Morley of Barnes and Mr C Alcock of the Forest club elicited great applause from the spectators of whom there were a large number present.' An interesting meeting: Morley, the 'father' of the FA, against Alcock, whose initiative would lead later to the birth of the FA Cup and international football.

Morley was a solicitor with chambers at 3, King's Bench Walk, Temple, but football was only one of his interests. He was a good enough oarsman to be in the London Rowing Club's eight for the Grand Challenge Cup at Henley in 1864; he was the founder and secretary (1862–80) of the Barnes and Mortlake Regatta; and he helped organise a big annual athletics meeting on the day of the University Boat Race. He kept a pack (12 couples) of beagles and for nearly 50 years he hunted with the Surrey Union Foxhounds and the Devon and Somerset Staghounds. He also built and equipped a small gymnasium at Barnes which was used by footballers and rowers. He represented Barnes on Surrey County Council (1903–19) and was a Justice of the Peace, a Conservator of Barnes Common and a supporter of working mens' clubs. He was often referred to as 'the grand old sportsman of Barnes'.

Barnes, the club formed by Morley, also deserves recognition as a primary force in the establishment of the FA. The first three secretaries of the FA were all men of Barnes – Morley, Robert Willis and RG Graham – and the first game under the Association's new laws was between Barnes and Richmond a week before Christmas in 1863. The success of the old Barnes club in the FA Cup was modest, however, and after losing many of its players to the Old Boys' clubs it took part in the tournament for the last time in 1886/7.

Ebenezer Cobb Morley is the man who set football on its long track around the world.

EC Morley should not be confused with Dr ES Morley of Blackburn Rovers who became an FA committeeman in 1882, a vice-president in 1885 and was an authoritative and witty champion of Lancashire football.

Ebenezer Cobb Morley (1831–1924) – the man who proposed the formation of the Football Association and became its first secretary. This is the only known photograph of Morley and the first time it has been published. Thanks are owed to historian Raymond Gill of South Croydon for unearthing it. A picture of Morley will now take its place at Lancaster Gate along with the other leading administrators who have shaped and guided the FA.

1

GENESIS
1863–70

The simple game of football is only one of the contributions England has made to the culture of our planet. It takes its place, with proper modesty, in a line which includes the English language itself, the authorised version of the Bible, Charles Darwin's *The Origin of Species*, Greenwich Mean Time and such ribs of modern society as the computer and the postage stamp.

But, while football is only a game, it is beyond doubt the most popular game on earth. More than 160 nations are affiliated to the Fédération Internationale de Football Association – even the United Nations Organisation cannot claim such a membership – and it was sanely estimated by FIFA that 2·7 billion television viewers, half the population of the world, watched the 1990 World Cup finals in Italy.

Figures, however, say nothing about the essence of the game. They do not reveal the charm of its history or the importance of its traditions; nor relish the art and science of great players; nor appreciate the filigree patterns and stormy conflict of a fine match; nor hear the heavy, rolling swell of a Wembley crowd beneath the hived towers of the old stadium on Cup final day; nor feel the aching melodrama of promotion and relegation; nor share the dreams of kids scuffing an old ball about under a street-lamp half an hour after curfew.

At its best, football is a rich and magnetic game to play or watch. At its worst, mangled by society, it has been the cause of death and disaster, hooliganism, cheating, jingoism, selfishness and insularity. Football reflects life faithfully, if sometimes reluctantly, and for better and worse it was manufactured in England.

The formation of the Football Association in 1863 – the year in which slavery was abolished in the United States, the International Red Cross was founded and

London's underground railway rumbled into life – was the first milestone in the history of organised football. Football before then was a good but wasted idea. The FA, with courage and inspiration, fashioned order out of chaos; it gave a confused and splintered pastime a new springboard, a new life-force. The FA framed the game's laws and provided it with shape, momentum and direction; and here, too, was the source of the broad river of Cup and international football which was to flow around the world. League football, professionalism, organised coaching, a code of discipline and an enduring sense of fair play were among its many tributaries.

The Football Association has been the game's pole-star. It has made mistakes and enemies, but its eminence and authority have remained constant; and in the huge family of FIFA, from Afghanistan to Zimbabwe, it is the one national association which does not require an identity tag. It is not the England FA or the FA of England. It is, simply, the Football Association.

But if England is the cradle and home of the game it cannot, honestly, be described as its birthplace. There is wholly acceptable evidence that man found pleasure in kicking a ball 2,000 years ago. The Chinese of the Han Dynasty, around the time of the birth of Christianity further west, called it 'tsu chu'. The Japanese knew it as 'askemari', the Greeks as 'episkyros', the Romans as 'harpastum'; and in Florence in 1530, with the city besieged by fearsome Hapsburg mercenaries, a game of football was played by the high-born. It was a handsome act of defiance which is still profitably celebrated by Florentines with pageantry, costume and, of course, their historical version of the game, an amalgam of football, rugby and martial mayhem.

Football is also the oldest of England's team sports, but its early form, from the 13th century onwards, was little more than an excuse for a riot, a violent thing of the streets and market-places. Games split towns and set village against village with, sometimes, hundreds on each side. The 'goals' could be several miles apart and the running battle carried on through stream and pond. Shops were closed and boarded, and dented heads and broken limbs were counted as minor mishaps. Regular attempts were made to suppress this popular violence – described by one contemporary observer as 'a bloodie and murthering practise'. But football had become a folk custom and it survived: in London's Smithfield, Strand and Cheapside, in Dorking, Manchester, Nottingham, Corfe in Dorset, Ashbourne in Derbyshire and Kingston-upon-Thames. Its roots were deep, its forms infinite.

Here was the strong, if primitive, seed of the world game – but the next stage in its development was one of the most important. England's rising middle class took a reforming interest in education; and the public schools, which had been coarse and often primitive kennels for the sons of the privileged, expanded healthily in the middle of the 19th century. Science found its way onto curricula which had been narrowly classical, and new attitudes developed towards manly decorum and a proper balance between work and play.

Muscular Christianity was a central plank of the reforms. The advantage of organised team games was recognised, and football, easily and naturally, found a new role. The game was no longer just a child of the streets. It had now been adopted by the ruling and professional classes of England with their genius for organisation. It had crossed a hugely significant bridge with perfect timing, because the old habit of playing in the streets was being broken by improved law and order and because the leisure time of the working classes was being smothered by industrialisation.

The schools developed their own styles of football, so it was difficult and sometimes impossible for one to play another. Variations were extensive and technical slang confused things even further. There was hacking, piggling, shinning, tagging and mauling. At Rugby the ball was handled at any time, at Eton not at all, with Harrow allowing 'a fair catch off the foot'.

There was a heated correspondence in *The Times* in which it was apparent that Etonians thought Rugby's version was 'plebeian', while Rugby regarded the Etonians as 'cowards'. Harrow's style needed practical explanation and one writer, with misty logic, pointed out that, in any case, there was a feud between Eton and Harrow. The style at Winchester, it was agreed, was simpler; while a dribbling game developed at Westminster and Charterhouse where lack of playing fields confined football to the cloisters.

The confusion became even more apparent when players moved from school to university. They still wanted to play football ... but which variation? Cambridge enthusiasts, to their everlasting credit, made the first move towards unification with meetings in 1846 and again two years later. They produced the 'Cambridge Rules' – and, while no copy now exists of them, here was the start of it all. Graduates spread the word, and the formation of clubs followed: Sheffield, Blackheath, the Forest club near Epping Forest (later the famous Wanderers), one or two of the big London hospitals, old boys' clubs and officers' messes. The spirit of the game was with them.

The game of football is a good one. It has a great claim to be considered an important one, because it is adapted to a special season when others are impracticable. When the trees are bare of leaves and the ground is saturated with the autumn rains, and the wind too cold to allow of inaction; when boating of all kinds, and swimming, and long country rambles, lose a great deal of their interest; when the cricket bat has to be put away, then it is that football comes to the rescue, providing an amusement for the dull days, better than any other known English game which can be played at this particular season.

John D Cartwright in The Field *on Saturday, 24 October 1863 – two days before the formation of the Football Association.*

Football was ready for a new dawn. JC Thring – an Old Salopian, a force behind the early Cambridge movement and later a master at Uppingham – made his mark again by producing a short and refined set of rules in 1862. There were ten in all – the basis of what he called 'The Simplest Game'. Only the ball could be kicked, no tripping, no 'out of play' movement in front of the ball – the early definition of offside. A new version of the Cambridge Rules followed in October 1863 – well-intentioned and clearly defined, but destined to split the game of football into two irreconcilable parts.

The newspapers of the day were largely unaware of the significance of what they were reporting – or, in some cases, not reporting – on the subject of football. Coverage of the game in many cases was sketchy and erratic. Cricket, racing, angling, wrestling, hunting and boxing were more to the fancy of the time. Much, for example, was made in that last week of October 1863 of the prize fight between Baldock and Gannon. 'The proceedings', according to one report, 'were more worthy of savages on the Zambezi than Englishmen encountering in the Metropolitan circuit.' *Bell's Life* threatened to stop being 'the organ of the ring' after describing how scoundrels drew knives to hack off the fingers of those who wore valuable rings.

Reports that 29 people had died of smallpox in London during that week were carried alongside advertisements championing miracle remedies – 'Dr Record's Essence of Life restores health and strength to the most shattered constitutions in four weeks. Failure is impossible.'

The Field – 'The Country Gentlemen's Newspaper' – was one of the few which liberally devoted space to the game; and, in John D Cartwright, they had a man who might properly be described as the first football writer. He was a tireless and trenchant enthusiast and, in *The Field* of 31 October 1863, he wrote a 4,000-word article, by no means his first, on the need for uniformity. He wrote:

That which is wanted is a headquarters for football, from which rules shall be issued and tried: and, if found wanting, revised again and again – a headquarters such as there is for cricket in the Marylebone club, and for all other sports which England claims as national. In our next paper we shall endeavour to show that such a 'headquarters' might be easily found.

Alas, history had overtaken Cartwright. In the same edition, in the very next column, a short report carried this headline: 'Formation of a Football Association'. As Cartwright commented the following week: 'Reform is apparently at hand (reported in last week's *Field*).'

Thus, without fanfare, the Football Association was born. On the evening of Monday, 26 October 1863, the captains, secretaries and other representatives of a dozen London and suburban clubs met at the Freemason's Tavern, Great Queen Street, Lincoln's Inn Fields, in the heart of a city of oil lamps and hansom cabs, top hats and beards, of rising prosperity and obstinate poverty. John Bull was at ease with himself.

They met 'for the purpose of forming an Association with the object of establishing a definite code of rules for the regulation of the game'. The clubs represented – among them names which have no modern relevance – were Barnes, the WO (War Office) Club, Crusaders, Forest of Leytonstone, No Names club of Kilburn, Crystal Palace, Blackheath, Kensington School, Percival House (Blackheath), Surbiton, Blackheath Proprietory School and – the only public school represented – Charterhouse.

EC Morley of Barnes proposed that Arthur Pember of the No Names club, a London solicitor, should take the chair; and it was Morley again who formally proposed the formation of the Football Association. The proposal was carried heartily, 11 of the 12 clubs present were enrolled as founder-members and Morley, the most influential voice, was named as secretary. Charterhouse alone stood back from it all, their captain BF Hartshorne insisting that he could not pledge himself until the attitude of the other schools became clear. Their absence has been attributed to lack of publicity for the meeting: the real reasons were stubbornness and suspicion.

This little group of mid-Victorians had, however, achieved their first target – the creation of an authority which, they hoped, would lead to the unification of a hopelessly fragmented game. They were very aware, too, that they had taken a position which might give them a spinal role in the control of the sport. Football, in the first place, had belonged essentially to the people; then to the schools and universities; and now, with the formation of the FA, the balance of power seemed to be in the hands of a small number of London clubs. But there can be no authority without laws – and six meetings took place in 44 days before the Association, a little unsteadily, was able to stand on its own feet.

The meetings led to confusion, bitterness and finally division; but the first three were peaceful enough. The FA was formed at the first, the rules of the Association were formulated at the second (subscription was a guinea a year, with an annual meeting every September, and alterations to rules or laws were to be advertised in the sporting papers) and a useful discussion on the drafting of the laws took place at the third.

The game, as they saw it, would be a blend of handling and dribbling. Players would be able to handle the ball – a fair catch accompanied by 'a mark with the heel' would win a free kick. The Cambridge Rules, which made no mention of clutching and running with the ball, were still strongly championed; but this was not the cause of the real friction.

The sticking point was 'hacking', or kicking an opponent on the leg. The Rugby men believed a few bruises on the shin enriched character and life. Advocates of the dribbling game considered the practice brutal. The battlelines of the argument were established at the fourth meeting and everything came into the open, painfully, at the fifth. Blackheath – on behalf of the Rugby code – argued that the attempt to ban hacking savoured 'far more of the feelings of those who liked their pipes and grog or schnaps more than the manly game of football . . .'

The hackers lost their argument, however, and at the sixth meeting of the FA – the final act in the birth of the Association – Blackheath moodily withdrew. The dribblers and the handlers went their different ways, and football was divided forever. Yet Rugby itself was soon to abolish hacking with the blessing of one of the founder-members of the Rugby Union in 1871 . . . Blackheath.

The Football Association wasted no time in publishing new laws – its first commercial enterprise. John Lillywhite of Seymour Street, Euston Square, London, was given sole rights to issue and sell them. They appeared in a 'neat little book' for the pocket at a shilling a time and in a larger 'roller' form for clubrooms at 1s 6d.

The new overlords of the game were also anxious to see their laws in action. An inaugural match was arranged for the second day of 1864 at Battersea Park, but impatience got the better of them. A game was played between Barnes and Richmond on Saturday, 19 December 1863 at Barnes, and *The Field* saw it this way: 'Very little difficulty was experienced on either side in playing the new rules, and the game was characterised by great good temper, the rules being so simple and easy of observance that it was difficult for disputes to arise.' Result: a goalless draw.

The FA's early influence on the game at large was not dramatic or even widespread. Its membership was small and its authority and laws were often challenged and sometimes ignored. But its motives and ambitions were so honourably based that, like growing ripples on a still pond, its standing grew perceptibly. It was a period of high ideals and ready compromise.

Two years after its formation, however, the FA still had only one provincial member. However, it was an important club, Sheffield, the oldest and one of the most influential in the game, and early in 1866 this Yorkshire arm of the Association suggested that a match should be played between the clubs of London and Sheffield. The FA quickly recognised the significance of the proposal and, the challenge accepted, the two cities met on 31 March in Battersea Park.

It was the first representative match played by the Football Association, the first in the history of the game and the forerunner of all representative and, in a sense, even international football. The match was comfortably won by London, with the distinction of scoring the first goal in a representative game falling to EC Morley, the secretary of the FA and, according to one account, a 'pretty and most effective dribbler'.

The FA accepted that here was something good and new. Other matches between the two cities followed and, in little more than a year, the FA began to organise inter-county matches, which helped hugely in spreading the gospel. Sheffield contributed a precious northern perspective to matters of policy and the FA, with growing range and budding confidence, was ready for its second step into the future.

The Football Association
Milestones

1863 Football Association formed.	1914 George V becomes first reigning monarch to attend an FA Cup final.
1871 Birth of FA Cup: 15 entries.	
1872 First international: Scotland 0, England 0.	1923 First FA Cup final at Wembley.
1873 Scottish FA formed and Scottish Cup launched.	1924 First international at Wembley.
	1928 Four British countries withdraw from FIFA.
1876 FA of Wales formed.	
1880 Irish FA formed and Irish Cup introduced.	1930 First World Cup: staged and won by Uruguay.
1885 Professionalism legalised.	1938 Laws rewritten by FA secretary Stanley Rous.
1886 International Board formed.	
1888 Football League formed.	1946 British countries rejoin FIFA. Walter Winterbottom appointed first England team-manager and first FA director of coaching.
1893 Birth of FA Amateur Cup.	
1895 FA Cup stolen in Birmingham and never recovered.	
1904 FIFA formed.	1950 England compete in World Cup for first time. United States 1, England 0 in Brazil.
1908 FA Charity Shield introduced.	
1910 Second FA Cup withdrawn because of duplication and replaced by a third.	1953 England's first Wembley defeat by foreign opposition: England 3, Hungary 6.

The Stanley Matthews Cup final: Blackpool 4, Bolton Wanderers 3.

1955   Birth of European Cup.

1958   Munich air disaster.

1960   FA recognises Sunday football.
Birth of Football League Cup.

1961   Maximum wage (£20 week) abolished.

1962   Sir Stanley Rous becomes president of FIFA.
Alf Ramsey succeeds Walter Winterbottom as England team-manager.

1963   FA centenary.

1966   England win World Cup.

1968   Manchester United become first English club to win European Cup.

1974   End of amateurism and FA Amateur Cup.
Don Revie replaces Alf Ramsey as England team-manager.
Joao Havelange (Brazil) succeeds Sir Stanley Rous as FIFA president.

1977   Don Revie leaves for United Arab Emirates and is replaced by Ron Greenwood as England manager.

1981   Tottenham Hotspur win 100th FA Cup final.

1982   Ron Greenwood retires after World Cup finals in Spain and is succeeded by Bobby Robson.

1984   Last British Home Championship.
FA National School opened at Lilleshall.

1985   Heysel disaster before European Cup final between Liverpool and Juventus.
English clubs banned from European competition.
Bradford fire tragedy.

1988   Football League centenary.

1989   Hillsborough disaster: 95 die at FA Cup semi-final between Liverpool and Nottingham Forest.

1990   England reach semi-finals for first time in an overseas World Cup (Italy).
Bobby Robson joins PSV Eindhoven and is succeeded by Graham Taylor.
English clubs return to European competition.

1992   FA Premier League launched (Football League reduced to three divisions).
First presentation of fourth FA Cup (third trophy withdrawn because of wear and tear).

①

②

① Seed of the World Game: the earliest form of football in England, from the 13th century onwards, was a primitive maul which split towns and set village against village. The Derbyshire market town of Ashbourne maintains the tradition – and games there on Shrove Tuesday and Ash Wednesday involve no referees or rules. The teams are known as the Up'ards and Down'ards and the aim is to 'goal' the ball at the opposite end of town. The battle takes in the River Henmore, fields, streets, car parks and all obstacles devised by man and nature. But it stops short of abrasive hooliganism – and a 'goal' is as highly prized as a winner at Wembley.

② London street football, circa 1820, etching by H Heath. Sporting mayhem – but its days were numbered. The Highways Act of 1835 prohibited football in the streets and fines of up to 40 shillings were levied.

①

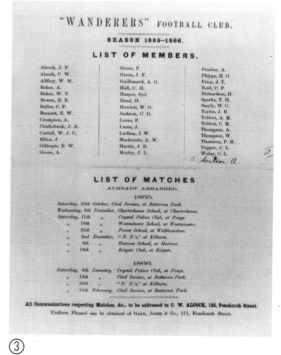

②

③

④

① The playing fields of Eton where, according to the Duke of Wellington, the battle of Waterloo was won. The Old Etonians Football Club, to mark its centenary, presented this picture to the FA in 1965. The Old Etonians FC was founded by the Hon Arthur Kinnaird and reached the FA Cup final six times (two victories) in nine seasons between 1875 and 1883. They were the last 'true blue' amateur side to win the tournament.

② The cloisters at Westminster School – one of the 'cradles' of football. A form of the game was played here nearly 300 years ago. Two gates acted as goals, three walls limited movement and matches sometimes took two or three days to settle. No holds were barred and injuries were sometimes extensive. The Chapter tried to suppress the game in 1710 and Abbey clergy regularly objected to the violence and noise so close to a house of worship.

③ The Wanderers were the first outstanding football club, winning the FA Cup five times in its first seven seasons, and membership was the ambition of nearly all the best players. Formed from Forest FC (1859–63), an Old Harrovian team which played at Snaresbrook on the edge of Epping Forest, it was the first club to set out, deliberately, to make the game popular. The Wanderers played their early football at Battersea Park, where matches were sometimes stopped because the gates had to be closed for the night, but they increasingly used opponents' grounds. Wanderers' players were university, public school and military men – and were the first Englishmen to play in Scotland. The Wanderers eventually lost their players to the old boys' teams and the club died in the early 1880s. This list of members in 1865 includes AG Guillemard who was to become 'the father' of the Rugby Union six years later.

④ The only statue in London depicting a football. The central figure is Quintin Hogg, founder of the Polytechnic and a member of the Scotland side which played England in the first 'unofficial' international in London in 1870. The group, in bronze by Sir George Frampton, has stood on a marble pedestal in Langham Place, beside the BBC's Broadcasting House, since 1906. Hogg is reading a book to two boys – one of whom is carrying a football. Hogg played for the Wanderers and the Old Etonians (Cup final 1876) and is said to have been 'a splendid back'.

①

②

Meeting held 26th October 1863 at Freemasons Tav.

Proposed by Mr Morley
Seconded by Mr Mackenzie
and Carried "That Mr Pember to take the Chair".

Prop'd by Mr Morley
Sec'd by Mr Steward
and Carried "That the Clubs represented at this
meeting now form themselves into an
Association to be called "The Football
Association"
whereupon the following clubs we
enrolled

Clubs	Represented by
N. N. Kilburn	Arthur Pember
Barnes	Ebr C. Morley
W. O. War Office	Ed. Mawn
Crusaders	H. T. Steward
Forest. Leytonstone	J. F. Alcock
Perceval House Blackheath	G. W. Shillingford

③

① The Freemasons Tavern, Great Queen Street, just off Drury Lane in central London, where the Football Association was founded on 26 October 1863. The meeting probably took place in a hall at the rear and, in the engraving, girls from a Methodist school at Euston are entering the room for a 'charity festival'. The Connaught Assembly Rooms now stand on the site – and have been used for meetings by the Football League.

② In the beginning was the word: the first page in the first minute book of the Football Association. The historic decision to form the FA is recorded in the meticulous copperplate writing of the proposer and first secretary – Ebenezer Morley.

③ The Thames-side home of Ebenezer Morley – 26, The Terrace, Barnes – where he drafted the FA's first laws of football in 1863.

2

LITTLE TIN IDOL
1871–84

The writing in the first minute book of the Football Association is fading now. There is a hint of gold in the paling ink – and so there should be. The two short minutes which record the beginning of Cup football and international football deserve to have been penned with something precious.

There is no embellishment, no pretension and no sense of high destiny in the minutes. The announcement of the birth of the Football Association Challenge Cup runs to just 29 words: 'That it is desirable that a Challenge Cup should be established in connection with the Association for which all clubs belonging to the Association should be invited to compete' – 20 July 1871.

International football was launched by an equally brief sentence: 'In order to further the interests of the Association in Scotland, it was decided that during the current season, a team should be sent to Glasgow to play a match v Scotland' – 3 October 1872.

Thus the game found its spring of life. The FA Cup – 'The Cup' – was football's first national tournament and has become the best-loved of all England's sporting institutions, a major strand of the nation's fabric and as much a part of its way of life as Sunday roast and a pint at the local. And the first international between England and Scotland carried football up to its top floor. Here is the dimension of the game which examines standards at the highest level, pulls together the pride of nations and crosses all the boundaries and obstructions devised by man.

The two notions provided football with inspiration and a strong heartbeat. They crossed the seven seas and, with only gentle adjustment, sold themselves to almost every nation on earth.

Both, moreover, were the idea of one man: Charles William Alcock. He was a big and principled Sunderland man of many parts – player, referee, administrator, committeeman, author and journalist – talented and respected enough as a player to captain England and organised enough as an administrator to be secretary of the Football Association and of Surrey County Cricket Club at the same time. He was secretary of the FA for a quarter of a century (1870–95) but, in this long period of progress and change, he contributed nothing more important to the game than his priceless ideas about Cup and international football. Men have been canonised for less!

Alcock was not quite 30 years old, and had been the FA's secretary for little more than 12 months when he first had his vision of a national knockout tournament. He had remembered playing in an inter-house 'sudden death' competition during his schooldays at Harrow – and his real triumph was in recognising that the idea could be employed on a much grander scale.

He put his proposal to six other FA men, all gentlemen and officers, all representatives of well-known clubs, in the offices of the *Sportsman* newspaper in Boy Court, just off the bottom of Ludgate Hill, in the old parish of St Bride. The place and occasion should now be marked by a brass plaque; but, alas, Boy Court no longer exists. It can be assumed that the meeting took place in the *Sportsman*'s office because Alcock was a regular contributor to the paper.

Alcock's proposal was swiftly agreed, and at another meeting – held nearly three months later – 18 rules were drafted and 15 entries accepted: Barnes, Civil Service, Crystal Palace, Clapham Rovers, Hitchin, Maidenhead, Marlow, Queen's Park (Glasgow), Donington Grammar School (Spalding), Hampstead Heathens, Harrow Chequers, Reigate Priory, Royal Engineers, Upton Park and the Wanderers. All were based in or near London with the exception of Queen's Park and Donington School. It was a disappointing entry because the FA by then had 50 members; but many felt that competition would lead to unhealthy rivalry and even bitterness.

A trophy was required, of course, and this was designed and made in silver by Martin, Hall and Company for about £20 – a stubby, heavily embossed pot, about 18 inches high, with two curved handles and the figure of a player on its lid. Here was the original FA Cup – soon to be known as the 'little tin idol'.

The first tournament was more skirmish than campaign. Fifteen clubs entered but, pruned by withdrawals and byes, only 12 played and only 13 games were required. Harrow Chequers, Reigate Priory and Donington School scratched without playing ... and Queen's Park, exempted until the semi-finals because of distance and cost, played only once. The celebrated Scottish club drew with the Wanderers but then, funded by public subscriptions and unable to remain in

London for a replay, they departed for home with dignity.

Thus the Wanderers were left to face the Royal Engineers in the first FA Cup final at Kennington Oval, then football's premier ground, on 16 March 1872. The game was attended by 2,000 spectators who paid a shilling apiece – and, for that then considerable sum, they saw a close and, according to the *Sporting Life*, 'most pleasant contest'. But it was not a game with which the modern fan would easily identify. Shirt colours were consistent – Wanderers, for example, usually wore orange, violet and black and the Engineers red and blue – but, with numbers not yet even imagined, players were distinguished by the colour of their caps or stockings. The 'crossbar' was a length of tape. Ends were changed every time a goal was scored. There was no heading of the ball. The throw-in was one-handed and taken by the side which touched the ball first after it had gone out of play (hence the term 'touchline'). And inside those touchlines the field was unmarked.

The game itself was based on dribbling, the longer the run the better, with most of the rest of the team 'backing up' the man in possession. Seven, even eight, forwards were still employed: defence was a lesser art. The passing game, however, was developing in Scotland (as Queen's Park had shown in their semi-final with the Wanderers) and the arrival of combined 'team' football was imminent. The Royal Engineers, in fact, had already made a move in this direction, and their 'better organisation and combination' saw them made firm favourites to beat the Wanderers in the first final.

But the Cup made it clear from the start that it was never going to be predictable. One of the Engineers players, Lieutenant Cresswell, broke his collarbone only ten minutes after the start and, although he remained on the pitch, the Wanderers made telling use of their advantage. They had strong sun and a breeze behind them and, in Robert Walpole Sealy-Vidal of Westminster, they had a future England international who was known as 'the prince of dribblers'. And it was Sealy-Vidal who provided 'AH Chequer' with the only goal of the game.

All records show, or should show, however, that Wanderers' winning goal in the first Cup final was scored by Morton Peto Betts of West Kent and the Old Harrovians, a member of the FA committee which had unanimously approved the birth of the tournament. 'AH Chequer' (a Harrow Chequer or Harrow old boy) was the name assumed by Betts for the final – a simple deceit which may have had something to do with the fact that the Wanderers were drawn against Harrow Chequers in the first round. The Chequers scratched – and Betts re-emerged for the final. Clearly everything was above board because the Wanderers were captained by none other than CW Alcock, secretary of the FA and 'father' of the Cup.

The first seven finals all involved the Wanderers or the Royal Engineers. The

Wanderers won the 'little tin idol' on five occasions, while the Engineers won it once and finished as losing finalists three times – again falling to the Wanderers in 1878. But here, also, were two clubs which drew together the three outstanding men of those early days of the Football Association.

One, of course, was Alcock: the others were Francis Marindin and Arthur Kinnaird. Their influence on the development of the game is incalculable and, together, they spanned a remarkable period of nearly 60 years, first as players and then as administrators or commanders-in-chief.

Major Marindin (later Sir Francis) was, in turn, a distinguished soldier; founder, captain, doughty full back and twice an FA Cup finalist with the Royal Engineers; then a goalkeeper with the Old Etonians; the outstanding referee of his time (taking charge of nine Cup finals); and president of the Football Association from 1874 to 1890. He was unfailingly courteous, impartial and diligent, a man of conscience and an amateur of the old school. He disguised his apprehensions at the coming of professionalism and the rising influence of the northern and Midland clubs during the 1880s, and steered the game deftly through a period of extreme turbulence. But once it was clear that the age of the amateur had passed forever, Marindin gracefully stepped down. He was a man of his time; and that time had passed.

Marindin's chair was immediately filled, however, by a man of even greater stature – Lord Kinnaird – who was to be president of the Football Association for the next 33 years. The length of his involvement with the FA, the range and weight of his contribution and his success as a player take the breath away even now.

Kinnaird became an FA committeeman at the age of 22 in 1869, two years before the birth of the Cup, and he died as president just a few months before the opening of Wembley in 1923. He played in the second Cup final in 1873 and nearly saw the 48th in its new and permanent home in north London. And Kinnaird himself played in nine of those finals, finishing on the winning side in five of them, three with the Wanderers, two with the Old Etonians – a record shared only with fellow Wanderer Charles Wollaston and James Forrest of Blackburn Rovers. Kinnaird was an FA committeeman for eight years and treasurer for 13 years before his presidency carried the game deep into the 20th century; and he was, too, president of the YMCA of England and Lord High Commissioner to the Church of Scotland.

Kinnaird is not only remembered for his remarkable work as an official and head of establishment, and for his outstanding success as a player, but he is also remembered, above all perhaps, as an exceptional man with a huge appetite for life as well as football. He was a mixture of fun and steely resolution, with contagious warmth and a buoyant spirit. He was large and muscular with a full auburn beard, broad brow and direct gaze – a man nobody missed and nobody forgot. Kinnaird was also an international – a Scottish international! This son of an old Perthshire family won one cap against England in 1873, the second official international, but he took a central role in pointing the game in its new and hugely important direction.

But this was after Charles Alcock had again pulled together some loose strands to formulate the good, basic idea. One of his first steps was a letter to the *Glasgow Herald* dated 3 November 1870 which announced that a game between England and Scotland – 'the best elevens at their disposal' – would take place in London 16 days later. 'In Scotland, once essentially the land of football, there still should be a spark left of the old fire . . .' Scottish players wishing to take part were invited to send their names to Mr AF Kinnaird, 2 Pall Mall East, London.

This 'unofficial' international proved to be a ragged affair at the Oval between players who lived in London. Kinnaird played for 'Scotland' and Alcock for 'England', who won 1–0 – and the form of 'Scotland', like its Scottish connection, was very thin in three other unofficial matches which followed. Alcock needed help and, in the absence of a Scottish Football Association, it was provided by Queen's Park. The illustrious Scottish club had proved their courage and fostered natural rivalry by travelling to London to play the Wanderers in the semi-finals of the first FA Cup and now they agreed to stage and organise the first full international between Scotland and England . . . a move which led to the FA's historic directive on 3 October 1872.

They were glorious days in the way of enjoyment, those of the late 1860s and throughout the 1870s. Then it was at least the game pure and unadulterated. No gates to speak of – down our way, at least. It was real sport, *sans* exes, *sans* records, *sans* everything. Those were the days primeval. To go to Glasgow – a railway journey of over 800 miles there and back – for an hour and a half's football and at one's own expense was not in a way grateful and comforting. How we did it is not as easy to say. But it was done, and plenty of fun it brought with it, even if one had to travel through the night in draughty carriages with hard seats – a severely economical style.

Charles Alcock, secretary of the Football Association 1870–95.

The game was played on Glasgow's biggest enclosed sportsfield, Hamilton Crescent, the Partick home of the West of Scotland Cricket Club, on Saturday, 30 November 1872. Alcock, having captained the Wanderers in the first Cup final, would undoubtedly also have been England's captain in the first international but for injury. It would have been a richly deserved 'double', but he damaged a leg so badly in a game between the Old Harrovians and Old Etonians a fortnight before that it was even feared his playing career was over. But he was still at Partick for the birth of international football.

That late November afternoon in 1872 was a pleasant one. Heavy rain had fallen for two or three days and there was some light drizzle on the morning of the match, but by the time the game kicked-off at 2·20pm (20 minutes late) there was limpid sunshine. The pitch was a little greasy but considered to be in 'good order'. The admission fee, as it had been for the first Cup final, was a shilling: a weighty sum set against the average industrial wage of about 20s a week. And this for a sport which had yet to capture the public imagination in Scotland – where the Rugby code had made impressive headway.

Scotland's side was selected by Queen's Park and, with Kinnaird not available and other clubs offering a narrow choice, they unhesitatingly plumped for their own players, or at least players with whom they had a strong connection. England's team was drawn from eight clubs and included four players from Oxford University.

The match itself was a goalless draw but a resounding success in almost every other way. The *North British Daily Mail* reported that it was played 'in the presence of the largest assemblage seen at any football match in Scotland – there being close on 4,000, including a good number of ladies . . . it will be readily admitted that the Association game is one which will commend itself to players who dread the harder work of the Rugby mode'. *Bell's Life* saw it as 'one of the jolliest, one of the most spirited and most pleasant matches that have ever been played according to Association rules'.

Queen's Park believed the fixture would be a springboard for the game in Scotland which, at the time, had only ten clubs. They were right. More than a dozen other clubs were soon born and, only four months after that first international, the Scottish Football Association was formed.

England and Scotland had by then already met for a second time – on 8 March 1873, London's first international – with England even holding a series of trial matches before making eight changes from the side which played in Glasgow. England won 4–2, but Scotland's first victory was only another year away. Already, earnest comparisons were being made between the close-knit passing style of the Scots and the dribbling forays of England's gentlemen. It even ceased to be a decent argument after Scotland had won ten of the first 16 meetings, sometimes with embarrassing ease, and England only two. But the English method was so deeply rooted in tradition and in the bullish inclinations of its public school old boys that there was no broad line of new thinking until the coming of professionalism and the adoption of the game by the working masses.

The expanding empire of the FA itself was one reason for the shift in power. County and District Associations, charged with fostering the game and organising clubs in their own areas, sprang into life all over the country between 1875 and 1885. They ran their own Cup tournaments, kindled enthusiasm and provided the framework for hundreds of new clubs. They lit a new fire and gave the FA – and the Cup – its national character. The contribution the County and District Associations made to the growth and development of football was of towering importance.

The golden age of the southern amateur was nearly over. The first ten finals of the FA Cup involved only six clubs: The Wanderers, Royal Engineers, Old Etonians, Oxford University, Old Carthusians and Clapham Rovers. But, in 1882, a club from the north reached the final for the first time. Blackburn Rovers travelled to the Oval with a large following and such high confidence that a Lancashire poet lauded victory long before the kick-off:

> The English Cup, by brilliant play
> From Cockney land they brought away;
> Let's hope in Blackburn it will stay
> To cheer the Blackburn Rovers.

But the zestful Old Etonians won 1–0 and Kinnaird celebrated their triumph by standing on his head in front of the Oval pavilion. He was not to know it, but the game itself was in the process of being turned on its head. The Cup was never again won by an amateur club.

Twelve months later another Blackburn club reached the final, Blackburn Olympic, and again their opponents were Kinnaird and the Old Etonians. Olympic had been formed five years before by the merging of two minor clubs and, after modest beginnings, their impact on the game was a powerful one. They were systematically trained, coached and organised; they even went to Blackpool for a week before the final to round off their preparations. The Old Etonians' style and resolution was as robust as ever, but they lost an important player, Arthur TB Dunn, an England captain of the future, early in the game. So when the final went into extra time, their ten men were painfully stretched by Olympic's ability to switch the ball from wing to wing with long passes. And it was one of those passes which gave Jimmy Costley, a spinner by trade, the chance to close in from the left and score Olympic's winner.

The Cup had found its first northern home, and another 18 years were to pass before it returned to London. Indeed, the Cup remained in Blackburn for another three years – kept there with consummate efficiency by the Rovers, whose standing in the town became so powerful that poor Olympic, having pointed the game in a new direction, found they had no future themselves and folded in 1889.

Blackburn Rovers won the finals of 1884–6 to emulate the success of the Wanderers a decade before, an achievement never since equalled. The people of Blackburn relished every moment with brass bands, bunting, fireworks, parties and processions. Thousands, too, followed their team to the Oval for the three finals, where they were described by a writer in the *Pall Mall Gazette* as 'a northern horde of uncouth garb and strange oaths'. A tribe of Sudanese Arabs let loose in the Strand, he added, would not have caused more amusement and curiosity. Blackburn could afford to smile. Some would even have known that the writer was the Lancashire-born son of a dedicated Rovers supporter.

But underlying Rovers' historic success were graver matters which the Football Association would now have to face.

FA Cup

Year	Date	Winners		Runners-up		Venue	Attendance	Referee	Entries
1872	16 March	Wanderers	1	Royal Engineers	0	Oval	2,000	A Stair	15
1873	29 March	Wanderers	2	Oxford University	0	Lillie Bridge	3,000	A Stair	16
1874	14 March	Oxford University	2	Royal Engineers	0	Oval	2,000	A Stair	28
1875	13 March	Royal Engineers	1	Old Etonians	1*	Oval	3,000	CW Alcock	29
Replay	16 March	Royal Engineers	2	Old Etonians	0	Oval	3,000	CW Alcock	
1876	11 March	Wanderers	1	Old Etonians	1	Oval	3,000	WS Rawson	32
Replay	18 March	Wanderers	3	Old Etonians	0	Oval	3,500	WS Rawson	
1877	24 March	Wanderers	2	Oxford University	1*	Oval	3,000	SH Wright	37
1878	23 March	Wanderers	3	Royal Engineers	1	Oval	4,500	SR Bastard	43
1879	29 March	Old Etonians	1	Clapham Rovers	0	Oval	5,000	CW Alcock	43
1880	10 April	Clapham Rovers	1	Oxford University	0	Oval	6,000	Major Marindin	54
1881	9 April	Old Carthusians	3	Old Etonians	0	Oval	4,500	W Pierce Dix	63
1882	25 March	Old Etonians	1	Blackburn Rovers	0	Oval	6,500	JC Clegg	73
1883	31 March	Blackburn Olympic	2	Old Etonians	1*	Oval	8,000	C Crump	84
1884	29 March	Blackburn Rovers	2	Queen's Park	1	Oval	4,000	Major Marindin	100

①

②

① Paternoster Row, London EC – No 28 was the first permanent home (1881–5) of the Football Association. The FA's room was reached by a rear staircase, and the account for furnishing it was modest: 'General furniture for new office, £29 18s 9d; washstand not to exceed £3. CW Alcock £3 office table. NL Jackson £3 0s 6d to include a clock £1.' JJ Bentley, president of the Football League (1894–1910) and a vice-president of the FA, remembered it as 'an unpretentious, badly furnished little room'. Paternoster Row, in the shadow of St Paul's Cathedral, was a quiet street and a centre of bookselling and publishing – but it was devastated during World War Two when around 6 million books were destroyed.

② Charles William Alcock, secretary of the Football Association for a quarter of a century (1870–95) and founding spirit of the FA Cup and international football. He joined the FA committee in 1866; captained Middlesex against Surrey and Kent in the first county match in 1867; founded the Wanderers and captained them to victory in the first Cup final in 1872; captained England against Scotland just a week before he refereed the Cup final in 1875; and was vice-president of the FA from 1896 to his death in 1907 at the age of 64. Cricket was another pillar of his life: he played for Essex and was secretary of Surrey County Cricket Club for 35 years (1872–1907). He organised the first Test match in England – against Australia in 1880 – at Kennington Oval which was also the home of the FA Cup final for 20 years. He was, too, the managing official at the birth of the 'Ashes', when Australia beat England for the first time in England in 1882. Alcock wrote of the occasion: 'Men who were noted for their coolness at critical moments were trembling like a leaf; some were shivering with cold; some even fainted. At times there was an awful silence.' Alcock's stylish use of words is not surprising, because he was also one of the most noted and industrious sports journalists of his time. He launched and edited the first 'Football Annual' from 1868, started two magazines, 'Football' and 'Cricket' (which he edited until 1905), wrote several books and contributed to many papers, including *The Sportsman* and *The Field*. A Sunderland man who was educated at Harrow, Alcock also helped found the Referees' Association and

was one of the first vice-presidents of the London FA and the Surrey FA. He was chairman of Richmond Athletic Association and vice-president of Mid-Surrey Golf Club, and was a Justice of the Peace. His place in the history of football, cricket and sports journalism and literature is indelibly secure ... but football's debt to him is greatest of all. A contemporary wrote: 'When the flashing meteors have come and gone, when the League tables are full and complete, and when the present fades into the past, the name of CW Alcock will stand out all the more prominently like a rugged rock in a sea of bubbles.'

③

④

③ John Charles Clegg – a member of England's first international team (v Scotland, Glasgow, 30 November 1872) and the first man to be knighted for services to football (1927). One of the FA's greatest and most formidable administrators. As a player he was a forward noted for his speed: he was a leading athlete who could run 100 yards in 10 seconds. As an administrator he was a man of dauntingly high principles, strong willed, confident and the dominant force at any meeting he attended. 'Nobody gets lost on a straight road,' he would say. Charles Clegg, a Sheffield man and a solicitor, joined the FA committee in 1886, became chairman in 1889 and was president from 1923–37. He also refereed the FA Cup finals of 1882 and 1892. His younger brother, William Edwin Clegg, also played for England (in the first international in London, v Scotland, 8 March 1873) and, like Charles, he was a solicitor who was knighted. William was Lord Mayor of Sheffield (1893–9). Charles was 87 when he died, William 80.

④ Sir Francis Arthur Marindin, KCMG – known as 'the Major' – founder of the Royal Engineers and distinguished president of the Football Association (1874–90) during years of great upheaval and change. He was captain and full back for the Royal Engineers in two Cup finals (including the first in 1872) and later kept goal for the Old Etonians, who he also helped found. He faced a division of loyalties when the Royal Engineers and the Old Etonians reached the 1875 final – a problem he solved by withdrawing. He later became the outstanding referee of his time – 'one of the very few referees who really know all the rules' commented a writer. Remarkably, he refereed nine Cup finals (1880, 1884–90 – including a replay in 1886). NL Jackson described him as 'the kindest and best of friends'.

① The proposal which launched football's first tournament. Committee meeting held at the Sportsman Office on 20 July, 1871.

Present. C. W. Alcock, C. W. Stephenson, J. H. Giffard, M. P. Betts, D. Allport, Capt. Marindin, & a Stair.

Resolved unanimously "That it is desirable that a Challenge Cup should be established in connection with the association for which all clubs belonging to the association should be invited to compete. The Secretary was instructed to communica[te]

②

① The proposal which launched football's first tournament. The signature at the top is that of Ebenezer Cobb Morley – the 'father' of the Football Association.

② The 'Little Tin Idol' – the original FA Cup and the first football trophy of all. Designed and made in silver by Martin, Hall and Company in 1872. Cost: £20. Height: 18 inches. Capacity: one quart. It was one of English sport's most coveted trophies for 24 seasons (1872–95) – and was then stolen.

③ Darwen, the first of the FA Cup's iconoclasts, the club which established the democracy of the tournament. The picture was taken in 1880 – the year after the Lancashire town's team of mill-workers had stretched the celebrated Old Etonians (led by the Honourable Arthur F Kinnaird) to three games in the quarter-finals. The first was drawn 5–5, with Darwen scoring four in the last quarter-hour and the Old Etonians refusing to play extra time and 'finish it there and then'. The second game was drawn 2–2 and it was only in the third encounter that the Old Boys' strength told: they won 6–2. But all three games were played at Kennington Oval – and Darwen were then tired by their long trips to London. Darwen's expenses were met by the townspeople who established a 'London Fund', the first example of that curious affliction known as 'Cup fever'. Even the FA contributed £10 to the fund; and a year later they also changed the regulation which ruled that the final three rounds should be played in London. Back row (left to right) – J Duxbury, S Fish, T Brindle, L Broughton, WH Moorhouse. Middle row – T Marshall, T Rostron, Dr Gledhill, Dr JC Holden, R Kirkham, T Bury. Front – Fergie Suter, an import from Glasgow, one of the first professionals and recognised as 'among the best backs in the kingdom'. Suter, however, was soon to join Blackburn Rovers and, according to the *Lancashire Daily Post*, the move stirred up 'the most bitter enmity between the officials and supporters of the two clubs' – a feud that was 'eventually settled through the instrumentality of the English Association after voluminous correspondence'. Tom Brindle and Tom Marshall are wearing England shirts – quickly won after Darwen's Cup success.

The cotton town of Blackburn dominated the FA Cup for a decade in the late 19th century in a way never since matched. Blackburn Rovers reached the final in 1882, Blackburn Olympic won the Cup in 1883 and Rovers kept it in the parish in 1884–5–6 and won it again in 1890 and 1891. Blackburn, the town, was involved in seven out of ten finals – winning six of them.

④ Blackburn Rovers: the first northern club to reach the final of the FA Cup, 1882. Back row – D Greenwood, R Howorth, J Hargreaves, F Suter ('professional'), W Duckworth (secretary). Middle row – J Duckworth, H McIntyre ('professional'), H Sharples, F Hargreaves, T Strachan, G Avery. Front row – J Brown, J Douglas ('professional'). The Rovers were beaten 1–0 at Kennington Oval, but the game marked the end of the southern amateurs' domination of the Cup. Fred Hargreaves, with headwear, was Blackburn Rovers' first England international – and his brother, John Hargreaves, was also capped. Their father was Blackburn's coroner. Acceptance of professionalism was still three years away but Suter, McIntyre and Douglas were undoubt-

③

④

⑤

edly paid – or, as one observer put it, 'considerable portions of Blackburn's funds were expended in securing their comforts'. Suter, an outstanding and much-admired full back, put it another way: 'We had no settled wage, but it was understood that we interviewed the treasurer as occasion arose.'

⑤ Blackburn Olympic: the first northern club to win the FA Cup, 1883 – 'a triumph for the democracy', as one contemporary observer put it, over the public school boys of the south. Back row (left to right) – W Bramham (secretary), G Wilson ('professional'), T Dewhurst (weaver), T Hacking (dentist's assistant), J T Ward (cotton machine operator), A Astley (treasurer). Middle row – J Costley (spinner), J Hunter ('professional'), J Yates (weaver), W Astley (weaver). Front – T Gibson (iron-moulder's dresser), SA Warburton (master plumber), A Matthews (picture framer). Jimmy Costley scored Olympic's winning goal against the Old Etonians (2–1) and Alf Warburton, their captain, is said to have observed on receiving the Cup: 'It'll have a good home, and it'll ne'er go back to Lunnon.' He was right. It would be another 18 years before the tournament was won by a London club – and by then the original trophy had been spirited away for ever by a thief.

① The first international, Scotland 0, England 0, Glasgow, 30 November 1872: drawings by W Ralston and published in *The Graphic* two weeks after the match. The dress and vigour of a famous occasion are nicely captured by this charming and deservedly popular woodcut. It was once kept at Twickenham, according to one authority, in the belief that it illustrated Rugby Union's formative days. It also emphasised that the art of football-making had not been perfected. Early balls often lost air and shape.

② Balance sheet for the first international in London – England 4, Scotland 2, Kennington Oval, 8 March 1873. The most expensive item is food.

3

FOOTBALL: A PROFESSION 1885–1900

Professionalism rolled up on football like a huge black cloud in an otherwise blue sky. Everyone could see it coming, but few were sure whether it would plunge the game into darkness or simply cast a passing shadow. Its arrival, however, was inevitable.

The clubs of the north, deeply smitten by the FA Cup, saw nothing wrong in profit and success, nor in paying a man for doing his job. They saw football as something more than an innocent diversion, a way of housing healthy minds in healthy bodies, and there was only one road they could take. It led them away from the south's cherished concept of amateurism – and came near to splitting the game in two.

The conflict lasted about six years. It began with a team from a Lancashire valley-town employing a couple of Scottish players to help them make a dramatic tilt at the Cup in 1879; and it ended on 20 July 1885 when the FA formally legalised professionalism. The formation of the Football League three years later was a natural sequel.

They were years of bitterness, division, hypocrisy and confusion – and the FA must shoulder its share on the blame. It shirked its responsibilities for too long and came close to losing its sovereign power.

The first source of the hostility was Darwen, a town cradled in the ridges of the Pennines, a place of more than 50 mills and mean streets, whose population of 30,000 took their pleasure wherever they could find it. Their football club played its part by reaching the quarter-finals of the eighth FA Cup and stretching the Old Etonians to their noble limits. It took three absorbing games at the Oval to settle the issue. The first was drawn 5–5, with Darwen scoring four in the last 15 minutes; the second was drawn 2–2 after extra time; and it was only then, drained after their third journey of 220 miles, that the publicly-funded Darweners were overcome.

Darwen's audacious swipe at Kinnaird and his Old Etonians was important for several reasons. The Lancashire club established the democracy of the tournament. So, the following season, properly responding to northern complaints about the unfairness of playing too many rounds of the Cup at the Oval, the FA grouped entries into regional groups to save time and money.

The presence of two Scottish players in the Darwen side was also highly significant. The club steadfastly denied that Fergie Suter and Jimmy Love – the spirit and backbone of their team – were paid for playing football. But the two men had much better jobs than those they had left in Glasgow, where they played for Partick, and Darwen did not wait long before arranging a benefit for them.

> Footballers at the present time are overdoing the short-passing game. Preston North End played it almost perfectly, but they were giants in skill and also powerful physically. But for the ordinary first-class team it is a mistake. It is harder work for your forwards, there is greater risk of injury, and to overdo passing is to give the defence more time. The game I would advocate would consist of open, swinging play, with pace and vigour. In this way play is more open, keeps opposing backs constantly on the trot, gives your forwards more chance of finding loopholes for a dash, and provides more cause of excitement. I don't want to discount science, but there is room for more of the punch and run style of play with less passing and repassing.
>
> *Fergie Suter of Darwen and Blackburn Rovers, one of English football's first professionals, comparing the game in 1900 with the 1880s.*

Here then were two of the game's first professionals, and it is difficult to accept that the dozens of other Scottish players who soon followed them to Lancashire and Yorkshire were only seeking a change in climate. There was even a proposal by one of the London clubs, just before Darwen travelled south for their first game against the Old Etonians, that 'no side which does not consist entirely of amateurs, as defined by the rules to be drawn up by the committee, be entitled to compete in the Challenge Cup competition'. It was a hand raised in vain against a gathering wind. Scottish players, with their close passing and tactical cunning, were much admired; and the ambitious clubs of England's industrial north beckoned them with generous offers.

Charles Alcock was again among the first to recognise a new and important movement. He wrote:

> There is no use to disguise the speedy approach of a time when the subject of professional players will require the earnest attention of those upon whom devolves the management of Association Football. It will be well for those who have the interest of the game at heart to recognise the existence of a problem that will in all likelihood have to be mastered before long.

More and more Scots moved south, as English clubs discovered that local talent was not enough to provide the success and entertainment which attracted profitable crowds. Rumour abounded and suspicion grew that accounts were being falsified. Official investigation seemed essential.

A new rule was thrown into the stew in 1882. It declared:

> Any member of a club receiving remuneration or consideration of any sort above his actual expenses and any wages actually lost by any such player taking part in any match, shall be debarred from taking part in either cup, inter-Association, or International contests, and any club employing such a player shall be excluded from this Association.

But nothing really changed, and the FA continued to turn a blind eye to the festering problem until late in 1882 when a sub-committee was formed 'to enquire into the rumoured importation and payment of professional players'.

The 'importation' of Scots, of course, was rather more than a rumour. The venerables of the FA had all seen the Old Etonians win the Cup that season by beating Blackburn Rovers – and among the Scots in Rovers' team was one Fergie Suter, who had joined them, gainfully, from Darwen. Kinnaird had special reason to remember him: the treasurer of the FA was playing for the Old Etonians.

The movement against the 'sin' of professionalism began slowly. There were protests and accusations by clubs, but proof was difficult. Accrington were expelled from the FA in 1883 for paying a player; but the first major breakthrough came early in 1884 when, after a Cup game in London, Upton Park accused Preston North End of having hired help. The FA committee met representatives of both clubs at Kennington Oval, prepared to chisel a verdict out of a mass of conflicting evidence. But they had overlooked the courage of one man.

Major William Sudell, Preston's chairman, admitted openly that he paid his players. Sudell was, in effect, the 'manager' of Preston – perhaps the first outstanding member of that uncertain profession – and he made no secret of his ambition to build a side capable of challenging the all-powerful Blackburn Rovers. This, he said, would be impossible without professional players – a common practice. In short, his plea to the surprised committee was self-defence. Preston were dutifully suspended from the Cup for a season.

The issue was in the open at last, but the FA was still divided. Men such as Kinnaird and Alcock were convinced that professionalism was inevitable and should be properly contained by legislation. Against them were men, a strong body, who were still in love with the notion of playing for health and fun. Alcock twice proposed that professionalism should be legalised, but, for a while, the tide of opinion was against him. Rules were even passed which restricted 'lost time' payments to one day a week, obliged clubs to produce receipts for all payments, made it necessary for all suspected clubs and players to prove their innocence and stipulated that only Englishmen could play in the Cup.

Here were repressive measures which goaded the north into action. Late in 1884, 31 clubs met in Manchester and were told it was counsel's opinion that the Football Association had exceeded its powers. A rival organisation to the FA was formed, called the British Football Association, and it seemed that English football was on the brink of even greater chaos.

It proved, in fact, to be the beginning of the end of the row: the threat of secession was the dam-breaker. For another six months there were heated meetings and harsh words, grim warnings and probing questionnaires, tentative resolutions, close votes and lengthy reports. But finally wisdom, or at least basic common sense, prevailed.

Professionalism was legalised on 20 July 1885 at Andertons Hotel in Fleet Street. There were stringent conditions: professionals could only play in the Cup, for example, if they qualified for their clubs by birth or by two years' residence within six miles of the ground. There was still bitterness, and even resistance, especially in the south and in Scotland, which did not sanction professionalism until eight years later. The strong Lancashire clubs even attempted to take over the running of the Football Association and switch its headquarters to Manchester.

A major problem, however, had been solved; but the game now needed a better structure. A season which consisted of friendly matches and a few Cup games was clearly not going to sustain the professional clubs of the north and Midlands. Their hunger demanded something more substantial. The game as a whole, moreover, was in a mess. Friendly fixtures were often cancelled at will, sometimes at the last minute if the weather was poor, or if transport presented a problem, or if players were injured, or if other more attractive opponents had been found. Spectators would arrive at grounds to find them deserted. Fixture cards were not worth the paper they were printed on. Professional clubs with pressing bills sometimes found themselves without a game – and income – for two or three weeks.

Football needed another good idea – and it was provided by a bearded and ample Scot called William McGregor. He was a Liberal of energy and humour, who had left his native Perthshire in his 20s to open a draper's shop in thriving Birmingham. He was no player himself. 'I tried it once when I was very young,' he was to confess, 'and had to take to bed for a week.' But the game intrigued and then captivated him and, after watching several other local sides, he was drawn to Aston Villa; and Villa and McGregor rose to prominence together.

McGregor was a natural leader, a man who loved to be involved, and his expanding contribution to the game was made as an umpire, district organiser, charity worker, Villa committeeman and as an FA stalwart who, after early misgivings, threw his considerable weight behind the cause of professionalism. He was among the first to recognise that football had a new and urgent need for an organised system of regular fixtures involving the best clubs in the country. There was a baseball league in the United States; but McGregor's real inspiration was much closer to home. Cricket's County Championship had begun in 1873, just a year or so after the birth of the FA Cup, and McGregor was convinced that its format would also work for football.

McGregor spent nearly a year championing and refining his idea and then, with a small but influential body of support behind him, he wrote a letter to just five clubs on 2 March 1888:

> I beg to tender the following suggestion . . . that ten or twelve of the most prominent clubs in England to combine to arrange home and away fixtures each season . . . my object in writing at present is merely to draw your attention to the subject, and to suggest a friendly conference to discuss the matter more fully. I would take it as a favour if you would kindly think the matter over, and make whatever suggestion you may deem necessary.

The immediate response was lukewarm. There were suspicions that the authority of the FA might be undermined; there was concern about expense and there was inevitably disagreement about which clubs should be invited to take part in the league.

But it took only two meetings to put the show on the road. The first was at Andertons Hotel on 22 March 1888, on the eve of the Cup final between West Bromwich and Preston North End, and the second at the Royal Hotel, Manchester, on 17 April which may be regarded as the birthday of the Football League. Twelve clubs were formally invited to be members – six from Lancashire: Accrington, Blackburn, Bolton, Burnley, Everton and Preston North End; and six more, broadly, from the Midlands: Aston Villa, Derby County, Notts County, Stoke, West Bromwich Albion and Wolverhampton Wanderers.

No southern club received an invitation because there was no professional football south of Birmingham; but the south showed little interest and certainly did not feel aggrieved. Membership of the League was set at £2 2s a year, every club was obliged 'to play its full-strength team in all matches' and McGregor was duly named as its first chairman.

> Next to being a City Alderman, one of the most pleasurable things of this life must be to have a seat on the board of the English Football Association or to be a leading member of some other leading Association body. There is no doubt that these big-wigs take full advantage of the various outings, feeds etc, etc, yet perhaps, after all, it is but natural.
>
> Athletic Journal, *1890.*

There were teething problems – fixtures, contracts, division of profits, discipline and lines of authority – but it was clear to most that the family of the Football Association had a strapping new member and that the professional player had an important new platform. The FA was the parent authority, but the League lived as a self-contained body within it. As the indefatigable William Pickford (FA president 1937–8) was to write: 'The power of the League strengthens the Association and the authority of the Association safeguards the League.'

> I made my first appearance (at an FA Committee meeting) on 5 November 1888. I remember it well. Up two flights of stairs to an upper set of rooms at 51, Holborn Viaduct, London, overlooking Farringdon Street. There was a room with one long table in it, reached through the office, and a tiny waiting room. The hour of meeting then and for some years was 5·45pm There was no late train back to Bournemouth so I had to stay overnight. After sampling various hotels north of the river I stayed, generally, near to the L & SWR station at Waterloo to catch the early morning newspaper train. I did this for years in order to be at the office as soon after 9am as possible, for having had the previous afternoon off I did not like to ask more favours. It was not at all a happy experience being knocked up by a night porter out of a sound sleep and having a hasty breakfast in a cold and

deserted room, and then travelling in an unheated compartment for several hours. In the very cold weather one could get a tin footwarmer from a railway porter for twopence, and that helped, but very soon I used to take a rug also. Major Marindin told me that he used to put his feet in a solicitor's brief bag and tie it above his knees when travelling in winter.

William Pickford in A Glance Back at the Football Association Council 1888–1938.

The first programme of League matches took place on 8 September 1888, five games in all, with Preston scoring the very first League goal in their 5–2 victory over Burnley before a crowd of 6,000. And Preston continued as they started. Major Sudell had made good his promise to build the best side in the country, and they won the FA Cup without conceding a goal and the League championship without losing a match. They were extravagantly praised and one writer of the time described them as 'the most perfect, the most consistent team in the history of the game'. Perhaps he was right; the game was young. But Preston were well named The Invincibles.

Other clubs were to emerge before the turn of the century. Sunderland – 'the team of all the talents' – won the League championship three times in four years, Blackburn Rovers re-emerged to win the Cup in successive seasons, West Bromwich Albion reached the final five times in a decade, and Aston Villa saw out the Victorian era by winning the League title five times in seven years, the Cup twice and completing the Cup and League 'double' in 1897.

Aston Villa even managed to win and lose the Cup in the same year. They beat West Bromwich Albion 1–0 in the first final to be held in the great natural bowl of the Crystal Palace in 1895. But, later that summer, Villa allowed the famous trophy to be exhibited in the shop window of William Shillcock, a football and boot manufacturer of 73 Newtown Row, Birmingham. A fortnight later, on 11 September 1895, it was stolen. Anxious crowds gathered outside the shop, police investigation was thorough and a sizeable reward of £10 was offered for the trophy's return. But the 'little tin idol' was never seen again. Its fate is still a mystery, although 63 years later, in 1958, an octogenarian claimed he had melted it down for counterfeit coins.

Villa had insured the Cup for £200 and it was proposed that this sum should be used to provide a replacement in gold. It was decided, however, that the next trophy should be 'as nearly as possible like the old cup', and this was provided by Vaughtons Ltd at a cost of £25. And Villa were fined that exact sum.

There was, however, one amateur club which flourished in this new world of the professional. They were called the Corinthians. N Lane 'Pa' Jackson, the assistant secretary of the FA and an unyielding opponent of professionalism, had been increasingly concerned by Scotland's early supremacy on the international field; and, as public school and university men formed the backbone of the England side, he reasoned that if they had 'plenty of practice together they would acquire a certain amount of combination'. The outcome was the formation of the Corinthians in 1882 and, over the next quarter of a century, they won themselves a remarkable place in the history of the game.

They were amateurs to a man, who played regularly for other clubs, mostly in the London area, but when they pulled on the white shirt of the Corinthians they stood apart. They were hugely successful as a team, with their dashing artistry, progressive passing and intelligent manoeuvring, but they were much more than that. They were a symbol of fair play and selflessness. They stood for an ideal. They championed the highest standards of sportsmanship. And as one Austrian international was to observe after the Corinthians had visited Vienna:

> I remember how they walked onto the field, spotless in their white shirts and dark shorts. Their hands were in their pockets, sleeves hanging down. Yet there was about them an air of casual grandeur, a haughtiness that was yet not haughty, which seemed intangible. And how they played!

The Corinthians gave the south something to be proud of between the decline of the old amateurs and the arrival of professionalism in London. They would surely have won the FA Cup but for one of their original rules: 'The club shall not compete for any challenge cup or prizes of any description.' At their best, they were certainly a match for the finest professional teams. Blackburn Rovers beat Queen's Park, Scotland's best side, in 1884 to win the FA Cup for the first time – and then lost 8–1 to the Corinthians. Bury beat Derby in the final of 1903 by a record margin of 6–0 – and Bury, with all but one of the same side, lost 10–3 to the Corinthians. Twice, too, against Wales in 1894 and 1895, England sent out a side consisting entirely of Corinthians. They were not always consistent, because their best players were not always available and, when they did start competing in the FA Cup in 1922, the halcyon period of the amateur was over. But to this day the word 'Corinthian' still has rare meaning.

The last years of the 19th century saw rapid change and progress. England won the fledgling Home International Championship six times in the decade which followed the formation of the League. The last of the old controls on professional players, who had been tied by birth and residence, were swept away. The FA

Amateur Cup was introduced to give the eclipsed amateur a new incentive and to stimulate the love of football for its own sake. The south grasped the nettle of professionalism, with Royal Arsenal bravely leading the way. The penalty kick was introduced and the prospering League took on a Second Division.

The popularity of the Cup was also greater than ever. Men even saved all year round – contributing weekly to 'Cup final outing' clubs – in case their team gave them the unmissable chance of 'going up for the Cup'. Their Slate Club paid for travel, admission, fluid, pork pies and everything else that was part of doing things properly. Meanwhile, the aldermen of the FA now sat 'in council' instead of on a committee. They were ready for the new century.

FA Cup

Year	Date	Winners	Runners-up		Venue	Attendance	Referee	Entries
1885	4 April	Blackburn Rovers 2	Queen's Park	0	Oval	12,500	Major Marindin	116
1886	3 April	Blackburn Rovers 0	West Bromwich Albion	0	Oval	15,000	Major Marindin	130
Replay	10 April	Blackburn Rovers 2	West Bromwich Albion	0	Baseball Ground	12,000	Major Marindin	
1887	2 April	Aston Villa	West Bromwich Albion	0	Oval	15,500	Major Marindin	126
1888	24 March	West Bromwich Albion	Preston North End	1	Oval	19,000	Major Marindin	149
1889	30 March	Preston North End	Wolverhampton Wanderers	0	Oval	22,000	Major Marindin	149
1890	29 March	Blackburn Rovers 6	Sheffield Wednesday	1	Oval	20,000	Major Marindin	132
1891	25 March	Blackburn Rovers 3	Notts County	1	Oval	23,000	CJ Hughes	161
1892	19 March	West Bromwich Albion	Aston Villa	0	Oval	25,000	JC Clegg	163
1893	26 March	Wolverhampton Wanderers	Everton	0	Fallowfield	45,000	CJ Hughes	183
1894	31 March	Notts County	Bolton Wanderers	1	Goodison Park	37,000	CJ Hughes	155
1895	20 April	Aston Villa	West Bromwich Albion	0	Crystal Palace	42,560	J Lewis	179
1896	18 April	Sheffield Wednesday	Wolverhampton Wanderers	1	Crystal Palace	48,836	Captain W Simpson	210
1897	10 April	Aston Villa	Everton	2	Crystal Palace	65,891	J Lewis	244
1898	16 April	Nottingham Forest	Derby County	1	Crystal Palace	62,017	J Lewis	213
1899	15 April	Sheffield United	Derby County	1	Crystal Palace	73,833	A Scragg	235
1900	21 April	Bury	Southampton	0	Crystal Palace	68,945	AG Kingscott	242

①

②

③

④

① Big reward: no response. The sum of £10 should be compared with the average weekly wage of a footballer in 1895 (£3 in season, £2 in summer), the average worker's wage (£1) and the price of admission to a game (6d). More than 60 years later it was claimed the first FA Cup had been melted down to make counterfeit coins.

② The Birmingham shop, at 73 Newton Row, from which the original FA Cup – the 'little tin idol' – was stolen on 11 September 1895. William Shillcock, the proprietor, wrote later: 'It was an incident which seemed to me at the time a great and unprecedented calamity. I pictured myself a ruined man. I seemed to see myself a hated individual – to see my business boycotted. What was this heinous offence of which I was guilty? Why, I was the man who lost the English Cup. It was on view at my establishment when the Villa won it in 1895, and apparently it was looked at with envious eyes by a festive Birmingham burglar. He and his colleague – for there must have been at least two – adopted time-honoured methods. They removed a portion of the shop roof, and the Cup disappeared, and has not since been heard of. I am not joking when I say that I believed that incident was destined to ruin my connection with football, but happily such has not been the case. But you see that I shall ever be a man with a record unique in the annals of football.' From *The Book of Football*, 1906.

③ NL 'Pa' Jackson, founder of the Corinthians and one of the busiest and most dedicated of the game's second wave of early legislators. The finest of his many ideas was that if public school and university players, the backbone of England's side, had 'plenty of practice together they would acquire a certain amount of combination'. His spur was the embarrassing success of Scotland against England – and his reward was the creation, in 1882, of a precious new dimension to the English game. The Corinthians were mightily successful but, more importantly, they became a shining symbol of fair play and sportsmanship. The word 'Corinthian' still has a noble ring. Jackson, a polished and unyielding champion of the amateur game, became a member of the FA committee in 1879, honorary assistant FA secretary in 1881, founder secretary of the London FA in 1882 and FA vice-president in 1895. He was an author, editor and journalist and one of the founders of the Lawn Tennis Association.

④ Corinthian programme: evidence of their strength – and the increasing commercial interest in football. Sheffield Wednesday won the FA Cup in 1896 and were one of the top six professional clubs in the country, but they lost 2–0 to the Corinthians at the Queen's Club in south west London. The Corinthians were amateurs to the last man, but they knew how to raise funds. Two of the advertisements mention the Corinthians. Note, also, the advertisements for embrocation and cherry brandy: new attention was being paid to simple remedies for strains and bruises – and tonics for energy and warmth. Football was developing a profitable 'spin-off' industry.

①

OFFICIAL MATCH CARD.

Marlow. *1 Goal, allowed 2 F.6 off side*

(*Royal Blue and White quartered.*)

M. H. ROUTLEDGE.

F. T. HANDSOMBODY.   G. MORTON.

J. SPINDLO.   J. ELLERTON.   E. SHAW (capt.)

W. DAVIS.   J. W. JANES.   G. H. JACQUES.   E. G. HATTON.   C. A. SHAW.

E. M. TRINGHAM.   C. D. HEWITT.   G. O. SMITH.   W. F. STANBOROUGH.   E. M. JAMESON.

E. C. BLISS.   C. WREFORD BROWN (capt.)   E. F. BUZZARD.

W. U. TIMMIS.   E. H. BRAY.

B. K. R. WILKINSON.

(*Dark Blue, Maroon and Pink Stripes.*)

Old Carthusians. *2 Goal allowed*

Referee : CAPT. W. SIMPSON (Royal Welsh Fusiliers).
Linesmen : MESSRS. H. C. PLATT & J. STARK (Referees' Association).

Maidenhead v. Chesham, in Kidwell's Park, immediately after this Match.

" ADVERTISER " PRINTING WORKS, MAIDENHEAD.

②

③

① The Invincibles of Preston North End, 1888/9: a unique picture. The presence of Morton Peto Betts, top right, an FA committeeman, gives this fading team group a place on its own. Betts scored the only goal in the first FA Cup final (Wanderers v Royal Engineers, 16 March 1872) – and (contemporary reports vary) either Jack Gordon, front left, or Fred Dewhurst, front row, fourth from left, scored the first League goal of all (Preston v Burnley, 5–2, 8 September 1888). This Preston team won the first League championship without losing a match, and completed the first League and FA Cup 'double' by winning the Cup without conceding a goal. Major William Sudell (back row, fifth from left) was both Preston's chairman and manager – the first outstanding member of a precarious profession. Sudell was also the leading force in the fight for professionalism, the man who proposed the title 'The Football League' and the League's first treasurer. MP Betts, the

outsider in the group, was a member of the FA committee which launched the FA Cup and international football, and played for England himself (v Scotland 1877). Betts used a pseudonym, AH Chequer, in the first FA Cup final because of a connection with another club, Harrow Chequers, in an earlier round. Back row (left to right): J Woods, A Robertson, RA Howarth, G Drummond, W Sudell, J Trainer, R Holmes, J Graham, MP Betts. Front: J Gordon, J Rose, J Goodall, F Dewhurst, S Thompson. John Goodall was the leader and star of the side, England's centre forward (14 caps) and a man described as 'the pioneer of scientific professional play'. Later he played for Derby County, and Derbyshire at cricket, and was often referred to as 'Johnny Allgood'.

② Match card for FA Amateur Cup semi-final, 1897. Old Carthusians won by two goals ('one decidedly offside') to

one (two given offside) – and went on to beat Stockton by 4–1 in a replayed final. Old Carthusians were the first winners of the FA Amateur Cup (1894) and, against Marlow, they included four full internationals, Smith, Stanborough, Wreford Brown (who is said to have coined the word 'Soccer' and was later an FA vice-president) and Wilkinson.

③ Winston Churchill, on his own admission 'an insignificant subaltern', with the winners of the 4th Hussars Squadron Challenge Shield in Bangalore, India, 1897. Polo was Churchill's game but, as Prime Minister during the Second World War, he quickly appreciated the role of football as a morale-raiser. For the wartime international between England and Scotland (2–0) at Wembley, 4 October 1941, Churchill was accompanied by seven Cabinet members. Football also made a major contribution to Mrs Churchill's Aid to Russia Fund.

① FIFA mark the centenary of the International Board, 1886–1986. The minutes of the first meeting, reproduced here on the cover of *FIFA Magazine*, are recorded under a Scottish letterhead; and Joseph S Blatter, general secretary of FIFA, reflects in the magazine: 'It is to the Board's credit that its way of functioning has often been questioned as well as its decisions. But how many changes would football have undergone if the International Football Association Board would not have incessantly and coldly rejected submitted novelties with a characteristic British tenacity?' The International Board is the guardian of football's Laws and any proposed alteration must receive a threequarter majority at its annual meeting in June. FIFA has four votes and the four British Associations have one vote each.

② The first FA tourists: a mixed representative team of professionals and amateurs visited Berlin, Prague and Karlsruhe in 1899. Four games were played, all won, with 38 goals scored and four conceded. Back row (left to right): J Cox, GS Sherrington (FA vice-president), GG Taylor (Corinthians), Wreford Brown (Corinthians), CJ Hughes (FA Council), WH Waller (Richmond), ED Brown (Clapton), JW Crabtree (Aston Villa and England), CW Alcock (FA vice-president, former FA secretary), Stanley-Briggs (Clapton), PA Timbs, E Chadwick (Burnley). Front row: GS Wilson (Corinthians), WI Bassett (West Bromwich and England), J Holt (Reading and England), P Bach (Sunderland and England), J Rogers (Newcastle), Fred Forman (Nottingham Forest). William Isiah 'Billy' Bassett (5 feet 5½ inches) and John Holt (5 feet 4½ inches) were two of the smallest men in English football; but Bassett was regarded as one of the finest wingers of his day and Holt, despite his lack of inches, was a centre half renowned for his jumping ability and tenacity. Bassett later became a celebrated and long-serving chairman of West Bromwich Albion and an FA councillor. Philip Bach became chairman of Middlesbrough, a member of the Football League Management Committee and an FA councillor. Fred and Frank Forman both played for Nottingham Forest and England, the only two brothers from the same professional club to have played together for England, with Frank becoming a Nottingham Forest committeeman for more than 50 years.

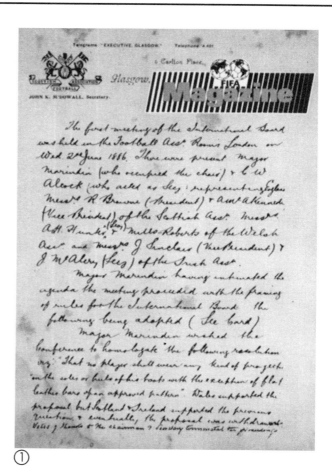

①

②

4

PEACE AND WAR
1901–22

The Cup knew where it stood on the first day of the 20th century: its life was well ordered. It had belonged to the patrician south for a decade and, from then until the end of the old century – a period of 18 years – it had lived with the professional yeomen of the north and Midlands.

Change was coming, however, and it came at the start of an age of enormous expansion which was also to see international football establish itself as the highest plateau of the game all over the world. The formation of the Fédération Internationale de Football Association (FIFA) in 1904 pointed football towards a new future and eventually, of course, the World Cup. FIFA's establishment filled a need. The growth of the game demanded regulation.

But, in the beginning, it was the Cup which gave football its competitive drive and, more than anything, inspired a love of the game among the English which they carried like missionaries to almost every inch of the map. English sailors exported the game to Brazil, cotton men to Russia, businessmen to Argentina, engineers to Spain, railway builders to Uruguay and Embassy staff to Sweden. Intrepid Scots, too, carried the word; and settlers, tourists, teachers, students and servicemen by the thousand also played their part.

The Cup, meantime, prepared to make a little journey of its own – back to its home town of London. And its timing was again inspired, because football, before the turn of the century, had split the country neatly into two. The playing standards of the south had fallen so far behind the professionals of the north and Midlands that many believed the gap would never be bridged.

What movement towards professionalism there was in the south was muddled and often veiled. Royal Arsenal (later Woolwich Arsenal) led the way in 1891, and were immediately barred from all tournaments by the London Association. Millwall and Southampton were next, two years later, and this was followed by the formation of the Southern League as a rival to the Football League. But the absence of Arsenal, who had now joined the Second Division of the Football League, was a serious blow to its standing. The Southern League was never more than a junior partner.

The north regarded the first hesitant steps towards professionalism in the south with amusement and even scorn. But in 1900 Southampton reached the final by way of a steep and rocky road: they beat Everton, Newcastle, West Bromwich Albion and Millwall before losing to Bury in the final. It was a powerful blow for the south. Its renaissance was under way and, 12 months later, Tottenham Hotspur stressed the point again in the best way possible – they became the first southern club to win the Cup since the days of Kinnaird and the Old Etonians.

Spurs had turned professional on the Monday before Christmas in 1895 and they won the Southern League championship in 1900 with the nucleus of the side that went on to bring the Cup back to London. They were rather patronised at the start of their run, but one writer who referred to 'Jack and his master' – Tottenham undoubtedly being Jack – would have been well advised to study the north London club's team. It included five Scots, two Welshmen, an Irishman and three Englishmen from above the Trent.

Spurs won the Cup in 1901, moreover, by beating the old Invincibles of Preston, Bury who were the Cup holders, Reading, West Bromwich who had reached the final five times and – by 3–1 in a replay at Bolton – Sheffield United who had nine full internationals in their side. The *Sheffield Telegraph* declared that United were 'manifestly outplayed' and the *Sheffield Independent* added that Tottenham had won with 'skill, pluck and keenness which showed that although the Cup has gone to a region which for long has not known it, it has fallen into worthy hands'.

But Tottenham's triumph was more than a trumpet blast for the south. It is still the only time the Cup has been won by a club from outside the Football League since its formation in 1888. Part one of the final, a 2–2 draw at the Crystal Palace, was watched by 110,820 spectators, which dwarfed the previous best of 73,833 (1899) and was a world record which stood until 1913. It is also doubtful if Tottenham's celebrations have ever been matched.

The party began as Lord Kinnaird presented the trophy and appears to have lasted for the best part of three days. The crowd was so dense when Spurs got back to north London that, according to one report, 'you could have walked on their heads'. There were fairy lights, Chinese lanterns, fireworks, horns, confetti, ostrich feathers, prancing processions, two bands, an 'animated picture show' of the final two games, a party for the players at which they honoured 'woman and wine' – and also, on the following Monday and Tuesday, two Southern League games against Luton and Kettering, the first won by Spurs, the second drawn. It said much for their stamina, and even more for the huge popularity of the Cup.

In the last dozen years there has been a great change in the character of the paid player. We now see him able to take his position in the best of company, and would have no hesitation in asking a lady to take a seat with him in his saloon. Why, it is a fact that the Manchester City team on our recent journey to London for the final of the English Cup, surprised the occupants of a station they were leaving by singing, and that too quite musically, 'Lead, Kindly Light'.

William (Billy) Meredith in Association Football and The Men Who Made It, *by Alfred Gibson and William Pickford, 1906.*

Football's format and nature fitted in well with the needs of social and industrial life. The game's professional structure appealed to the working man and its simplicity attracted children who could play happily in park and street. It was already a significant dimension of urban existence. But it was also a period of death and greed, rift and dissension for the game. The work of the Football Association was rarely tranquil or untroubled.

The Ibrox disaster of 2 April 1902 confronted the FA with a new and grim reality: it was, then, the worst tragedy in the history of the game. Six minutes after the start of that year's international between Scotland and England, a wooden stand split and collapsed under pressure from a swaying crowd and hundreds fell, one on top of another, through a 70-foot hole. Twenty-five people were killed and more than 300 injured; although the match was eventually resumed (and drawn), it has never counted as a full international. It was re-staged a month later at Villa Park and the proceeds, around £1,000, were given to the Disaster Fund. The FA contributed another £4,000 and worked closely with the Scottish FA as it met every claim for damages – which did much to unite the two bodies after years of barely disguised mistrust that went all the way back to their early differences over professionalism. Very quickly, too, the FA became a limited company as a protection against personal liability.

In a period of rapid development of organised labour that led to the birth of the Labour Party, the professional players followed suit and formed a Union in 1899. It claimed the right to bargain and freedom of contract for its members, but it was a poor, unrepresentative body to begin with: the League and the clubs knew they had its measure and the aldermen of the FA believed that their own ability and machinery could settle all disputes. The Union foundered and all but died, its life weakly sustained by a few pounds tucked away in a bank account, and it took them another 10 years to establish their collective strength.

The FA set a maximum wage of £4 a week (double that of the average skilled working man) for season 1901/02 but this meant an immediate proliferation of undercover payments by some of the greedier clubs. The FA made several attempts to find an answer to the thorny problem, even suggesting a sliding scale of wages, but its competence in this field was aggressively challenged by the League. And, in 1904, the FA wilted under the pressure and agreed that the League should be responsible for all financial matters between clubs and players. It was a significant moment in the history of the English game.

But the FA felt obliged to act when, a year later, Sunderland sold Alf Common, a talented forward, to Middlesbrough for £1,000: the first four-figure transfer fee and a major sensation. The FA decreed that from 1 January 1908 there would be a limit of £350 on transfer fees. The clubs had plenty of time to devise ways of cheating and this they did so successfully that the rule was quickly recognised as worthless. It lasted three months.

The Players' Union found a new heartbeat in 1907, led from the front by Manchester United's Charlie Roberts, their captain and centre half, a strong and articulate man who had learned much about life from steelworkers and trawlermen in his native north-east. The FA gave the Union its formal blessing in 1908 and its consent to a match between Manchester United and Newcastle United in aid of Union funds.

The easing of one problem, however, always seemed to be followed by the arrival of another. The Players' Union considered becoming members of the General Federation of Trade Unions, which might have meant industrial action on behalf of other workers. The FA, the League and the clubs were uniformly horrified at the prospect and the leaden weight of all their authority fell heavily on the Union. The players, in turn, threatened to strike and the clubs armed themselves with lists of uncommitted footballers who would have been willing to keep the 1909/10 season afloat.

The players did not have one voice or opinion, though, and compromise was reached before the brink. The authority of the FA was accepted and the Union was again recognised; but while the players emerged with a better financial package, they had made no progress towards the freedom they wanted. They would have to wait 50 years and more for that.

There were, by now, 400 professional clubs and 6,000 professional players; but they were mightily outnumbered by 12,000 amateur clubs and 300,000 amateur players. The professionals' contribution to the popularity and development of the game was still growing rapidly, however, and this was openly and often fiercely resented by many old-guard amateurs including, of course, the redoubtable 'Pa' Jackson. Their voice was strident, their attitude intractable; and it led to the 'amateur split' which lasted from 1906 to 1913.

These champions of a lost era cared little for innovation, commercialism and the increasing power of the game's tradesmen. The final indignity, it seemed to them, was an FA resolution that County Associations should affiliate the professional clubs within their areas. Most counties happily accepted the proposal, but Surrey and Middlesex, the heartland of the amateur game, decided enough was enough. They would not open their doors to unwanted guests.

The 'split' followed. A rebel body defiantly called the Amateur Football Defence Federation – soon to be renamed as the Amateur Football Association – was formed and its broad object was to make a stand against the 'corruption' of the game. It did not stand a chance. The self-exiles found they were expressively cold-shouldered, both at home and abroad, and the quality of their fixture lists deteriorated alarmingly. They were not taken seriously, and both their support and playing standards declined.

This was inevitable from the moment that Frederick J Wall, who had succeeded Charles Alcock as FA secretary, made it clear that the breakaway clubs and their players would not be able to play 'with or against' clubs and players under the jurisdiction of the FA; and this meant, among other things, no FA Cup and no Amateur Cup. It is surprising that the division lasted seven years but, in the end, it only reinforced the authority of the FA.

Wall took over from Alcock in 1895 and found himself with a difficult act to follow, but by the early years of the 20th century his eye for detail, his urbanity and his stamina had earned him great respect. He was a lawyer, an experienced administrator at club and county level and, in his younger days, he had been a useful, if not outstanding, goalkeeper. He held the job for 39 years and, like Alcock before him, he helped guide the Association and the game through a long period of growth and change.

There is no trace of the slipshod, the sloven or of the least irregularity about the machine. It runs on oiled wheels, and is as well regulated and as accurate as Big Ben itself. There is a metal clip ready whenever two or more documents relating to the same subject need to be kept together. Everything is docketed, dated, scheduled and indexed in the most prosaic and business-like manner. Anything that the most urgent councillor may want to put his hands on is producible at a moment's notice. No speck of dust is allowed to remain long enough in evidence to collect a germ, and the Council have hardly vacated their seats after leaving the tidy chamber a litter of shreds and loose documents than it is at once attacked by some member of the staff whose duty it is.

Frederick Wall on life at the Football Association's headquarters at 104 High Holborn, London, 1902–10.

But the FA did not always have a clear view of the road ahead. It certainly had no early vision of the growth of international football, and a letter from the Dutch association in 1902 suggesting European unity, an international championship and uniformity of the laws in all countries was met with cool indifference. A year later the French suggested a European federation and received this remarkable reply: 'The Council of the Football Association cannot see the advantages of such a Federation, but on all matters upon which joint action was desirable they would be prepared to confer.'

The FA's attitude to this new dimension of the game was blinkered at best, and monumentally insular at worst. An FA team had visited Germany in 1899, the Corinthians had been to South Africa, and Sunderland and Southampton had also played abroad. But, essentially, when the FA talked about international football it was referring to the British Home Championship. The need for a broader structure became so evident, however, that Wall was instructed to arrange a conference in England. But this was something the rest of Europe had heard before and, on 21 May 1904, they took things into their own hands.

In answer to Berks and Bucks FA, the Council decided that there could be no objection to a player with a wooden leg taking part in the game, provided he did not play in a manner dangerous to his opponents.

Minute 21 of FA Council meeting, 1907.

Representatives from Belgium, Denmark, France, Holland, Spain, Sweden and Switzerland met in Paris – and, with accord, they founded the Fédération Internationale de Football Association. A few FA men were surprised that something so progressive had been achieved without their help; but a committee, under Lord Kinnaird, was quickly appointed to review the new situation and early in 1905 an international conference was at last held in London at which the FA formally approved the existence of FIFA.

Doubts persisted about FIFA's definition of amateurism and its policy on the laws of the game, and there were regrets that the FA had not taken an active interest right from the start. But the FA quickly made up lost ground when a powerful delegation attended a FIFA conference in Berne in the summer of 1906. The senior association became a member of a bigger family and DB Woolfall, a Lancashire man and the FA's treasurer from 1901–18, was elected president. He held the post for 12 years and his shrewdness helped FIFA establish itself on solid and democratic lines.

There were murky waters ahead. England and the other British nations withdrew from FIFA for four years after the 1914–18 war, refusing to play against Germany and her allies, and there was even talk of forming a new international organisation. There was to be another, much longer, period in which the FA stood outside FIFA's door; but that, like the World Cup, belongs to a later chapter.

New powers were emerging in the professional game. Liverpool won their first League championships in 1901 and 1906 and twice again soon after the Great War; and Manchester United were champions for the first time in 1908 and again in 1911 and Cup-winners for the first time in 1909. And, while Blackburn Rovers had long ago left an indelible print on the Cup, it was not until 1912 and once more in 1914 that they won the League – the first and last time they were to manage to do so.

But the outstanding club of the period was Newcastle United, who won the League championship three times (1905, 1907 and 1909) and reached the Cup final at Crystal Palace five times in seven seasons, although they won it only once (1910). They were a side of character and rare ability, strong, well-organised and unpredictable, an attraction wherever they played. Their only weakness seemed to be an aversion to the Crystal Palace itself. The turf there was thick and strong and perhaps it did not suit United's smooth patterns in the way their own fine surface did at St James's Park; but, whatever the problem, Newcastle never won a game on the south London ground. Even their one triumph in a final, over the doughty Second Division men of Barnsley, was completed in a replay at Everton. How Tyneside celebrated! Led by a pipe band, the team moved through the main streets of Newcastle in eight landaus – with the elusive Cup held high.

It was the last time that particular pot – the second FA Cup – was competed for. The FA discovered its design had been extensively copied in Manchester and it was decided that the trophy should be presented to Lord Kinnaird to mark his

21 years as FA president.

Fifty guineas were earmarked to buy a third FA Cup – and dozens of designs were submitted by leading silversmiths from all over the country. Messrs Fattorini and Sons got the job and this Bradford firm, founded by a travelling pedlar who had arrived in England at the time of the Napoleonic wars, produced the familiar and handsome trophy which is still the star of every FA Cup final. Its first winner in 1911, properly, was Bradford City – the only time this Yorkshire town has been involved in the Cup final.

The years just before the Great War were a little golden age for the game. The northern clubs were still the overlords of a prosperous Football League, which now consisted of two divisions of 20, but the Midlands recovered its voice in 1913 when Aston Villa won the Cup for the fifth time before a world record crowd of 120,081. There was a record entry of 476 clubs for the Cup in 1914, when the final between Burnley and Liverpool became the first to be watched by a reigning monarch. George V was the patron of the Football Association and, mindful that the Crystal Palace belonged to Lancashire for the day, he wore a red flower in the buttonhole of his overcoat.

This, too, was the last of the 20 finals to be played at the Crystal Palace. Three months later, war was declared and Lord Kitchener, pointing his finger at the nation's young men, urged them to volunteer for a very different kind of contest. There was no conscription to begin with. The defence of freedom was a sensitive matter of conscience and, when the FA permitted the Cup to run its course during season 1914/5 and the League did not stop its own programme, there was a storm of criticism. A letter to *The Times* accused football clubs of actively contributing to a German victory and the Dean of Lincoln, in a letter to the FA, wrote witheringly of 'onlookers who, while so many of their fellow men are giving themselves in their country's peril, still go gazing at football'.

These broadsides were undeserved. The FA had taken advice from the War Office and the League believed that football would provide a precious antidote to the poison of war. The FA, moreover, gave its money to war charities: its resources were £15,000 in 1914, but less than £1,000 by 1918. Except on match days grounds were used as drill centres, and the FA's own headquarters at 42 Russell Square became a storehouse for equipment and welfare goods. Cup and League games proved to be valuable recruiting occasions, with well-known personalities urging fans to enlist and the players themselves signing on in front of stands and terraces.

The response of the people's game was remarkable and, by early in 1915, it was claimed that Association Football and its clubs had encouraged 500,000 men to join the forces. No other section of the community matched this contribution.

Inevitably, attendances tapered away and, as the horror of the war unfolded, football's last major occasion for four years was the 1915 Cup final between Sheffield United and Chelsea at Old Trafford. The crowd was subdued, the day wet and gloomy, and the joyless affair is remembered as the 'Khaki Cup final'. Lord Derby presented the Cup to Sheffield United, and his parting words touched the resolute heart of the game and the nation: 'You have played with one another and against one another for the Cup. It is now the duty of everyone to join with each other and play a sterner game for England.'

The work of the FA almost ground to a halt: football was regional and recreational. Wages and bonuses were forbidden and, when it was discovered that Leeds City had rewarded many guest players for helping them win wartime tournaments, they were summarily disbanded. Football also became subject to Entertainment Tax in 1916, a 'temporary' measure designed to help the war effort which proved so profitable it lasted until 1957.

The war changed football along with everything else. The feeling persisted, unjustly, that rugby players had been more patriotic in 1914, and this was one reason for a small but significant swing away from football. The number of rugby clubs increased and, with many public schools switching to rugby, there was a decline in the number of those gentlemen footballers who had played such a dominant role in the creation of the modern game. There was a new, professional emphasis in football which became, more than ever, a working-class game. It continued to flourish at its amateur level, but the professionals provided its image and momentum. The game boomed, the League expanded and the work and authority of the FA grew healthily. The country would soon know depression, but football provided hope and diversion.

The first three Cup finals after the war were played at Stamford Bridge, the home of Chelsea, which meant the character of the event was immediately changed. Finals at the Crystal Palace, with its little 'flower pot' stands and open areas of grass, had been social occasions. There was room to parade and picnic, although some fans only saw the ball when it was kicked 20 feet into the air. The Bridge, however, was essentially just a football ground, and its big banks enabled everyone to see all the play. The minimum charge was three shillings and, for that, the cloth-capped supporters were offered a football match and nothing much more. And, in keeping with the hardening mood of the period, nothing more was demanded.

FA Cup

Year	Date	Winners		Runners-up		Venue	Attendance	Referee	Entries
1901	20 April	Tottenham Hotspur	2	Sheffield United	2	Crystal Palace	110,820	AG Kingscott	220
Replay	27 April	Tottenham Hotspur	3	Sheffield United	1	Burnden Park	20,470	AG Kingscott	
1902	19 April	Sheffield United	1	Southampton	1	Crystal Palace	76,914	T Kirkham	226
Replay	26 April	Sheffield United	2	Southampton	1	Crystal Palace	33,068	T Kirkham	
1903	18 April	Bury	6	Derby County	0	Crystal Palace	63,102	J Adams	223
1904	23 April	Manchester City	1	Bolton Wanderers	0	Crystal Palace	61,374	AJ Barker	252
1905	15 April	Aston Villa	2	Newcastle United	0	Crystal Palace	101,117	PR Harrower	274
1906	21 April	Everton	1	Aston Villa	0	Crystal Palace	75,609	T Kirkham	280
1907	20 April	Sheffield Wednesday	2	Everton	1	Crystal Palace	84,584	N Whittaker	305
1908	25 April	Wolverhampton Wanderers	3	Newcastle United	1	Crystal Palace	74,967	TP Campbell	348
1909	26 April	Manchester United	1	Bristol City	0	Crystal Palace	71,401	J Mason	361
1910	23 April	Newcastle United	1	Barnsley	1	Crystal Palace	77,747	JT Ibbotson	424
Replay	28 April	Newcastle United	2	Barnsley	0	Goodison Park	69,000	JT Ibbotson	
1911	22 April	Bradford City	0	Newcastle United	0	Crystal Palace	69,098	JH Pearson	403
Replay	26 April	Bradford City	1	Newcastle United	0	Old Trafford	58,000	JH Pearson	
1912	20 April	Barnsley	0	West Bromwich Albion	0	Crystal Palace	54,556	JR Schumacher	410
Replay	24 April	Barnsley	1	West Bromwich Albion	0*	Bramall Lane	38,555	JR Schumacher	
1913	19 April	Aston Villa	1	Sunderland	0	Crystal Palace	120,081	A Adams	457
1914	25 April	Burnley	1	Liverpool	0	Crystal Palace	72,778	HS Bamlett	476
1915	24 April	Sheffield United	3	Chelsea	0	Old Trafford	49,557	HH Taylor	454
1920	24 April	Aston Villa	1	Huddersfield Town	0*	Stamford Bridge	50,018	JT Howcroft	445
1921	23 April	Tottenham Hotspur	1	Wolverhampton Wanderers	0	Stamford Bridge	72,805	J Davies	674
1922	29 April	Huddersfield Town	1	Preston North End	0	Stamford Bridge	53,000	JWD Fowler	656

①

②

MR J. T. HOWCROFT

③

① Bob Crompton, captain of Blackburn Rovers and England – a model professional. Crompton, a full back, was strong enough to have kicked any winger over any stand, but he was also fair, disciplined and an admirable craftsman. Played 528 League games for Blackburn (1896–1920) and 41 matches for England (1902–14). A member of the Blackburn side which won the League championship in 1912 and 1914 – their first and last titles.

② Albert Wilkes, industrious wing half for Walsall, Aston Villa, Fulham and England – and one of the first photographers to specialise in football. Wilkes won five caps for England (1901–2) and played in the tragic match against Scotland at Ibrox in 1902 when a stand collapsed and 25 people were killed and more than 300 injured. A fire destroyed his studio in 1909 and he decided to retire as a player and concentrate on rebuilding his business as 'The Football Photographer' in West Bromwich.

③ Jack 'Jimmy' Howcroft, English football's most respected referee in the years after World War One. A Bolton man, he was noted for his firmness but was also popular with players. 'Howcroft, the greatest of them all,' wrote Billy Walker of Aston Villa and England who played in the 1920 FA Cup final, against Huddersfield at Stamford Bridge, which Howcroft refereed. 'What a referee Howcroft was! A few moments after the teams were out on the field he would walk with the greatest dignity imaginable out into the centre, place the ball and then bow right and left like royalty. There was no rough play when Howcroft was about because the players knew he knew all about it, and that there was no chance of their getting away with anything.'

7th' June 1901.

Sir,

    I have the honour to inform you that I have submitted to The King your letter of the 16th' Inst: and in reply I am commanded to say that His Majesty is pleased to accede to the request contained in it, to grant his Patronage to The Football Association.

    I am Sir,

       Your obedient Servant,

               General.
       Keeper of H. M's Privy Purse.

The Secretary,
    The Football Association.

①

②

① For the first time a ruling monarch – King Edward VII – becomes Patron of the Football Association. An FA request for Royal patronage in 1882 (19 years after the Association's formation) was politely refused.

② History assembled: many of the great figures of the English game are in this earliest picture of the Council of the Football Association, 1905. Standing (left to right) – JW Carter, John Lewis (one of the founders of Blackburn Rovers), WH Haskins, F Styles, J Albert, Nat Whittaker, W Kemp, SA Notcutt, N Malcolmson, WJ Wilson. Seated (left side of table) – RP Gregson (one of the committee which approved professionalism in 1884), John McKenna ('Honest John', an outstanding figure in Liverpool's early history and later the Football League's longest serving president 1910–36), RE Lythgoe, Daniel B Woolfall (first English president of FIFA 1906–18), Frederick Wall (FA secretary 1895–1934), JC Clegg (later Sir Charles Clegg, played for England in first international against Scotland, 1872, and president of FA, 1923–37), Charles Crump (first president of Birmingham FA when formed in 1875), CS Sherrington, CJ Hughes, John J Bentley (member of original Football League Committee, 1888, and League president 1894–1910). Right side of table – WH Bellamy, HS Radford, AG Hines (later FA chairman 1938), Arthur Kingscott (Cup final referee 1900 and 1901 but suspended as treasurer of the FA after controversy over selection of the ball for the 1933 final, a profitable advertisement for the chosen manufacturer), MT Roberts, William Pickford (who served the FA for nearly 50 years and FA president 1937–9), Alfred Davis, William McGregor ('father' of the Football League), GW Simmons.

③ Menu for the Football Association's 50th anniversary banquet in the King's Hall, Holborn Restaurant, London, Monday, 3 November 1913. Fourteen courses build up to Shakespeare's theory about the 'Good life'. A bottle of the claret they drank would now cost £50, the port £80 and the brandy £100.

③

TO ENGLAND
WINNER of FIRST PRIZE
FOR
AT·THE·OLYMPIC·GAMES·LONDON·1908·

THE PARTING OF THE WAYS.

AMATEUR F.A.: "Look here! I don't want to play with you any more; and I'm not going to."
THE FOOTBALL ASSOCIATION: "All right, little man. I dare say I can worry along without you."

③

England, the first Olympic football champions, 1908 – and champions again four years later. England won the Olympic title when football was included in the Games for the first time, at the White City, London, 1908; and England (again representing Great Britain) retained the title in Stockholm in 1912.

① The 1908 winners' certificate: only six teams took part, including two from France, and England beat Sweden (12–1), Holland (4–0) and, in the final, Denmark (2–0).

② The England team which finished first in 1912: back row, left to right – HC Littlewort (Glossop), RG Brebner (Darlington and Chelsea), A Berry (Oxford University and Everton), H Walden (Bradford City), VJ Woodward (Chelsea), G Hoare (Glossop), I Sharpe (Derby County), AE Knight (Portsmouth). Front row – J Dines (Ilford), TC Burn (London Caledonians), E Hanney (Reading). There were 11 entries in 1912, and England beat Hungary (7–0), Finland (4–0) and, in the final once again, Denmark (4–2). Vivian Woodward, England's captain and centre forward at both Olympics, was one of the finest amateur players English football has produced. He played for Tottenham when the north London club was new to League football and White Hart Lane, and then joined Chelsea (1909–15) because it was nearer his home. He would not accept even the cost of his bus fare to matches.

③ Establishment view of 'the split' in 1907. Champions of the amateur game objected bitterly to an FA ruling that all County Associations should permit the affiliation of professional clubs. The rebels, led by the Surrey and Middlesex Associations, decided to break away and form their own governing body – first called the Amateur Football Defence Federation, but later renamed the Amateur Football Association. Unity was not restored for seven years.

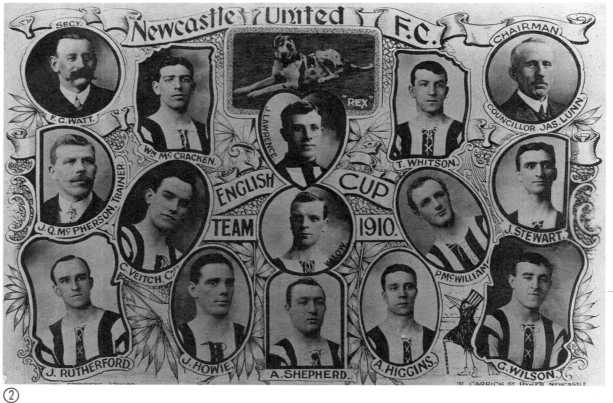

CUP FINAL AT MANCHESTER. "THE WINNING GOAL".

①

②

① Made in Bradford ... won by Bradford. JH Speirs scoring the only goal of the 1911 FA Cup final replay against Newcastle United at Old Trafford. They were playing for a new FA Cup – the third, and present, trophy – which had just been made by a Bradford firm, Messrs Fattorini and Sons. And Bradford City won it in their first and only Cup final.

② Newcastle United: FA Cup winners for the first time, 1910. They were the outstanding side of the first decade of the 20th century, winning the League championship three times in five seasons (1905–7–9) and reaching the FA Cup final at Crystal Palace five times in seven seasons. But they did not win a single game on the south London ground: their one Cup final victory (1910) was gained in a replay at Everton, Newcastle 2, Barnsley 0. They were a side of character and humour as well as quality – the best, perhaps, in Newcastle's history.

③ Nothing to smile about. Billy Minter who scored seven goals for St Albans City against Dulwich Hamlet in an FA Cup fourth qualifying round replay on 2 November 1922 – and still finished on the losing side. Final score: Dulwich Hamlet 8, St Albans 7. His record is one of the least envied: 'The player who scored most goals for a defeated side in the FA Cup ...'

④ Harry Hampton, fourth from left, scored both Aston Villa's goals against Newcastle in the 1905 FA Cup final at Crystal Palace. Hampton – ' 'Appy 'Arry' – was a legendary figure in Birmingham football during the decade before World War One. His style was uncomplicated and muscular: he gave the ball to a winger and then, by any way possible, looked to bully the return into the net – including, if necessary, the opposing goalkeeper. The method worked: Hampton (career 1904–20) and Billy Walker (1919–34) are still, jointly, Villa's leading scorers.

③

④

5

WEMBLEY
1923–33

The Football Association took on a new recruit in 1923. It was 890 feet long, 650 feet wide, 76 feet high and built with 25,000 tons of concrete, 2,000 tons of steel and 500,000 rivets; and it was constructed on a north London hillock at a cost of £750,000. They called it the Empire Stadium.

Here was the mightiest stadium on earth, a source of curiosity, as well as pride, throughout England and a cause of immediate concern to the 4,500 people who lived in the pleasant and then rural suburb of Wembley, six miles from Marble Arch. It was larger than the Colosseum in Rome, that wonder of the ancient world, and, according to one excited and obviously well-read official of the time, it was 'as big as the Biblical city of Jericho'. It was also a gamble by the FA, who needed a new home for the Cup final. Stamford Bridge had only been a temporary residence, its capacity was too small, and the FA considered going back to the Crystal Palace which was free at last of its war duties. Discussions on the daunting cost of this project were under way when another suggestion was put to the FA.

A plan to hold a British Empire Exhibition had been floated before the war and, by early in 1921, with royal support and government backing, things were moving quickly. Wembley had been chosen as the site and the FA were told that the centre-piece of the exhibition would be 'a great national sports ground'. Were they interested?

Frederick Wall visited Wembley Park and found a golf course, a metropolitan railway station and the ruins of one man's dream. Sir Edward Watkin had chosen the Park, long before the war, as the site for a tower that would be 1,150 feet high and a major tourist attraction. He saw it as a rival to the Eiffel Tower in Paris, but discovered the best he could hope for was another version of the Leaning Tower of

Pisa. The foundations proved to be chronically unstable and Sir Edward, beset by costs and disappointment, simply abandoned the project – known for a generation as 'Watkin's Folly'. The legs of the tower stood where the pitch is now, while the lift-shaft is buried beneath the royal entrance.

Wall and a quickly convened Ground Committee were impressed by the site and the plans, and so, in May 1921 – seven months before the Duke of York (later King George VI) cut the first piece of turf – the FA signed an agreement to stage the final at Wembley for the next 21 years. It was an act of faith, courage and far greater significance than the FA or anyone else realised. It made the building of the stadium possible, it ensured the staging of the British Empire Exhibition and it changed the whole character of the suburb of Wembley.

The exhibition project had raised little enthusiasm or money to begin with. The memory of the war was still fresh and Wembley, in any case, was considered 'too far out of town' to attract people in big numbers. But, when it was revealed that a new 'home' for football would be at the heart of the exhibition, the attitude of the country suddenly changed. Money and guarantees flowed in. The people of Glasgow alone raised £105,000 in two months. The general appeal fund was over-subscribed.

Shortage of time meant the opening of the exhibition itself had to be put back a year, but this did not affect the plan to hold the 1923 Cup final on its new stage. The stadium rose swiftly and dramatically on the north London skyline, a marvel in reinforced concrete, its two domed towers representing pride and confidence. It took 300 working days to build, from first sod to final rivet, and it was completed with just four days to spare. The last act was a safety test by a uniformed battalion of infantry. They lined up on the terraces and, for nearly an hour, with rhythmic enthusiasm, they stamped their heavy boots – a basic examination of the stadium's structure. It survived.

The official capacity of Wembley was 127,000, and Frederick Wall declared with pride that 'at last we have a ground for everybody who wants to see the Cup final'. The finalists were Bolton Wanderers and West Ham United and, on the morning of 28 April 1923, the Wembley authorities ran up the flags, buttered the buns, adjusted their best bibs and tuckers and opened up their 104 turnstiles. The day was fine, a London club was involved, the mighty white-walled stadium had aroused intense curiosity and there was no limitation on numbers by ticket. The FA and Wembley waited confidently.

And the people came . . . enough to fill two Wembley stadiums. By one o'clock the ground was full and, by 1·45, when the gates were eventually closed, nearly 200,000 were inside; tens of thousands more were still queuing at the turnstiles, flowing up the broad approach to the stadium, spilling out of trains or jammed in traffic. Every available policeman from every station in north London was frantically summoned but the situation was beyond mortal law and order. Turnstiles were climbed, gates broken down and walls scaled. The pressure inside built up from the rear and middle sections of the stands and terraces, and thousands of those who had arrived early and settled down in their seats found themselves swept forward. Some even offered attendants money to find them a route to safety. But the only people with a choice were those at the front, and more and more escaped from the crush by spilling onto the pitch.

The playing area was soon black with people, but somewhere in the middle the Grenadier and Irish Guards' band bravely played on. One newspaper reporter claimed that 'police were whirled away like twigs in a Severn spate' and another, having closely observed the scene through his field glasses, wrote: 'How could people bring women into such a crush?'

King George V arrived at 2·45 and Frederick Wall, in his book *Fifty Years of Football* (published in 1935), recalled that he said to His Majesty immediately: 'I fear, Sir, that the match may not be played. The crowd has broken in. The playing-ground is covered with people.'

As His Majesty caught a glimpse of the massed crowd at the end of the tunnel leading to the Royal Box he said: 'Whose fault is that?' I felt I could only bow and smile. What could I do or say? The King, seeing the predicament, simply said: 'What do you want me to do?' I replied: 'If Your Majesty will kindly go to the Royal Box we will see what we can do to clear the ground'.

As soon as King George was seen there, every face was turned towards him. The great assembly remained silent and still while the band played the National Anthem. I felt that there was a possibility of order. I murmured to myself: 'The King will save the situation'. The police made an effort to clear the ground. The teams were brought out ... all to no effect. His Majesty waited ... then, as if by the magic of telepathy, I saw the eyes of thousands of trespassers directed towards the Royal Box. Then, all at once, the people grasped their opportunity of seeing their King at closer quarters ... they surged in the direction of the Royal Box. They could not turn back. They passed within a few yards of His Majesty ... and each person, having had his own private 'close-up' strolled on through the tunnel which led from the stadium to the exhibition ground. Tens of thousands passed by in this way, the playing area was

①

②

① The first football book – in the FA's library at Lancaster Gate. The first minute book of the Association covered the period 1863–75, measures 8×6 inches and has been rebound in green (although the original covers in black still exist).

② The Charles Alcock Scroll, 1881. It was the year in which referees were first mentioned in the Laws of the game and the year in which the FA first moved to a regular home, in Paternoster Row ... but Alcock's contribution to the development of football was already recognised. A silver inkstand, candlesticks and 300 guineas was a remarkable testimonial.

①

②

③

④

⑤

① Lord Kinnaird: football's answer to WG Grace – unless Grace was cricket's answer to Kinnaird. Arthur Fitzgerald Kinnaird (1847–1923) was football's first outstanding personality, an earthy, fearless, rumbustious player and a much-loved administrator who once said: 'I believe all right-minded people have good reason to thank God for the great progress of this popular national game.' Played in nine FA Cup finals (five won) for the Wanderers or Old Etonians and was an FA administrator for 54 years (33 as president). *Vanity Fair* supplement: 'Men of the Day', Number 2289.

② FA commemorative badges, worn by players and officials on their blazers

at the turn of the century. These are all for home games against Scotland: 1899 (Villa Park), 1901 (Crystal Palace), 1903 (Bramall Lane, Sheffield) and 1905 (Crystal Palace).

③ To the Football Association – with love from the Sappers. The Royal Engineers made a major contribution to the early development of the FA and football. They set standards in technique, organisation and sportsmanship.

④ John Goodall's England cap for the matches against Scotland 1888–95 – a run which began when he was helping Preston North End complete the first League and FA Cup 'double'. NL Jackson, founder of the Corinthians, first

proposed that caps should be awarded in 1886. The first colour was royal blue, but later a tassel was added, colours varied and three lions replaced the rose.

⑤ Winners only: FA Cup and FA Amateur Cup medals. Top (left to right): FA Amateur Cup – Clapton (1907), Walthamstow Avenue (1952), Clapton (1924). Centre: FA Cup – Wanderers (1877), Blackburn Rovers (1886). Bottom: FA Cup – Sheffield Wednesday (1907), Wanderers (1876), West Ham United (1940 – War Cup).

G. O. SMITH, Corinthians,

①

C. B. FRY, Corinthians,

②

CB Fry and GO Smith: two great talents – and both were born in Croydon in 1872. The artist's impressions of them were used in the Herriot series of 'Famous Footballers' by William Collins and Sons, circa 1905, one of the earliest postally-used series of cards.

① Gilbert Oswald Smith – recognised as the finest centre forward of his time and described by RC Robertson Glasgow as 'the greatest hero of them all'. Played football for Oxford University, Old Carthusians, Corinthians and England (20 caps, 1893–1901) – and CB Fry, in his role as author, wrote of Smith: 'A genius in football he was.

Like all geniuses he rose on stepping stones of his real self by taking infinite pains in terms of his natural gifts ... what made him was his skill in elusive movements, his quickness in seeing how best to bestow his passes, his accuracy and his remarkable penetrative dribbling ... he was as straight and hard a shot as I have ever met except perhaps only Steve Bloomer of Derby County, on one of Steve's special days. GO's was every day.' Smith was also a first-class cricketer for Surrey, a headmaster and an author.

② Charles Burgess Fry – first claimant for the title 'England's finest all-

rounder'. Footballer, cricketer, athlete, Rugby Union player, classical scholar, schoolmaster, author, editor, journalist, Parliamentary candidate, sailor and grandee: his range, achievements and style set him apart. He scored more than 30,000 runs (including 94 hundreds) for Surrey, Sussex, Hampshire and England; he was a full back for the Corinthians, Southampton (1902 FA Cup final) and England (one cap, 1901); he held the world long jump record (1893) and was a fine sprinter; he played Rugby Union for Oxford University and Surrey; and he won Blues for football, cricket and athletics. He also claimed to have turned down the throne of Albania.

gradually cleared and those who had seen their King were gratified and satisfied.

When the King came to one of the finals some years later I ventured to remind him of the opening of the stadium and added: 'Had you not been here, Sir, the match would not have been played'. His Majesty, with a spice of fervour, answered: 'I know it. I know it would never have been played'.

King George stood patiently for nearly an hour, watching chaos turn slowly into order; and he would have admired the firm discipline of the police in general and one officer and his horse in particular. Other mounted policemen did a wonderful job, but only one horse was white. His name was Billy, and he and his rider, constable George Scorey, were always at the heart of the confusion on the pitch. 'Energetic, undaunted, resourceful, at once decisive and good-tempered,' observed the *Daily Mirror*, 'he dominated the crowd by the sheer force of his personality, and wherever he appeared he received willing obedience.' The handsome, 13-year-old Billy nosed his way into history: the first final at Wembley is remembered, above all, as 'the White Horse final'.

The game itself started 45 minutes late and was a cramped and difficult affair with spectators, shoulder to shoulder, forming a human wall all round the touchlines and goallines. The ball and players regularly disappeared into the crowd, which often had to be asked to pull back from the lines. Sometimes, too, the ball would hit a spectator and stay in play. The teams did not even leave the pitch at half time, which was reduced to five minutes. Surprisingly, perhaps, the final was completed without mishap. Bolton became the first club to win the Cup at Wembley (2–0) and that most graceful of centre forwards David Jack, who later moved to Arsenal, became the first player to score a goal in the stadium.

The official attendance was given as 126,047, with gross receipts of £27,776. The FA's share was £6,365, of which they refunded nearly £3,000 to ticket-holders who had not been able to claim their seats. They were the only figures which could be given, but they reveal nothing of a chaotic occasion which stopped only just short of disaster.

Who was to blame? The FA quickly issued this statement: 'Under the agreement between the Football Association and the British Empire Exhibition the arrangement for the sale of tickets for admission to the stadium, the provision of police and the control of the crowd generally were in the hands of the British Empire Exhibition. The Football Association deeply regrets the incidents and inconvenience caused to the public . . .' The *Bolton Evening News* was not so sure:

'The FA are merely begging the question. The public look up to the FA, and indeed to every football body, to keep faith with them, and such a debacle as this will do unquestionable harm to the game.'

Pointed questions were asked in the House of Commons, the Home Office enquired into the management of crowds on big occasions ('It is safe to leave the matter to football's governing bodies,' it concluded) and the FA decided that admittance to all future Cup finals would be by ticket only. The British Empire Exhibition authorities carried the can. Nobody, however, raised doubts before the game and nobody could have known that the marriage of the Cup final and the game's new Mecca would be so successful.

> My greatest honour came when I was chosen to play for England against Scotland in the first international between the two countries at Wembley. It was curious how I found out I was to play. I was walking home from business when a friend stopped me in the street. 'Congratulations, Charlie,' he said, 'and may the ball run kindly for you.' Very surprised, I asked him what it was all about. 'Don't you know?' he asked. 'You're England's centre forward at Wembley. I've just heard it over the air.' The first announcement had been made by radio. I boasted only a 'cat's-whisker' set in those days and, more often than not, it failed to work.
>
> *Charles Buchan on hearing about his last selection for England in 1924. From* A Lifetime in Football, *1955.*

It was the first major trophy that Bolton, who were one of the Football League's founder-members, had won; but they were to become the outstanding Cup side of a decade which saw familiar names emphasise the strength of the north but also, significantly, a robust challenge from the south. Bolton won the Cup again in 1926 and 1929, and in the three finals they used only 17 players. They were a steady and dogged side, nerveless and wholesomely Lancastrian, for whom Wembley held no fears. As Jimmy Seddon, their captain and centre half, a Bolton man through and through, was to say later: 'We always kept our heads.'

Newcastle won the first all-ticket final in 1924, just a few days before the British Empire Exhibition was opened by the King, and the old warriors of Sheffield United and Blackburn Rovers soon enjoyed the ritual of victory at Wembley as well, but two new names were also to be inscribed on the Cup: Cardiff and Arsenal. They met in the 1927 final and Cardiff's 1–0 victory, which meant the trophy left England for the only time in its history, was heard by the nation – the first final to be broadcast by BBC Radio. Cardiff's star was at its highest in the 1920s, a side of zeal and cunning which reached at least the quarter-finals five times in seven seasons.

It was Arsenal, however, who had really arrived as a fresh power in the land. The north London club had been one of the flyweights of the First Division, but they added a rounded but dapper Yorkshireman to their pay-roll in 1925, and Arsenal and football were never the same again. His name was Herbert Chapman.

Chapman's modest career as a player with half a dozen clubs was notable only for the yellow boots he wore; but, as a manager, he influenced the game like no other before or since. He shaped modern football management and the two clubs which benefited most from his genius were Huddersfield Town and Arsenal. At each club Chapman built a side good enough to win the League championship three seasons in a row – a feat which only Liverpool (1982–4) have matched.

Huddersfield was a club beset by financial problems and erosive frustration in a town devoted to rugby league when Chapman took over in 1920. He sought and bought with care and, two years later, with a team that had a heart of granite, he guided them to Cup victory over Preston in the last final to be played at Stamford Bridge – the first and only time Huddersfield have won the trophy. Chapman then led them to their first two League championships (1924 and 1925) but, before they began their third successful tilt at the title, he was gone.

Arsenal had beckoned and Chapman recognised their potential immediately. The Highbury club was short of pedigree, but it was a club close to the heart of one of the world's great cities and success would mean high reward and acclamation. He was right on both counts. Chapman wasted no time. He bought Charlie Buchan from Sunderland for £2,000 plus £100 for every goal he scored in season 1925/6. The craggy Buchan, a master footballer who was then 33 years old, did both clubs a favour. He scored 19 League goals and two more in the Cup, which earned Sunderland another £2,100 and helped lift Arsenal, who had just avoided relegation the season before, into second place behind Chapman's old club Huddersfield.

Buchan's arrival at Highbury and a modification of the offside law in 1925 enabled Chapman to give Arsenal the most successful years in their history and, at the same time, to alter the face of English football. The change in the offside law was a calculated and overdue attempt to encourage attacking play. The offside trap was constipating the game, with Bill McCracken, Newcastle's brilliant Irish international full back, widely recognised as its principal exponent, although he had retired by the time the rule change came into operation. It was not uncommon for games to be riddled by 30 and even 40 free kicks for offside.

The International Board, meeting in Paris on 13 June 1925, decided that the answer to the problem was to reduce from three to two the number of defenders who could put an attacker offside. It was a simple change, but its ramifications were profound and the controversy it created rumbled on for years.

Nets everywhere billowed with goals. In the last season under the old offside law 4,700 goals were scored in the Football League. In the first season after the change there were 6,373. Vulnerable defences were embarrassed, records tumbled, pace became more important than skill. Crowds relished the glut of goals, but more perceptive observers saw a sudden decline in the quality of the game. One problem had again been replaced by another.

It was Chapman, inevitably, who produced a solution. He changed the role of the centre half. Instead of using him as an all-purpose player in midfield, Chapman plugged the hole in his defence by employing his centre half as an extra defender. The 'stopper' had arrived. Other teams followed and, like Arsenal, they withdrew an inside forward to make good the link between attack and defence. The standard 2–3–5 formation (two full backs, three half backs and five forwards) became 3–3–4.

Chapman properly takes the credit for evolving and refining the system, but the idea was Charlie Buchan's. Right at the start of the 1925/6 season he urged his manager to use Jack Butler, Arsenal's centre half, simply as a defender. Buchan raised the idea at every team meeting for the next five weeks, but Chapman continued to demur – until Newcastle, inspired by the firefly artistry of Scotland's Hughie Gallacher, beat the north London club by 7–0 at St James' Park in early October. Chapman capitulated immediately. He and Buchan had a long talk before catching the train back to London – Chapman openly describing the proposed system as 'your plan, Charlie' – and they decided to make the radical change for the very next game. Two days later, Arsenal beat West Ham at Upton Park by 4–0.

That was the start of Arsenal's revival. Chapman's nose for talent, his unorthodoxy as a businessman, his instinctive understanding of men's strengths and weaknesses, his grasp of tactics, his ability as a motivator, his steely belief in discipline and his flair for publicity were all single-mindedly directed at making his club the greatest in the land. Chapman built his side with courage and money: there were no half-measures about the man. Buchan retired in 1928 to become a highly respected journalist, and Chapman replaced him by spending £10,890 – the first five-figure transfer fee – on David Jack who had already made his mark on the history of the game with Bolton. Chapman also invested £9,000 on a little midfield genius called Alex James. Preston saw it as good business. Chapman knew he had a bargain.

Jack, that most elegant of predators, and James with his buttoned-down sleeves and baggy shorts, fitted smoothly into the Arsenal pattern. Cliff 'Boy' Bastin, a phlegmatic prodigy from the rolling acres of Devon, and Joe Hulme, perhaps the fastest man in English football and a celebrated Middlesex cricketer, were on the wings – men who could pick the lock of most defences. And behind them were men of the quality and fibre of Herbie Roberts, a red-haired giant who was bought from Oswestry to become the most talked-about centre half of his day; Bob John of Wales, a wing half to count on, who played for the club for 15 years (1922–37); Tom Parker, bought from Southampton to be the club's captain and right back, straight of figure and purpose, never quick in action, but somehow never late on the ball; and the immaculate Eddie Hapgood, known as the 'Ambassador of Football', a left back of such polish and confidence that he was sometimes accused of conceit.

Arsenal's first major success was the FA Cup in 1930 and, almost symbolically, it was Huddersfield they beat by 2–0 in a final of invention and breathless action. Chapman watched his old club hand the baton on to his new one. And Wembley, in turn, was watched by the huge German airship the *Graf Zeppelin*, which cast its shadow over the stadium – a dark symbol of another rising power.

Chapman's team crushed on. They were League champions five times (1931, 1933–5 and 1938), runners-up in 1932 and third in 1937; and they won the Cup again in 1936 and were beaten finalists in 1932. They were the sovereign power of English football, their success envied and even resented by all but their own, their methods studied and copied but never emulated. Here, at last, was London's riposte to the north and Midlands. The Football League was middle-aged and, for the first time, the capital had a champion club.

It needed the Cup, however, to remind Arsenal that they were only mortals. They were beaten 2–0 by Walsall of the Third Division North at Fellows Park in the third round on 14 January 1933. It is said the voices of BBC newsreaders trembled with surprise when they delivered the score to the nation that evening. And at Highbury, where Arsenal's reserves were playing, the result was greeted with roars of laughter. They thought it was a leg-pull. Walsall's win was instant history, arguably the most celebrated act of giantkilling in the story of the Cup, and it split the Black Country town into two quite separate factions: those who had seen the match and those who hadn't. The right to say 'I was there' conferred new status in the community and, over the years, the constant repolishing of the facts have given them a lovely patina.

> Of all the players, I think I felt the effects of the defeat most deeply. At 20 years old, I was the youngest of the side, so perhaps this was only natural. On my way home to my lodgings that night, in the Underground Railway, I felt positively suicidal. Visions of the Arsenal goals that might have been

rose up before my eyes; hopes that the events of the afternoon had been nothing but an evil nightmare would delude me for a brief moment, only to be banished away by the cold, grim reality. Walsall 2, Arsenal 0. Nothing could change those figures.

Cliff Bastin on Arsenal's FA Cup defeat by Walsall in 1933. From Cliff Bastin Remembers, *1950.*

'The Swift' of the *Walsall Times* was there, of course, and we should accept his report as a fair and honest account of how Arsenal and their internationals, who were on their way to the first of three successive championships, were squarely beaten by a club 54 places below them in the League:

Is it true? Is it not a dream that I shall awake and smile at? No! Even now I cannot quite grasp that my little Walsall – the team I gaze upon so anxiously every week – has had the cheek, the impudence, to wipe the great and mighty Arsenal out of the English Cup and send them back to the Metropolis bewailing a whipping at the hands of an insignificant club in the Northern Section of the Third Division. And yet – it must be true, for I saw them with my eyes – I watched Alsop and Sheppard do the things that made their names famous throughout the football world – heard the mighty roars that followed these actions. Indeed, did I not so far forget my complete impartiality as to give vocal praise as the Saddlers left the field – triumphant!

Here is the essence of the Cup. It is beyond logic, beyond measure, beyond price.

A year later, before Arsenal looked towards Wembley again, Chapman was dead. He insisted on watching his third team (with a 16-year-old called Denis Compton on the left wing) play in a biting wind at Guildford, a chill turned to pneumonia and he died in the first week of 1934. But Chapman was a man who was ahead of his time, and his reputation and many of his ideas still endure. The Football Association knew him as a painfully direct critic, but also as a powerful ally. He railed at the Association about many subjects, from floodlighting to numbered shirts, but he was among the first to applaud a scheme for coaching public schoolboys, to whom he offered all the facilities at Highbury.

Chapman was also put in charge of England's team before their first international with Italy in Rome in 1933 – the first time a professional manager had been granted such royal responsibility. He gave the players a talk before the game, misplaced the key to the dressing room at half time and seemed content enough with a 1–1 draw. But it was not, of course, Chapman's team. England sides were then the creation and property of the FA's International Selection Committee – a fact which was certainly not to Chapman's liking, as he wrote soon afterwards:

> The idea may be startling, but I would like the English selectors to choose 20 of the most promising young players in the game and arrange for them to be brought together once a week under a selector, a coach and a trainer. The object of this would be to enable them to go out and practise with definite schemes planned . . . If this proposal were carried out, I think the result would be astonishing . . . I may say I have no hope of this international building policy being adopted . . . But it is on these new lines that some of the Continental countries are working.

Chapman's lack of confidence was wholly justified: there was 'no hope' of anyone even considering his suggestion. The 14 members of the International Selection Committee were happy to back their intuitive opinion against the game's professionals and millions of fireside selectors. But they did not make things easy for themselves. Selectors who belonged to clubs showed open preference for their own players; the final choice from four or five candidates for one position would be decided by vote; each position was considered separately, with little thought given to the shape and balance of the side as a whole; and one good club game (especially if it was a Cup tie) could win a man selection, one bad game could mean international doom. Teams were stuck together with optimism and wrapped in confusion.

In 1924, for example, 37 players figured in five internationals, and not one took part in all five. The first international at Wembley (a 1–1 draw with Scotland) took place on 12 April that year and, for an obviously auspicious occasion, the selectors altered their team in seven positions – and then made nine changes for the next game. Nineteen different goalkeepers were tried between 1923 and 1933. The *Athletic News* reported in 1930 that in the 11 seasons after the Great War 66 players had won just one cap each. Among them, remarkably, was Clem Stephenson, whose verve and subtlety inspired Huddersfield to their three successive League championships in the 1920s. Charlie Buchan described Stephenson as 'a great schemer and tactician who brought the best out of his colleagues' – but Stephenson played against Wales on a snow-covered pitch at Blackburn in 1924 and was never again asked to represent his country.

England did well enough against Continental nations of variable quality, but the definitive test was still Scotland and the Home International Championship. The record speaks for itself. England won only six of their 20 matches against

Scotland between the wars (1920–39) and, in the same period, they were outright winners of the Home Championship on only three occasions. Scotland's attitude to their game against England may well have been a contributory factor. The fixture, for the Scots, was a form of national expression, an extension of the country's character, a match which struck chords of deep pride and identity. Victory over England mattered above all – and one triumph still stands above all.

Scotland beat England in 1928 with such disarming ease and style that from Wick to Dumfries it elevated the fixture to cult status. Scotland won by 5–1 at Wembley and their players have been known ever since as the 'Wembley Wizards'. Their forward line, none of whom stood more than 5 feet 7 inches, is still recited like a litany: Jackson, Dunn, Gallacher, James and Morton. They strung passes together like beads on a string and, on a wet and uncertain surface, they allowed the heavy England players nothing more than a minor supporting role. The *Glasgow Herald* spoke for a nation: 'The success of the Scots was primarily another demonstration that Scottish skill, science and trickery will prevail against the less attractive and simpler methods of the English style ...' It was an opinion that had echoed down the years.

The first World Cup, held in Uruguay in 1930, might have provided the quality of English – and British – football with a relevant examination; but the Home Associations had by then once more withdrawn from FIFA over the old and vexed subject of amateurism. FIFA wanted amateur players to be compensated for the loss of regular earnings – 'broken time' payments – but the FA believed this would tempt amateurs to put sport before work and open the door even more to 'shamateurism', thinly veiled professionalism and under-the-counter rewards.

FIFA had already forced the organisers of the Olympic Games to accept the principle of 'broken time' payments by threatening to withdraw its members from the 1928 tournament in Amsterdam. The four Home Associations, however, did not yield: they withdrew from the Olympics and resigned from FIFA. The decision was conveyed to FIFA in a tartly worded letter from Frederick Wall which informed the game's ruling authority: 'The great majority of the Associations affiliated with FIFA are of comparatively recent formation, and as a consequence cannot have the knowledge which only experience can bring.'

One important link was maintained – FIFA's representation on the International Board which had been the guardian of the game's laws since 1886. It consisted originally of eight members, two from each of the British Associations, but two FIFA representatives were added in 1913 and their retention after the split guaranteed the continuing authority of the Board and kept an important channel open for future negotiation. It was not until 1948, however, that the British

Associations rejoined FIFA and by then they had missed three World Cups – 1930 in Uruguay, 1934 in Italy and 1938 in France. 'Our isolation was in no sense splendid,' observed Stanley Rous, who became secretary of the FA in 1934. 'It was a matter for regret and a constant cause of difficulty.'

FA Cup

Year	Date	Winners		Runners-up		Venue	Attendance	Referee	Entries
1923	28 April	Bolton Wanderers	2	West Ham United	0	Wembley	126,047	DH Asson	548
1924	26 April	Newcastle United	2	Aston Villa	0	Wembley	91,695	WE Russell	555
1925	25 April	Sheffield United	1	Cardiff City	0	Wembley	91,763	GN Watson	548
1926	24 April	Bolton Wanderers	1	Manchester City	0	Wembley	91,447	I Baker	570
1927	23 April	Cardiff City	1	Arsenal	0	Wembley	91,206	WF Bunnell	552
1928	21 April	Blackburn Rovers	3	Huddersfield Town	1	Wembley	92,041	TG Bryan	544
1929	27 April	Bolton Wanderers	2	Portsmouth	0	Wembley	92,576	A Josephs	520
1930	26 April	Arsenal	2	Huddersfield Town	0	Wembley	92,488	T Crew	525
1931	25 April	West Bromwich Albion	2	Birmingham	1	Wembley	92,406	AH Kingscott	526
1932	23 April	Newcastle United	2	Arsenal	1	Wembley	92,298	WP Harper	529
1933	29 April	Everton	3	Manchester City	0	Wembley	92,950	E Wood	543

Progress

1866 Duration of game fixed at 90 minutes.
1872 Corner kick.
Size of ball defined (average circumference 27–28 inches).
1874 Shinguards.
1875 Crossbar replaces tape.
Ends changed only at half time, not with every goal.
1878 Whistle.
1882 Two-handed throw-in.
1891 Umpires (two) become linesmen, referee has full control.
Penalty kick.
Goal-nets.

1925 New offside law.
1933 Players numbered 1–22 in FA Cup final.
1939 Numbering compulsory in Football League.
1951 White ball.
1955 Floodlighting for competitive games.
1958 Electric undersoil heating at Everton.
1965 One substitute allowed for injured player – and for any reason one year later.
1981 First artificial pitch by League club – Queen's Park Rangers.
1986 Two substitutes.

April 29, 1923

SUNDAY PICTORIAL

CUP FINAL CHAOS THAT WAS NEARLY A DISASTER

PAGE 5

Stadium Gates Stormed by 100,000 People—Pitch Overrun and Play Interrupted.

DOCTORS TREAT CLOSE ON 1,000 CASUALTIES

Broken Limbs and Serious Injuries in Great Rush and Struggle With the Police.

THE KING'S PART IN SAVING THE SITUATION

How near was chaos to disaster at Wembley yesterday, at the first Cup final to be played in the arena of the new Stadium, can be judged from the toll of casualties revealed last night.

Nearly 1,000 people were treated for injuries, there were sixty hospital cases, and many broken bones. There were 200,000 people on the ground, estimated to hold 127,000. Barricades were stormed, and 100,000 people rushed through. For forty minutes unmanageable thousands surged over the pitch.

When the King arrived he gave directions which relieved an ugly situation, and—big Police reinforcements being summoned, the pitch was cleared.

Again the crowd burst on to the field, and stopped play for twelve minutes, but it was resumed, and Bolton won the Cup, which was presented by the King.

It was a deplorable opening of the "finest sports arena in the world." It could not cope with the biggest football crowd ever assembled. The F.A. disclaim responsibility for the arrangements, which were in the hands of the Stadium authorities.

①

① Constable George Scorey and 13-year-old Billy – the stars of 'the White Horse final', 1923. Scorey, a former Scots Greys trumpet major, recalled afterwards: 'Funnily enough, I didn't expect to be at the match and I wasn't bothered as I wasn't keen on football. I was in a detachment of mounted police kept in reserve about four miles from the stadium, just in case anything out of the ordinary happened, and I was thinking about my wedding and not about football. About 2.30 we got an order to go to Wembley as soon as possible. We arrived at kick-off time and were given orders to clear the pitch. Clear the pitch indeed! You couldn't see it. I felt like giving it up as hopeless because nobody seemed in charge and I didn't know where to start. Anyway, Billy knew what to do and it was the first time he really behaved himself. He pushed forward quietly but firmly and the crowd made way for him. He answered all my orders beautifully and, although it was hard work, the crowd (and they were good natured) seemed to respect the horse. I told them to link hands and push back, and I remember telling one chap with one leg to get in the goal and stay there.

In half-an-hour the job was done and the match started. I stayed, of course, but I can't remember much about the game. As I say, I wasn't very keen on football.' Billy died on 15 December 1930 at the age of 20.

② Worm's-eye view of Dick Pym, Bolton's goalkeeper, making a save in 'the White Horse final'. There are fans on the roof and straying feet on the pitch.

③ The man who had one of the toughest jobs of all on Wembley's opening day: referee Dave Asson of West Bromwich. He called the captains together after the game had been delayed for 45 minutes and said: 'We are three men in the wilderness. But let's make a start. The game must go on.'

① A rare picture of Herbert Chapman as a player – a modest reserve with Tottenham before starting his managerial career with Northampton in 1907.

② The birth of organised coaching. Herbert Chapman of Arsenal, left, the man who shaped modern football management, talks with GN Foster, a champion of the amateur game, at Highbury, 6 September 1933. They were discussing a coaching scheme for schoolboys, initiated by the Corinthians and sponsored by Arsenal. Chapman commented: 'This scheme has enormous possibilities but unless its scope is extended, a golden opportunity will be missed. The Corinthians' scheme should be extended to cover the whole country.' Chapman suggested that 'working-class youths' everywhere should have professional coaching, and that the FA should distribute a coaching film nationwide and also open a football school. 'I shall consider the scheme has failed,' he added, 'unless the FA can be persuaded to father coaching on a grand scale throughout the country, catering for every class of player.' One month later the FA appointed a seven-man committee 'to consider the desirability of inaugurating instructional classes for boys in Association Football'. GN Foster, a member of a celebrated sporting family, was a former England amateur international and FA councillor. Four months after the picture was taken, Chapman was gone. He died of pneumonia in the first week of 1934.

③

④

When Scotland named their side to play England at Wembley on 31 March 1928, it was criticised for having too many 'Anglos' and the smallest forward line in international history. Scotland, however, won by 5–1 with a performance of legendary brilliance: they strung passes together like beads on a string and, on a wet and tricky surface, they allowed the heavy England players (including Dixie Dean) no more than a minor supporting role. Scotland's players earned immortality as the 'Wembley Wizards' ... and their five goals were scored by two men, Alec Jackson (three) and Alex James (two). Both helped sides built by Herbert Chapman win the League championship three seasons in succession.

③ Alex James of Arsenal, training with his dog 'Gunner' outside Highbury, December 1931. The style was unmistakable: he wore baggy shorts, and his gadfly runs and body swerves often made opponents look ridiculous and crowds roar with laughter. Sir Frederick Wall, after 60 years of watching football, wrote: 'I am confident I have never seen another James. By the deceptive daring of his manoeuvres he makes spectators laugh. Nature's bounty and his own industry have made him the footballer he is. I despair of ever again looking on his like.' James was a Preston player when the 'Wembley Wizards' gave Scotland their finest hour and a half and, after joining Herbert Chapman at Highbury for £9,000 in 1929, he helped Arsenal win four League titles (1931 and 1933–4–5) and two FA Cups (1930 and 1936).

④ Alec Jackson, at 5 feet 7 inches the tallest member of the 'Wembley Wizards' forward line. Debonair and audacious, he was a celebrity off the field as well as on it. His artful finishing and shimmying runs made a telling contribution to Huddersfield's completion of their hat trick of League titles (1924–5–6). Jackson also helped Huddersfield reach two FA Cup finals – but finished a loser in both, against Blackburn Rovers in 1928 and Arsenal (with Alex James) in 1930. He began his first-class career at Aberdeen and ended it at Chelsea. Jackson's admiration of Herbert Chapman never wavered: 'Chapman knew when to blow you up and when to blow you down, when to be the Big Boss and when to be the Family Friend. He was a genius and that's the fact of it.'

(1) 'Dixie' (William Ralph) Dean scoring for Everton in their 3–0 victory over Manchester City in the 1933 FA Cup final – the first final in which players were numbered: Everton wore 1–11 and Manchester City 12–22. The immortal 'Dixie' (centre, white shirt) is often described as the finest centre forward English football has produced: he is certainly a natural starting point for any such argument. Dean was a warrior of 5 feet 10 inches and 12 stone, with a brow and heart of steel, whose place in the history and affections of the game will always be secure. He played for Tranmere, Everton, Notts County and England (18 goals in 16 internationals, 1927–32). He scored 473 goals (including 37 hat tricks) in 502 League, FA Cup, representative and international matches – and, at the age of 21, he scored 60 League goals in season 1927/8, a record which is unlikely to be broken. Dixie died, aged 73, while watching Everton play Liverpool at Goodison Park on the first day of March 1980.

(2) Why is the captain on the left touching his head? Why is the referee carrying a flag? This was the start of an 'international' for deaf and dumb players representing England and Wales at Southampton, 9 September 1925. The Welsh captain is calling 'Heads' and the players would not, of course, have heard a whistle. England won 2–1.

(3) The first FA party to tour Canada leaves Euston en route for Southampton and the CPR liner 'Empress of Scotland', 17 May 1926. The schedule was astonishingly busy by modern standards. Twenty games were played between 24 May and 15 July and all were won. Goals for 105, against 18. Major FA 'missionary' tours of this kind, to South Africa, Australia, New Zealand and then Canada, began in 1910 and one or two were even undertaken in the early 1950s.

(3)

① Howard Baker, an amateur all-rounder from the highest plateau. He was an unorthodox but brilliant goalkeeper who played League football for Everton, Chelsea and Oldham and won two full caps for England. He was an Olympic high-jumper who held the British record (6 feet 5 inches) for 26 years, a discus thrower and hurdler of high note, a water-polo player of international standard and a cricketer for Liverpool CC. He died in 1987, aged 95.

② The Corinthians of 1924. Back row (left to right): EKM Hillary, RG Jenkins, FH Ewer, JG Stephenson, F Hartley, RG Capel-Slaughter. Front row: AG Doggart, AG Bower, JSF Morrison, Howard Baker, CT Ashton. Six of the team won full international caps for England: Freddie Ewer, Frank Hartley (who turned professional with Tottenham when he was 32), Graham Doggart (who scored 160 goals in 170 games for the Corinthians and later became chairman of the FA), Alfred 'Baishe' Bower, Howard Baker and Claude Ashton.

6

CHANGING TIMES
1934–45

English football moved bumpily but complacently through the 1930s, outside the broadening mainstream of the game in Europe and South America but sustained by a lofty conviction that English was best. The decade was tormented by political unrest, undermined by recession, and soured by its dole queues; but football continued to enrich and reassure. The game provided a focus for local pride and its passion answered an emotional need. Its wintry terraces bristled with hope. It touched, still, the heart of the nation.

Arsenal continued to move in a social circle of their own despite the death of Herbert Chapman. Provincial England saw the club as a symbol of the affluence and privileges of London, a club to envy and resent: their team, above all, was the one to beat. But Arsenal were also a powerful stimulant. They set new standards which breached convention and challenged complacency. They dominated the English game, but they also changed it.

The pursuit of success acquired a sharper edge: the game became more competitive, more combative. Higher levels of fitness and commitment were demanded, 'hard' players who left their consciences in the dressing room were a cornerstone of every team, transfer fees continued to spiral upwards and scouting systems at all levels developed a tighter mesh.

Radio and, later, television offered the game an important new dimension. The style – and demands – of the press became more robust. Gambling and the pools widened interest and invited controversy. 'Much as I admire and love the game,' wrote the Dean of Durham to *The Times*, 'I would sooner football died out altogether than it should become the tool of the gambling fraternity.'

English football stood firmly on its own feet, its confidence unbruised, its health strong, its following big and satisfied. But it stood alone. The FA showed no wish to rejoin FIFA, and the press showed little or no interest in the World Cup or anything else outside its own traditional experience. Reality was suspended. The English game kept its eye on the ball . . . a ball which in 1934 was inherited by the son of a Suffolk village grocer.

Stanley Rous succeeded Sir Frederick Wall (knighted in 1931) as secretary of the Football Association and continued an astonishing chain of service by three men. Charles Alcock was secretary for 25 years (1870–95), Wall then held the post for 39 years (1895–1934) and Rous continued for nearly 28 years (1934–62) until he became president of FIFA and one of the most influential men in the history of world football. Their service as secretaries of the FA spanned 91 years. They took the game from the year of the death of Charles Dickens and the start of the Siege of Paris to the year in which the Beatles had their first hit single and the Americans sent a spacecraft to explore Venus.

Rous had been only a moderate player in his village home of Mutford – a goal-keeper by right of height – and after artillery service in the Middle East and study-ing at St Luke's College, Exeter, he became a master at Watford Grammar School. He became a member of the Council of Hertfordshire FA and for eight years was one of English football's most celebrated referees. He officiated in 34 international matches and refereed the 1934 Cup final in which, to the accompaniment of thunder and lightning, Manchester City beat Portsmouth 2–1. By then Rous had already introduced the diagonal system of refereeing which is now universal.

Six days after the 1934 Cup final, Rous was one of six candidates interviewed at 22 Lancaster Gate for the job of FA secretary – 'commencing salary £800 per annum with residence'. Rous knew all the members of the FA Board, but was still disconcerted by the opening remark of its chairman William Pickford: 'The presi-dent [Sir Charles Clegg] is deaf and unlikely to hear your answers, but may ask you questions. Direct your replies to me but don't shout because I have a heart condition and mustn't be upset.'

Rous knew how to make himself understood by lip-readers because, during his time at Watford, he had taught games once a week at a nearby school for the deaf and dumb. So when Sir Charles asked if he had any questions, Rous framed his lips carefully: 'Is the post pensionable?' Sir Charles, to the surprise of his colleague, answered immediately: 'You don't have to worry. Your predecessor was well rewarded.'

'My predecessor? Am I appointed then?' asked Rous.

'Not so fast, young man,' said the FA president. 'It was a slip of the tongue.'

Sir Charles returned home to tell his sister that the new secretary of the FA was 'a nice young chap who was the only one I had any conversation with'. Two months were to pass, however, before Rous received confirmation of his appointment – and the press and BBC Radio knew about it first.

Rous inherited a staff of five who began their day at 10am, carried out their precisely defined responsibilities at an even but leisurely pace and decided what was important and what could safely be delayed or shelved. Rous allowed time to settle in and establish himself but, department by department, he then improved and stream-lined the FA's routine and procedure. Work began at 9am; letters were answered the same day whenever possible and the style of reply became simpler and more helpful; time was set aside for discussion; and Rous himself was accessible and directly involved.

> Before Council meetings the tradition apparently had been for £20 to be given to Sir Frederick Wall so that he and his wife could do the catering. They cut sandwiches the night before, provided the coffee, saved what they could and sent out to a nearby cafe for more cakes if the food ran out. That did not appeal to me as part of the Secretary's job, and I arranged instead for members to eat in the Merchant Navy Club restaurant which adjoined the FA. A full meal there cost only 7s 6d a head, so they ate better for less money and trouble.
>
> *Sir Stanley Rous on Lancaster Gate catering soon after succeeding Sir Frederick Wall as FA secretary in 1934. From* Football Worlds, *1978.*

Courses were developed for referees and coaches (a new idea which had teeth-ing problems before the right format was discovered and certificates were issued) which soon had a beneficial influence in clubs, colleges, schools and youth organis-ations. A County Youth championship was started and instructional books were produced. Rous also remembered that when he refereed the 1934 Cup final he and his linesmen had been obliged to change in an office and later bathe in one of the players' dressing rooms. So Rous wrote a comprehensive guide to Cup final day which covered everything from Royal Box protocol to the duties of the ball boys and ensured, among a multitude of other things, that the referee and his linesmen were properly looked after and accommodated and, like the players, received their medals from the guest of honour. Rous's guide became the standard key to a com-plex day.

Rous also used his expertise to rewrite the laws of the game – a long overdue task. The old codification was disjointed and confusing, a muddle without headings, which cried out for clarity and order. Rous realised he would have to tread softly after mentioning his intention to William Pickford, who had been a member of the FA's Rules Committee for more than 40 years. 'Don't you dare tinker with *my* laws,' Pickford said. 'Don't dare alter the meaning of one of them.' But Rous went ahead, of course, and his clear view of the 17 laws of football was accepted by the International Board in 1938. The simplicity of these laws are one of the enduring strengths of the game.

There were some things, however, that Rous could not change. A picture appeared in a newspaper of the FA secretary wearing a sporty pair of plus-fours at a game. Sir Charles Clegg was quickly in touch: 'I would remind you that Sir Frederick Wall went to matches in a top hat and frock coat.' Rous settled henceforth for a lounge suit and bowler.

England's list of international fixtures grew gently in the 1930s, despite its isolation from FIFA. One or two more games against European nations were played each season and representative teams made regular 'missionary' tours of Australia, New Zealand, Canada and South Africa. And, while none of the home countries belonged to FIFA, Great Britain was allowed to enter the Berlin Olympics in 1936. The Selection Committee was cumbersome and less than impartial; and, although Britain began the tournament as joint favourites with Germany, they never looked like winners. They beat China with difficulty by 2–0 and then lost 5–4 to Poland.

Maurice Edelston, who was 17 and still at school when he was picked for the 1936 Olympic squad, was to observe in later years that those games against China and Poland were among the earliest indications that the rest of the world was 'coming up in the fast lane'. Edelston, who became a much respected BBC Radio commentator, said the two games were 'a nasty blow to our pride and understanding of what the game was all about'.

There had been other pointers. England had suffered their first defeat abroad, losing 4–3 in Spain in 1929, after leading 2–0 at half time – but the *Athletic News* observed stoically that 'the English players did wonderfully well considering the tremendous handicap of playing after our heavy season at home and of renewing their activities in intense heat.' And Austria provided English football with a nasty cultural shock in 1932. The Austrians were widely recognised as the finest side in Europe and were known as the 'Wonder Team'; and, although they lost 4–3 at Stamford Bridge, they played football which charmed a crowd of 40,000 and perplexed their opponents. David Jack was in the England team and he commented afterwards: 'Austria's ball control, positioning and combination were reminiscent of the true Scottish footballer . . . if only they knew how to finish!'

English football's high opinion of itself was not easily bruised, however, and when Italy arrived in London is mid-November 1934, the game was humbly billed as 'the most important football match that has been played anywhere in the world since the Great War'. Italy had just won the World Cup with home help from feverish nationalism and intimidated referees; and England, despite mounting evidence to the contrary, still regarded themselves as the game's natural overlords.

The game was to be played at Highbury and Arsenal's stake in the occasion was increased by the England selectors, who included five of the champions' players in their team: Cliff Bastin, Ray Bowden, Wilf Copping, Eddie Hapgood and Frank Moss. And, when there were two late withdrawals because of injury, the selectors called on two more Arsenal players, George Male and Ted Drake. The reaction of the rest of the country to an England team with seven Arsenal players was mixed: there were sneers and sarcasm and, at worst, double-barrelled abuse. But there was more. Hapgood was made captain for the first time, Arsenal's Tom Whittaker was named as trainer and those who followed the game on the radio found the commentary was provided by Arsenal's secretary-manager George Allison.

Italy lost their mighty centre half Luisito Monti early on with a broken toe and, apparently convinced that his injury was the result of a deliberate kick, the world champions resorted to assault and battery. England, with artful combination and bold finishing, scored three in 15 minutes through Eric Brook (two) and Drake; but, after Hapgood's nose had been broken by an elbow, the game deteriorated into what is remembered as the 'Battle of Highbury'. As Hapgood said later, it was 'a bit hard to play like a gentleman when somebody closely resembling an enthusiastic member of the Mafia is wiping his studs down your legs'. One or two players relished the combat – above all the dark-jowled Copping, whose tackling and shoulder-charging might have won him a medal on a real field of battle.

The Italians simmered down later in the game and, with Giuseppe Meazza scoring twice, England's 3–2 victory proved little. Italy contributed hugely to their own downfall and the reasons, it was to be claimed, were the bonuses – money, a car and exemption from military service – offered their players by Mussolini, who wanted to use the occasion to add to the prestige of his Fascist country. But, despite their fall from grace, Italy's football team did enough to show why they were world champions and would be again in 1938.

Football, along with almost everything else, was affected by the political troubles of the 1930s. Germany, as well as Italy, saw sport as a natural vehicle for propaganda; but so, too, though less systematically, did the British Foreign Office. It was made clear to the FA what countries they should avoid visiting and what countries should always face the strongest side England could muster.

The match against Germany in the Olympic Stadium in Berlin on 14 May 1938 was one of high sensitivity. Germany had swallowed Austria, the world was moving quickly down the path to war and nobody – least of all the FA – pretended they were facing just another game of football. Sport had become another dimension of the game of war.

The England party was told in Berlin that the Germans would stand to attention for the British National Anthem and that in return the England team would give the Nazi salute during the playing of *Deutschland über Alles*. Stanley Rous and Charles Wreford Brown, the old Corinthian who was in charge of the FA party, sought advice from the British ambassador in Germany Sir Neville Henderson. 'When I go to see Herr Hitler I give him the Nazi salute because that is the normal thing,' Sir Neville said. 'It carries no hint of approval of anything he or his regime may do. And, if I do it, why should you or your team object?'

The players had mixed views, but took Rous's word that their decision would decide whether the game was played in a friendly or hostile atmosphere. They gave the salute and, although there was extensive press reaction at home – by no means all against the gesture of diplomacy – the game itself was played in front of a 110,000 crowd which was thunderously noisy but even-tempered. Politics were forgotten for that one sunny afternoon in Berlin. The game was the thing and this England won by 6–3, with 19-year-old Jackie Robinson of Sheffield Wednesday scoring twice.

Hapgood, who had argued strongly against giving the Nazi salute, confirmed afterwards that the incident made England's players 'doubly determined', and described the win as 'one of the finest and most satisfactory' of his career. English improvisation and stubbornness overcame a German side which had been carefully selected, rigorously drilled and methodically prepared. The contest would soon be continued on a larger field.

The FA Cup, meanwhile, was always full to its brim. Year by year, it injected new life into winter, its democracy unruffled, its charm unchallenged, its traditions inviolate, its final act at Wembley still the game's day of days.

It was Arsenal's decade, of course: in their two bleakest seasons they finished third and fifth in the League. But others, too, remember the period with affection. West Bromwich Albion won the Cup and gained promotion from the Second Division in 1931. Newcastle beat Arsenal in the following final with the help of their 'over the line' goal: was the ball out of play when Jimmy Richardson hooked it over for Jack Allen to score? Everton won the Second Division championship in 1931, the League championship in 1932 and the Cup in 1933. Manchester City (1933 and 1934) and Preston (1937 and 1938) reached the final two years in succession, with both sides losing the first and winning the second, Preston with a penalty by George

Mutch only 60 seconds from the end of extra time against Huddersfield.

Walsall were not the only side from below stairs to leave their print on the times. In 1937, heroically, Millwall became the first Third Division club to reach the semi-finals of the Cup. They beat Aldershot, Gateshead, Fulham, Chelsea, Derby County and Manchester City, who won the League title that season. On a rising tide of passion the modest south London club played every tie except the first in their own tight enclosure at Cold Blow Lane – and then, obliged to travel to Huddersfield for the semi-final, they went down narrowly to Sunderland who went on to win the Cup for the first time.

The last word, before the country drew its curtains, put on its gas masks and headed for the air-raid shelters, belonged to Portsmouth. Jack Tinn (with his famous white spats) led them to an 'impossible' Cup final victory over the universally fancied Wolves, who had also finished runners-up to Everton in the League. The Cup stayed in Portsmouth's keeping until 1946.

Sport knew its duty when Neville Chamberlain formally declared war on 3 September 1939: 'The concentration of Britain's whole effort on winning the war makes its continuance undesired and inappropriate,' said the *Daily Mail*. There was none of the well-meant but misguided confidence which allowed football to continue for a season after the start of the Great War. But it was immediately recognised that the game could still make a potent contribution to the war effort: morale and fitness were central to everything as the nation's conscripts prepared to fight the good fight.

The Football Association used its authority and weight in many ways. It cooperated energetically with the War Office and the Board of Trade, the armed forces, Civil Defence, the Red Cross and St John's Ambulance and the Central Council of Physical Recreation. Coaches, trainers and players knocked the nation's young men into combat shape. Nearly 200 football grounds became centres for a Fitness for Service campaign, organised by the FA and the CCPR, in which more than 40,000 took part. The FA, with Stanley Rous tirelessly involved, made a handsome contribution by way of money and effort to many charities.

There was also football: knockout tournaments of every size, district and regional leagues, service competitions, charity matches, representative and international games ... the stream was endless. It all took place on the implicit understanding that it did not interfere with the rather more serious business of winning the war and there were, of course, restrictions. Gates, travelling, wages and bonuses were all limited; but the small print was to be frequently changed.

The standard of the football was variable. So many players were on service duty that clubs often struggled to field full sides – without a 'guest' system the game would have ground to a halt. The big clubs continued to be a magnet for the brightest talents; but for many, it was on with the motley, a mixture of professionals who were stationed locally (or just passing through), local part-timers, youngsters and volunteers who were sometimes conjured out of the crowd shortly before kick-off. Some teams consisted entirely of 'guests'; many of the best players wore different colours week by week and wandering stars appeared in the most unlikely contexts. Players frequently arrived late and programmes, where they existed, were merely declarations of hope. And a few clubs sent out the finest sides in their history. Aldershot of the Third Division, from within the home of the Army, were able to call on men such as Stan Cullis, Joe Mercer, Tommy Lawton, Cliff Britton, Frank Swift and Jimmy Hagan.

Football followers did not like much of what they saw in the early days of the war: they were used to better things. But, as confidence slowly rose, football developed a surer footing. Its standing and worth grew perceptibly and handsome crowds flocked to watch a series of Victory internationals when sanity returned to the world at last. Football during the war had not been, essentially, about trophies and medals. Its role was more important than that. It helped bond the spirit of the nation. And 75 professionals gave their lives.

FA Cup

Year	Date	Winners		Runners-up		Venue	Attendance	Referee	Entries
1934	28 April	Manchester City	2	Portsmouth	1	Wembley	93,258	SF Rous	554
1935	27 April	Sheffield Wednesday	4	West Bromwich Albion	2	Wembley	93,204	AE Fogg	573
1936	25 April	Arsenal	1	Sheffield United	0	Wembley	93,384	H Nattrass	571
1937	1 May	Sunderland	3	Preston North End	1	Wembley	93,495	RG Rudd	563
1938	30 April	Preston North End	1	Huddersfield Town	0*	Wembley	93,497	AJ Jewell	574
1939	29 April	Portsmouth	4	Wolverhampton Wanderers	1	Wembley	99,370	T Thompson	556

①

②

① First impression – Reception at 16, Lancaster Gate.

② The Centenary Room at the Lancaster Gate home of the FA in west London. The panelled room is on the first floor and was fitted and furnished by the Football Associations of Scotland, Wales and Northern Ireland, and the Football League. The painting was presented by the Soviet Union and the trophy is an exact replica of the second FA Cup – the original of which was presented to Lord Kinnaird in 1911 for services to the game. The duplicate was commissioned by Manchester United after they had won the tournament for the first time in 1909 and was presented to JH Davies, the president-chairman of United for 25 years and the man who moved the club to Old Trafford. It was United's copy, however, which helped make the FA decide there should be a new and third trophy – the present one.

①

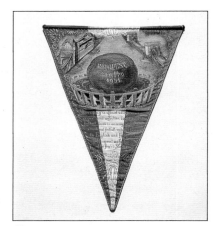

②

① Famous silverware. Back row: FA Vase, FA Cup, FA Trophy. Front: Rous Cup, FA Youth Cup, FA Sunday Cup, FA County Youth Cup.

② The finest pennant, perhaps, that England have received before an international. Hand stitched in satin, it was presented by Hungary in the Nep Stadium, Budapest, 1954. Hungary then gave England the biggest hiding in their history – 7 – 1.

③ The Class of '66.

Left to right: Jack Charlton, Nobby Stiles, Gordon Banks (half hidden), Alan Ball, Martin Peters, Geoff Hurst, Bobby Moore, Ray Wilson, George Cohen and Bobby Charlton. Roger Hunt missed the frame.

③

① SAY BILL—WE'VE LOST THE BALL ! OH, NEVER MIND THE BALL, LET'S GET ON WITH THE GAME.

② FOOTBALL JOTTINGS. FOOTBALL COMMITTEE "A CHARGE"

① ② A funny old game.

Toast List.

THE KING
Proposed by The Chairman

NATIONAL ANTHEM - Solo: Mr. Webster Booth.

THE QUEEN,
QUEEN MARY AND OTHER MEMBERS OF THE
ROYAL FAMILY
Proposed by The Chairman.

OUR GUESTS
Proposed by W. W. Heard, Esq.
Responded to by The Hon. Sir Ernest Bruce Charles, C.B.E.
The Right Hon. Lord Mottistone, P.C.
and M. Jules Rimet (F.I.F.A.)

THE FOOTBALL ASSOCIATION
Proposed by The Right Hon. Lord Purcell, D.S.O., M.V.O.
Responded to by The Chairman.

CONTEMPORARY SPORTS
Proposed by B. A. Glanvill, Esq.
Responded to by Maj. Gen. B. A. Hill, C.B., D.S.O.
(President Rugby Football Union)
The Lord Burghley, M.P. (A.A.A.)
The Rt. Hon. Viscount Hailsham,
G.C.V.O., K.C.B., G.M.G. (M.C.C.)

THE CHAIRMAN
Proposed by A. G. Hines, Esq.

Artistes.

GRACIE FIELDS
—
WEBSTER BOOTH
(Tenor)
—
SHERKOT
(Continental Eccentric)
—
THREE CANADIANS
(Acrobatic Comedians)

At the Piano:
Mr. GEORGE PIPER.

①

②

③

① ② Another birthday: speakers and artistes for the FA's 75th anniversary banquet at the Holborn Restaurant, 26 October 1938. William Pickford, with nearly 50 years' service to the FA, presided over 450 guests. The cover of the menu is signed by Johnny Goodall, centre forward and star of the Preston 'Invincibles' who won the League championship and the FA Cup in 1888/9.

③ Stanley Rous, left, succeeds Sir Frederick Wall as FA secretary, 4 August 1934. Rous was to record later that he received little help from Wall who said: 'The job's straightforward. You can read up the files. There is nothing much I can tell you.' Wall held the post for 39 years and Rous for nearly 28 years before becoming president of FIFA in 1961.

①

②

③

① Leg show at the Den: Millwall supporters astride the barriers for an FA Cup third round tie against Manchester City, 8 January 1938. Result: 2–2 – and City won the replay 3–1. City were then relegated from the First Division and Millwall became champions of the Third Division South. Millwall, in 1936/7, had become the first Third Division club to reach the semi-finals of the FA Cup.

② Billy Walker carries the FA Cup out of Wembley by the back gate after managing Sheffield Wednesday to a 4–2 victory over West Bromwich Albion in the 1935 FA Cup final. Walker was also in the Aston Villa team which won the Cup in 1920 and was Nottingham Forest's manager when they won the trophy in 1959. Walker, an inside forward of verve and high skill, won 18 caps for England (1920–32).

③ The famous Mutch penalty. George Mutch of Preston North End wins the 1938 FA Cup final against Huddersfield Town with a penalty in the last minute of extra time: the ball went into the net off the underside of the bar. It was the first Wembley final to be decided by a penalty – and the first full final to be transmitted live on television by the BBC. The TV audience was estimated at less than 10,000.

① Doctor's orders: Johnny Arnold, of Fulham and England, strengthens an injured knee by cycling around the pitch at Craven Cottage, November 1935. The club's doctor ordered him to cycle five miles every day – and the club paid for the bike. Arnold, an aggressive outside left for Fulham and a batsman who scored 37 centuries for Hampshire, was a double international: he won one cap for England at football (v Scotland, 1933) and one at cricket (v New Zealand, 1931).

② Football manager, 1939-style. George Allison of Arsenal addressing the Highbury crowd, Arsenal v Chelsea, 18 February 1939. Subject: 'Moral rearmament through Sport'. A month later Hitler's troops occupied Czechoslovakia. Allison was also a journalist and BBC Radio's first football commentator.

③ God before Joy. God (dark shirt), Poland's inside left, rises above Bernard Joy, Great Britain's centre half, to score in the 1936 Olympics in Berlin. Poland won 5–4 and Britain, joint favourites with Germany, were out of the tournament. Joy, who played for the Corinthians and the Casuals before joining Arsenal (1935–47), was the last amateur to win a full international cap for England, v Belgium 1936. Joy later became a highly respected journalist with the *London Evening Standard*.

①

②

③

④

④ An RAF depot 'somewhere on the East coast', April 1940. Ted Drake (Arsenal and England), centre, and Sam Bartram (Charlton) are instructed in the finer points of guard duty. Drake, a hammer of a centre forward, helped Arsenal win the League championship in 1935 and 1938 and the FA Cup in 1936. He scored seven goals against Aston Villa in 1935, won five caps for England and managed Chelsea to the League championship in 1955 (the first man to play in and later manage a League championship side). Bartram was considered the best goalkeeper of his era not to win an international cap, but he won countless admirers during his 22 years (1934-56) with Charlton. He was an FA Cup finalist in 1946, a Cup-winner in 1947 and later managed York and Luton. Drake and Bartram were old adversaries on the field.

⑤ Heart of England: World War Two international half-back line of Cliff Britton (Army and Everton), Stan Cullis (Army and Wolverhampton Wanderers) and Joe Mercer (Army and Everton). All three 'guested' during the war for Aldershot ('home of the British Army') who sometimes fielded sides of almost full international strength. Other England internationals who played for Aldershot included Tommy Lawton (Everton), Frank Swift (Manchester City), Wilf Copping (Leeds) and Jimmy Hagan (Sheffield United). Cullis (with Wolves and Birmingham) and Britton (Burnley, Everton, Preston and Hull) became managers after the war; and Mercer played for Arsenal (League champions 1948 and 1953, FA Cup-winners 1950) before managing Sheffield United, Aston Villa, Manchester City, Coventry and, for a short period, England.

⑤

7

THE WORLD GAME 1946–52

The nation's obsession with football, once the Second World War was over, suggested the game was the key to almost everything. Was it a coincidence that the world was created in the shape of a football? Hundreds of thousands of men, with six lost years behind them, saw the game as an antidote to austerity, a torch to follow in those half-tone days of coupons and licences. Football's appeal was intoxicating; it offered excitement, distraction, and a new focus for commitment. It was a virile symbol of normality.

Some men from Stalin's Soviet Union whetted the appetite. Moscow Dynamo arrived at Croydon airport in the bleak mid-winter of 1945, the first Soviet footballers to play in England, and they brought with them a long list of demands – one of which was that they must play Arsenal – and a cargo of talent. Their first game was against Chelsea at Stamford Bridge, and a crowd of 85,000 (of which at least 10,000 forgot to pay) laughed as the Dynamos came out in blue shirts decorated with a large white 'D', long blue shorts with a white hem – and bouquets of red and white flowers which they then presented to an embarrassed Chelsea.

Their football, however, was no laughing matter. They played with entrancing elegance and invention; and in 16 days they drew 3–3 with Chelsea (who had just bought England's centre forward Tommy Lawton from Everton for £14,000), mortified Cardiff by 10–1, beat Arsenal 4–3 (an Arsenal bolstered by Stanley Matthews and Stan Mortensen) and drew 2–2 with Glasgow Rangers at Ibrox. Their four games were watched by a total of 270,000 people. Dynamo insisted on using substitutes – another of their demands – and in the games against Arsenal (played in thick fog) and Glasgow Rangers they were quicker at sending players on than pulling them off. For a spell in each game they had 12 men on the field.

If this can be termed the century of the common man, then soccer, of all sports, is surely his game. This has been seen no more clearly than in the multiple expansion since the war of international fixtures at all levels. The recent series of matches arranged to celebrate the Festival of Britain entailed visits by teams from no less than 15 countries, to the land of soccer's birth. In a world haunted by the hydrogen and the napalm bomb, the football field is a place where sanity and hope are still left unmolested.

Sir Stanley Rous writing in The FA Year Book 1951–52.

The Russians complained about their accommodation, food, transport, venues and opponents, but they helped re-launch the game in Britain with memorable style. Bernard Joy, Arsenal's centre half against Dynamo and one of the few modern amateurs to win a full England cap, later wrote:

> Dynamo played brilliant attacking soccer based on the short ground pass ... and so the wheel had turned full circle. This was the style we had given the world earlier in the century and had abandoned in the negative football era of the 1930s. The Russians were but the ghosts of our past glories – the 'Wembley Wizards', the Corinthians, Newcastle's team of all talents and the Invincibles of proud Preston.

There were certainly few hints of old glory, real or fondly imagined, in the football which settled the first FA Cup tournament after the war. The conflict had stolen the best years of many players' careers and most of the sides which looked towards Wembley again in 1945/6 were generously laced with old heads and young but untried muscle. Even the tournament itself had a different look for this one season. Because of 'special circumstances' – which meant a pressing need for money – the FA decided that every round up to the semi-finals would be played over two legs, home and away, which promised to undermine the 'sudden death' essence of the Cup's attraction.

But the crowds still flocked in and it was, indeed, the second leg of a sixth round tie which produced the worst disaster British football had then known. On 9 March 1946 Bolton faced Stoke City at Burnden Park and, with Bolton leading by 2–0 from the first leg, most of the people in the old cotton town decided to see their club reach the semi-finals. Stoke also had Stanley Matthews – the 'Wizard of Dribble' and the biggest attraction in English football.

The turnstiles closed soon after 2·30pm, with 65,000 inside the ground and another 15,000 outside but determined, somehow, to get in. Some found their way onto an adjacent LMS railway track and from there they scrambled down to push over a fence. Thousands followed them, and the crush inside got worse. A brick wall toppled, so did three barriers, and a father – deciding to get his son out of the ground – picked the lock of another gate. Thousands more gratefully poured in. The game had started by now, with the players and many of the crowd unaware that anything was wrong. In fact, 33 people were dead or dying and another 500 were injured. The game was stopped for a few minutes, but then restarted at the request of the police who feared panic or riot.

A Home Office report described the tragedy as 'the first example of serious casualties inflicted by a crowd upon itself'. There had been no major structural collapse; but, with huge crowds stamping into elderly grounds which were in generally poor condition after the war, the tragedy threw stark light on an old problem.

The Moelwyn Hughes report into the disaster called for limited crowds and licensed grounds after stricter and more scientific examination. Football's response was not enthusiastic: there was talk of interference and high costs. A voluntary system of licensing for grounds holding 10,000 or more was started by the FA in 1948 and, while it lacked definition and firm guidelines, it was a small step in the right direction. The Government let things rest.

A mourning Bolton moved on to the semi-final, but the finalists in 1946 were to be Derby County and Charlton Athletic. The day was leaden, the dress utility, yet a Wembley crowd of more than 98,000 relished a game that was boldly won by Derby and which made its mark on the history of the tournament in several little ways. Charlton's Bert Turner became the first finalist to score for both teams: an own goal and an equaliser from a free kick less than 60 seconds later. The ball then burst as Derby's burly centre forward Jack Stamps attempted a shot which might have settled the match. But Stamps had better luck with the new ball in extra time, scoring twice in Derby's 4–1 win, although the two men who contributed most to their success and image that season were their inside forwards, Raich Carter and Peter Doherty.

Carter of England, and once of Sunderland, was small, neat and silver-haired, a player of disarming calmness and natural authority whose technique was expertly precise and broad in range. Doherty of Ireland, and once of Manchester City, was taller, more angular and red-haired, a player of pace and indomitable fire who hounded the ball as if he owned it. Perhaps nothing less than a union of Carter and Doherty could have won the Cup for Derby. Sixty years before, the club had evicted some gypsies from a camping site, and one old harridan had not only cursed the club but prophesied they would never win anything again. She was right, too, until Derby took Carter and Doherty to Wembley for a final that signalled a new beginning for the game.

The curtain rose on the first post-war League season on Saturday, 31 August 1946 – and the game seemed to be answering a call from the nation. Queues wrapped themselves around grounds like huge mufflers and terraces were often full a couple of hours before kick-off. The fixture list was identical to that for the bluntly curtailed programme of 1939–40 and crowds totalling 35,604,606 for the season 1946/7 shared an illusion that nothing much had really changed. The crowds kept on growing until – an undentable record – they reached 41,271,414 in 1948/9. The aggregate for the last four seasons of the 1940s was over 157 million. Absenteeism was a major problem, but the Government had to set this against the contribution football was making towards the spirit of the nation. Staggered working hours were introduced.

The boom could not last; and it began to fade as a dash of colour, new hope and material evidence of prosperity arrived with the 1950s. But football's crowds were still rudely healthy, that barometer of confidence known as the transfer market was buoyant and, although problems lay ahead, they would not be sharply defined for many years yet.

By this time, too, the FA had already pointed firmly to the future. In 1946 it offered help to clubs and associations at all levels with coaches, courses, text books, publicity and – as and when funds became available – loans and grants. The decision was also taken to rejoin FIFA again, a decision made easier by a new sense of European unity which was one of the few fruitful legacies of the war. The formal process took several months to complete, with meetings in Zurich, London and Luxembourg, and there was still argument about the thorny old problem of 'broken time' payments; but the need for strong and broad unity overrode all other considerations and the FA – who also negotiated on behalf of the other British associations – moved back into FIFA with enthusiasm and no major qualification. And the four home nations retained their places on the International Board.

The re-entry of the British led to a remaking of FIFA. The international body was in serious financial trouble and Stanley Rous suggested a celebration match between Great Britain and the Rest of Europe, with the proceeds to be given to FIFA. Early in May 1947 a crowd of 134,000 saw the British side win by 6–1 at Hampden Park and £30,000 – life-blood – went to FIFA.

The significance of the victory was happily magnified. It was described as 'The Match of the Century' and the result was held to be crowning proof that Britannia still ruled. In fact, the selection of the two teams gave the ad hoc selectors nightmarish problems – 'never again' muttered one – although the British side, a creation of careful compromise, was full of outstanding players. It included five from England (with Stanley Matthews, Tommy Lawton and Wilf Mannion in the forward line), three from Scotland, two from Wales and one from Ireland. The Rest of Europe, captained by Johnny Carey of Manchester United and Eire, consisted of players from nine different countries: they were characters in search of an author. But the game was fun.

> Scene: a cramped BBC Radio studio in the Blackpool Tower building after Blackpool's 1–0 victory over Fulham in the quarter-finals of the FA Cup 1951. Don Davies ('Old International' of the *Guardian*) has Stanley Matthews with him but, before interviewing the Blackpool and England winger, he has to deliver an account of the match for 'Sports Report' on the Light Programme.
>
> 'About 45 seconds before I was due to begin, all the lights fused. Everybody was beginning to walk over everybody else in the search for the prime cause when a quiet voice said: 'Stay put, chaps. Take your matches out and empty them on to the table.' Then, picking the matches up a dozen at a time, he lit them in relays, and I had the novel experience of reading to the world a glowing tribute to a master winger from a script illuminated by the glow of matches lit by the master himself. The circle of faces leaning over that pocket of light in the velvety blackness was a subject fit for a Rembrandt.'
>
> *Don Davies in* Sports Report, *1955. Davies was one of eight journalists who died in the Munich air crash in 1958.*

The FA also made a new appointment in 1946 that was to have a profound influence on the future of English football. Walter Winterbottom became Director of Coaching and, soon afterwards as well, the first manager of England's national team. He was a tall and personable man from Oldham, articulate, good-humoured, a devoted enthusiast, practical but also a visionary, a natural teacher but always a student, a man with broad vision but with a passion for detail as well. He was to need all these qualities.

He had been a promising half back with Manchester United in the late 1930s and 'guested' for Chelsea during the war until back trouble ended his career. He was a Wing Commander in charge of physical training at the Air Ministry and was a candidate for the post of principal at Carnegie College when the offer came from Lancaster Gate. He was then 33 years old.

Winterbottom's appointment ended a long campaign by Stanley Rous, who was convinced that the FA needed an expert coach on its staff. There was resistance from Council members on the grounds of cost on top of a more general objection to the whole concept of coaching. But Rous had his way – as he usually did – and as soon as Winterbottom had begun to make his mark, the FA secretary made another proposal. Why not appoint Winterbottom as the manager of the England team?

The idea, again, had a frosty reception. England's management had been shared by alternating Council members, each of whom usually plumped for the trainer of his own club to help him, and there was reluctance to change a popular and comfortable system. Cost would have been an immediate objection once more had Rous suggested a new man for the job – but his suggestion that Winterbottom should do two jobs for one salary was a winning card.

Winterbottom began his coaching job with an empty canvas and an army of doubters. 'Unless this coaching monster is seized firmly by the throat it will strangle the living grace out of our game,' observed one old England international. 'Winterbottom is a don who believes too much in words and diagrams.' Winterbottom, nonplussed, went on to build a national coaching scheme which became the envy of the world of football. He built a network which, by way of new standards, enlightened technique and an ever-widening circle of coaches, reached into schools, clubs and associations in every corner of the country. He also had a major influence on a new generation of managers – one of whom, Ron Greenwood, a future manager of England himself, was to write: 'Many people in the game now have no idea how much English football owes to Walter ... his influence has reached on down through the years and it certainly touched many of the clubs from which England called on players to win the World Cup in 1966.' Winterbottom opened a new door for English football; but what he could not do, of course, was to guarantee the quality of coaching at all its levels.

The post of England manager was a very different and, in many ways, an impossible one. The team was still picked by a committee, although Winterbottom was able to argue his preferences, and the introduction of a more professional approach could not be hurried. There was always a stubborn pocket of resistance to any change from 'the old days'. Pre-match training sessions and players' meetings were viewed with suspicion; so, too, were analysis and experiment. The attitude of players to Winterbottom varied enormously. Billy Wright liked him immediately – 'here was a man who thought deeply and skilfully about the game.' Alf Ramsey, a little later on, said Winterbottom's 'tactical knowledge and outlook left a lasting impression'. Others accused Winterbottom of using jargon which had nothing to do with the earthy world of professional football, or railed against the idea of polishing basic techniques, or protested that extra training would take the 'steam' out of them. When blazers were introduced for the England team, there was even a bleat that they were being forced to dress like schoolboys.

Winterbottom's grasp of his subject was apparent to most, however, and with many peerless players at his disposal his early record was above criticism. In the four seasons between the end of the war and the start of the 1950 World Cup finals in Brazil, England played 29 games, won 22, lost four, scored 90 goals and conceded 31; and four goals or more were managed on 13 occasions.

On 25 May 1947, a fortnight or so after Great Britain had scored six against the Rest of Europe, England ran in ten against Portugal in Lisbon with a forward line of Stanley Matthews, Stan Mortensen, Tommy Lawton, Wilf Mannion and Tom Finney. Lawton and Mortensen each scored four – and the Portuguese players were so embarrassed they refused to attend the post-match dinner. A year later the same five forwards faced Italy, the reigning world champions, in Turin, a match of lofty prestige which England won 4–0, with goals from Lawton, Mortensen and Finney, who scored twice in three minutes in the second half and who later described it as 'the finest performance by any team I played for'. Shop windows in Turin displayed pictures of the England team with captions which said simply 'Made in Britain'.

England were deemed ready to win the Jules Rimet trophy when the World Cup reached its first post-war climax in 1950. Scotland, too, should have gone to Brazil, but pride got in the way. The British championship was classified as a qualifying group, with the top two to make the trip to South America, but Scotland decided they would go only as champions. A goal by England's Roy Bentley beat them at Hampden Park and Scotland perversely stuck to their word.

England felt they could cope by themselves, however, although the international days of Tommy Lawton and Frank Swift were over; and Neil Franklin, the distinguished Stoke centre half and an automatic cornerstone of Winterbottom's team, had secretly joined the wealthy but non-affiliated Santa Fe club in Colombia – a move which left his career in ruins. But England still had Wright, Finney, Mortensen, Mannion and, eventually, the ageless Matthews, who travelled to Rio from Toronto. The FA had included Matthews in a party that was touring Canada and – by way of an afterthought prompted, to some degree, by media pressure – he was asked to leave the gentle business there and help England's cause in Brazil. The system was far from perfect.

England made a modest but adequate start in the mighty bowl of Rio's Maracana stadium, beating Chile by 2–0 and, for their next game, against the United States in Belo Horizonte, nearly 300 miles to the north, Winterbottom felt there should be one or two changes. So did Stanley Rous, who urged that Stanley Matthews should be included. But Arthur Drewry, the tour leader and principal selector, insisted that 'a winning team must not be changed'.

Drewry may well have been right but, in any case, they all shared the belief that England were going to win. England were one of the favourites, along with Brazil, and the United States were rank outsiders – a 500–1 curiosity whose players originated from half a dozen countries, a collection of international greenhorns whose goalkeeper was a former baseball player. Bill Jeffrey, a Scot, the Americans' manager, happily conceded to every microphone and notebook that his team had no chance, and several of his players contemplated defeat darkly through the bottom of their glasses until the small hours of match day.

The record books, however, are quite explicit: the United States beat England 1–0 on Thursday, 29 June 1950. It is still the most embarrassing result in the history of English international football, a defeat beyond analysis and enquiry, an enduring reminder that in football a moment of luck can be worth a volume of logic.

It is true that the ground was cramped and the pitch rutted and stony. It is a reasonable estimate that England hit post or bar 11 times and had 90 percent of the play. It is a matter for regret that a header by Mortensen sent the ball over the line before it was scooped away, and that England should have been awarded at least one penalty. But the one fact worth a bootlace was that the United States managed the game's only goal. It was scored by the Americans' centre forward Joe Gaetjens, who came from Haiti, in the 37th minute. The details of his famous goal, in keeping with the shape and result of the game, are hazy. Walter Bahr, the USA's left half, put the ball into the English penalty area; some reports say it was a long clearance, others claim it was a centre or a shot. Some accounts say that Gaetjens ducked and the ball hit him on the back of the head or, more precisely, his left ear – 'a million-to-one freak' according to Alf Ramsey, England's right back, who was not given to exaggeration. Others say that Gaetjens jumped for the ball and that his final contact was calculated. What is certain is that the ball finished in England's net.

'Bloody ridiculous. Can't we play them again tomorrow?'

Wilf Mannion of Middlesbrough after England's 1–0 defeat by the United States in the 1950 World Cup finals.

England's first attempt to win the World Cup really ended there. Stanley Matthews was recalled for the final game against Spain in Rio, but England again lost 1–0 and, still bewailing their bad luck, everyone left for home – every official, every player, every reporter. England were out: the rest was irrelevant. Just one

Englishman still had a contribution to make: George Reader of Southampton refereed the final match in which Uruguay, against all expectation, beat Brazil 2−1 to become world champions. And he did the job well.

The Brazilian experience rocked the English game at every level and the FA quickly set up a technical committee which trawled opinion from directors, managers and players, past and present, at a series of meetings. Coaching, training, preparation, the development of young talent, systems, tactics and refereeing were among the subjects they tackled: there were no inflexible guidelines, and the FA found itself among the targets for pointed criticism. The result was a better relationship between Lancaster Gate and the clubs and a greater awareness of the problems and priorities of each side. But, undermining the earnest talk was a conviction that only outrageous fortune had scuppered England in Brazil and that, subject to fine tuning, all was well in the home of football.

The FA Cup was still a thing apart, of course and, after Derby County's dramatic victory over Charlton had helped re-open the road to Wembley after the war, the tournament continued to delight and surprise. In the League, too, familiar names made their mark, with Manchester United, above all, reaching for the stars under the new stewardship of Matt Busby. His inheritance was unpromising, because United had a hefty overdraft and no ground. Old Trafford had been badly blitzed and for a few seasons United shared Maine Road with Manchester City. But Busby and United did have some very good players.

Manchester United finished runners-up in Division One in four of the first five seasons after the war before winning the championship for the first time in 41 years in 1952. They also beat Blackpool 4−2 at Wembley in 1948 in a Cup final which is regarded as one of the finest of all. Blackpool, with Matthews and Mortensen giving them guile and fire, took the lead twice; but United, with players of the calibre of Johnny Carey, Jack Rowley and the irrepressible Jimmy Delaney, forced the game to new, exhilarating heights and towards a climax which gave them two goals in the last 12 minutes. It had been a gloriously sunny afternoon, a classic final and a royal occasion; once again the Cup was full.

Ten months later, however, United and the city of Manchester reminded football that there is more to the Cup than the pomp of Wembley. A Maine Road crowd of 81,565 saw United beat Yeovil Town of the Southern League 8−0, but the score was not important. That huge crowd, one of the largest ever to watch an FA Cup-tie outside a final, gathered to pay tribute to a team of part-timers from the green and pleasant acres of Somerset that had captured the respect of the nation. The cheers which rolled around the ground at the end were for little men who had dared.

Yeovil's chances of winning the Cup had been assessed by the bookmakers at

5,000–1, but they then proceeded to beat Lovell's Athletic, Romford, Weymouth, Bury of the Second Division and – a victory which has become the stuff of legend – Sunderland of the First, who were known as 'the Bank of England club'. Their history was adorned with great names and achievements, and their spending on players had people inside the game, as well as outside, shaking their heads in disbelief. Yeovil, for their part, were a small club in a small town whose main business was beer, food and gloves.

But Yeovil Town had one or two things going for them. Their Huish pitch had a famous slope, which was regarded as the 'Boot Hill' of the game. They also had in Alec Stock a popular, intelligent and articulate player-manager whose career would take him to Leyton Orient, Arsenal, AS Roma, Queen's Park Rangers, Luton, Fulham and Bournemouth. The Yeovil team was not a collection of country bumpkins either, as some papers portrayed them: some had played the game at a higher level. Sunderland, for their part, may have been undermined by complacency but on a day of fog and tension, in front of a crowd of 17,000 – remarkable for a town of less than 23,000 – there was no doubt that Yeovil's victory by 2–1 was honestly earned. 'Argus' of the *Sunderland Echo*, who reported the game from a schooldesk on the touchline, wrote: 'Occasionally a bugle sounded. Whether Sunderland thought it sounded the retreat I don't know.' Yeovil had established themselves as an *enfant terrible*. Down through the years no club has relished a Cup date with the men from Somerset.

Portsmouth won the League championship in 1949 and again the following season, a 'double' managed by a team of intelligence and crushing consistency; but Newcastle soon matched them with a 'double' of another kind. Newcastle became the first side of the 20th century to win the Cup two seasons running (1951 and 1952) and Jackie Milburn, their buccaneering centre forward and a Tyneside folk-hero, was to claim that 'you have to be a Geordie to understand what the Cup means in these parts: it's glory, glamour, drama, excitement and, above all, it's instant . . . to us only the Cup matters.' And, just for good measure, Newcastle won the Cup again in 1955.

But Wembley did not belong only to the professional. The FA Amateur Cup was still a tournament of great character, and no club represented its appeal and spirit more perfectly than Pegasus, a combined side of Oxford and Cambridge University players, which passed through the history of the game like a bright comet. Pegasus won the Amateur Cup twice, in 1951 and 1953, each time before a Wembley crowd of 100,000, but it was what the club stood for, as much as their success, which so endeared them to the nation as a whole. Pegasus inherited the role of the old Corinthians. They represented simpler times and championed a grander code of ethics. They touched old and sweeter chords before the demands and quarrels of modern life crushed them. Pegasus 1948–63. RIP.

FA Cup

Year	Date	Winners		Runners-up		Venue	Attendance	Referee	Entries
1946	27 April	Derby County	4	Charlton Athletic	1*	Wembley	98,000	ED Smith	294
1947	26 April	Charlton Athletic	1	Burnley	0*	Wembley	99,000	JM Wiltshire	438
1948	24 April	Manchester United	4	Blackpool	2	Wembley	99,000	CJ Barrick	510
1949	30 April	Wolverhampton Wanderers	3	Leicester City	1	Wembley	99,500	RA Mortimer	617
1950	29 April	Arsenal	2	Liverpool	0	Wembley	100,000	H Pearce	617
1951	28 April	Newcastle United	2	Blackpool	0	Wembley	100,000	W Ling	615
1952	3 May	Newcastle United	1	Arsenal	0	Wembley	100,000	A Ellis	478

England's Full International Record 1872–1993

(Up to end of season 1992/3)

	HOME						AWAY					
					Goals						**Goals**	
	P	W	D	L	For	Agst	P	W	D	L	For	Agst
Albania	1	1	0	0	5	0	1	1	0	0	2	0
Argentina	5	3	2	0	10	6	5	1	2	2	5	5
Australia	–	–	–	–	–	–	5	3	2	0	5	2
Austria	5	3	1	1	18	9	10	5	2	3	36	16
Belgium	4	3	1	0	17	3	14	10	3	1	50	21
Bohemia	–	–	–	–	–	–	1	1	0	0	4	0
Brazil	7	2	4	1	9	7	9	1	2	6	5	14
Bulgaria	2	1	1	0	3	1	3	2	1	0	4	0
Cameroon	1	1	0	0	2	0	1	1	0	0	3	2
Canada	–	–	–	–	–	–	1	1	0	0	1	0
Chile	1	0	1	0	0	0	3	2	1	0	4	1
CIS	0	0	0	0	0	0	1	0	1	0	2	2
Colombia	1	0	1	0	1	1	1	1	0	0	4	0
Cyprus	1	1	0	0	5	0	1	1	0	0	1	0
Czechoslovakia	5	4	1	0	13	6	7	3	2	2	11	8
Denmark	5	4	0	1	8	3	8	4	4	0	18	8
Ecuador	–	–	–	–	–	–	1	1	0	0	2	0
Egypt	–	–	–	–	–	–	2	2	0	0	5	0
FIFA	1	0	1	0	4	4	–	–	–	–	–	–
Finland	2	2	0	0	7	1	7	6	1	0	27	5
France	8	6	2	0	23	4	14	9	1	4	39	23
Germany, East	2	2	0	0	4	1	2	1	1	0	3	2

	HOME						AWAY					
					Goals						Goals	
	P	W	D	L	For	Agst	P	W	D	L	For	Agst
West Germany/ Germany	8	5	0	3	15	9	12	4	4	4	21	17
Greece	2	1	1	0	3	0	3	3	0	0	7	1
Holland	6	2	3	1	14	8	5	2	2	1	4	4
Hungary	7	6	0	1	18	9	11	6	1	4	29	18
Iceland	–	–	–	–	–	–	1	0	1	0	1	1
Ireland, Northern	49	40	6	3	169	36	47	34	10	3	150	44
Ireland, Republic of	6	3	2	1	11	6	7	2	4	1	8	6
Israel	–	–	–	–	–	–	2	1	1	0	2	1
Italy	6	3	2	1	9	5	11	3	3	5	16	17
Kuwait	–	–	–	–	–	–	1	1	0	0	1	0
Luxembourg	3	3	0	0	18	1	4	4	0	0	20	2
Malaysia	–	–	–	–	–	–	1	1	0	0	4	2
Malta	1	1	0	0	5	0	1	1	0	0	1	0
Mexico	2	2	0	0	10	0	4	1	1	2	4	3
Morocco	–	–	–	–	–	–	1	0	1	0	0	0
New Zealand	–	–	–	–	–	–	2	2	0	0	3	0
Norway	3	2	1	0	9	1	5	3	0	2	17	6
Paraguay	–	–	–	–	–	–	1	1	0	0	3	0
Peru	–	–	–	–	–	–	2	1	0	1	5	4
Poland	4	2	2	0	7	2	5	2	2	1	5	3
Portugal	6	5	1	0	12	4	9	3	4	2	23	13
Rest of Europe	1	1	0	0	3	0	–	–	–	–	–	–
Rest of the World	1	1	0	0	2	1	–	–	–	–	–	–
Rumania	3	0	3	0	2	2	5	2	2	1	4	2
San Marino	1	1	0	0	6	0	–	–	–	–	–	–
Saudi Arabia	–	–	–	–	–	–	1	0	1	0	1	1
Scotland	53	25	11	17	115	87	54	18	13	23	73	81
Spain	6	5	0	1	19	6	10	5	2	3	16	13
Sweden	4	2	1	1	9	6	10	4	3	3	15	10
Switzerland	5	3	2	0	12	3	10	7	0	3	25	9
Tunisia	–	–	–	–	–	–	1	0	1	0	1	1
Turkey	4	4	0	0	18	0	4	3	1	0	11	0
USA	–	–	–	–	–	–	5	4	0	1	29	5
USSR	4	2	1	1	10	5	7	3	2	2	9	8
Uruguay	3	1	1	1	3	3	5	1	1	3	5	9
Wales	49	32	9	8	126	46	48	30	12	6	113	44
Yugoslavia	7	4	3	0	15	7	7	1	2	4	8	13

①

②

③

① Navy signal, ship to shore, on the Road to Wembley, 1946.

② The first goal in the first FA Cup final after World War Two, 1946. Bert Turner of Charlton Athletic (on ground, centre) deflects the ball into his own net to give Derby County the lead after 80 minutes – but just 60 seconds later Turner equalised with a free kick to become the first player to score for both sides in an FA Cup final. Derby County went on to win by 4–1 in extra time with Jack Stamps (white shirt, right) scoring twice.

③ Stamford Bridge: part of the crowd of 85,000 which saw Moscow Dynamo start their celebrated tour of Britain in 1945 by drawing 3–3 with Chelsea. The country was hungry for top-class football. Safety was not a factor.

④ Trooper WJ Charles receives the Army Cup from Lt Gen Sir Philip Balfour, 1952. John Charles also played for Leeds United, Juventus, Roma, Cardiff and Wales – splendidly built, magnificently gifted, a grand master in the air,

④

equally effective at centre forward or centre half and never sent off or cautioned. The greatest years of his career (1948–66) were with Juventus in Turin (three Italian League championships and two Cups) where he was known as the 'Gentle Giant'. The Army Cup, won in 1952 by 67 Training Regiment RAC, has been competed for since 1888 – the year in which the Army FA (and the Football League) was formed. The Inter-Services Championship and the Kentish Cup (a triangular tournament between, originally, the British, Belgian and French Armies) began after World War One. The sun never sets on British Forces' football.

①

②

③

④

① ② Romance ... and reality. Alec Stock, the player-manager of Yeovil Town, scoring the first of the two goals which gave the Somerset club their famous FA Cup victory over Sunderland – the 'Bank of England' club – on 29 January 1949. The notorious Huish slope is very apparent. But, in the fifth round, Yeovil of the Southern League met Manchester United at Maine Road – Old Trafford was still a war casualty – and their defeat by 8–0 is recorded with affection.

③ Donald Carr scores his second and Pegasus's sixth and last goal against Harwich and Parkeston in the 1953 FA Amateur Cup final. Pegasus, a combined Oxford and Cambridge University side, inherited the mantle of the old Corinthians and illuminated the game in the early 1950s. It was their second FA Amateur Cup triumph at Wembley in three years and each game was watched by 100,000. Of their victory over Harwich and Parkeston, Geoffrey Green wrote in *The Times*: 'To see Pegasus on this sunlit day was to admire the inner workings of some Swiss watch. Everything and everyone hung together. The mechanism worked perfectly.' Carr also played first-class cricket for Oxford University, Derbyshire and England (two Tests), managed three MCC tours and became secretary of the Test and County Cricket Board.

④ But sometimes during the dullest play
Something comes back from an earlier day
A fleeting moment, a hint of grace,
Brings back a feeling, a time, a place ...

Gordon Jeffrey, 'Men on the Terraces'

'Blue' Wanless, aged 75, watching Middlesbrough play in 1951 – 53 years after helping the club win the FA Amateur Cup. Because of a smallpox epidemic in lower Teesside in 1898, Middlesbrough's semi-final with Thornaby was secretly switched from Darlington – where people were afraid of the epidemic spreading – to the remote hill village of Brotton in the Clevelands. It was the last time Middlesbrough won a national knock-out tournament.

①

① Roy Bentley of Chelsea scores for England at Hampden, 15 April 1950. It was Bentley's first international goal and the only goal of the game – and it meant Scotland did not take part in the 1950 World Cup finals. The Home International Championship was classified as a qualifying group for the finals, with the top two countries going to Brazil, but Scotland decided they would go only as champions – and, when they finished runners-up, they kept their word. A crowd of 134,000 saw Scotland's goalkeeper Jimmy Cowan vainly get a hand to the ball. Bentley was immediately identified as 'the man who robbed Scotland of Rio'.

② Joe Gaetjens – the man from Haiti who gave the United States victory over England in Brazil, 29 June 1950. Joe (sometimes referred to as Larry) is carried off triumphantly after scoring the goal which ended England's first attempt to win the World Cup. Alf Ramsey, who was England's right back, described the goal as 'a million-to-one freak' – but it is still the most embarrassing result in the history of English international football.

③ A Brazilian cartoonist's view of English football after the 1–0 defeat by the United States in Belo Horizonte during the 1950 World Cup finals.

① Crowd control at Stamford Bridge 1947 – and a major police presence.

①

②

② Bill Nicholson who scored after 19 seconds of his first international for England – and was never picked again. England beat Portugal 5–2 at Goodison Park, 19 May 1951 – 'We kicked off, the ball came to me and I lobbed it forward,' remembers Nicholson. 'Stan Pearson nodded it back and I ran on to let go a first time shot which, from the moment I hit it, I knew was going in. But for the next game they brought back Billy Wright and I accepted that because he was a better player.' Nicholson was a versatile and effective player, but it was as a manager that he made his mark on the history of the game. He built the Tottenham Hotspur side which, in 1961, became the first club to complete the League and Cup 'double' in the 20th century and which, in 1963, became the first English club to win a European trophy.

③

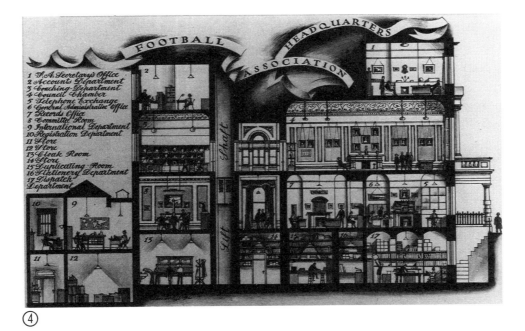

④

③ The first Schoolboy International to be played at Wembley, England 8, Scotland 2, 15 April 1950. Johnny Haynes of Edmonton (white shirt, scoring England's third goal) was the star of the game – a fact anticipated by the match programme which said of Haynes: 'Plays for London and Middlesex and in his third season with Edmonton. Smallest player in the side but a natural ball-player with style. Splits defences wide open with uncannily directed passes. Age 15. Height 5 feet 1 inch. Weight 7 stone 5 pounds.' Haynes, a natural ring-master, had already been watched by a herd of professional clubs for more than a year but, surprisingly perhaps, he chose Fulham, with whom he stayed for 19 years. He also won 56 caps for England (22 as captain) and became English football's first £100-a-week player when the maximum wage was removed in 1961.

④ Number 22, Lancaster Gate, London W2, the home of the Football Association, 1952. This former hotel was the FA's headquarters for 43 years (1929–72).

8

MATTHEWS, MAGYARS – AND MUNICH 1953–65

There were not many spare days for making history in 1953. It was a year which demanded everything; and, by and large, it got its way. It was the year of the Coronation, the conquest of Everest, Josef Stalin's death and the end of the Korean War. Sir Gordon Richards won the Derby for the first time with his 28th and last attempt; England won the Ashes for the first time since the Bodyline tour of 1932/3; Ben Hogan, at the age of 40 and only four years after being hit by a bus and left for dead, won the Open, the US Open and the Masters; and Maureen Connolly – 'Little Mo' – became the first woman to complete the Grand Slam of tennis.

Football, too, made its mark. In the year of the FA's 90th birthday, Stanley Matthews earned a Cup-winners' medal at last, at the age of 38 and at the third attempt; and Hungary became the first Continental side to beat England on English soil. Wembley witnessed both games: the first would have delighted the old grey stadium, because Matthews was also a national institution, while the defeat by the Hungarians would have saddened but not surprised it. Matthews, then and always, was the 'Master', but England were patently no longer the masters – even though Stanley himself played against the Hungarians. Matthews' medal and England's comeuppance were surely divined by a higher authority.

Matthews himself had contributed in no small way to the English arrogance about football – not because he was arrogant himself, far from it, but because the country knew that since the dawn of the game there had only been one like him. He was the first and only professional to be knighted while still playing, a Commander of the Order of the British Empire, the first man to be named Footballer of the Year (an award which he won again 15 years later in 1963) by the Football Writers' Association, the first man to be voted European Footballer of the Year, an honorary freeman of the City of Stoke and in Ghana he was formally made a chieftain. He played his first game for Stoke on 19 March 1932 and his last – a First Division match at the age of 50 years and five days – for Stoke again on 6 February 1965. By this time, for Stoke and Blackpool, he had played around 800 League and Cup games (including three FA Cup finals) and represented his country on 84 occasions, including war and Victory internationals, the first when he was 19, the last when 42.

Matthews did not score many goals – although he managed a hat trick against Czechoslovakia in 1937 – and he rarely headed the ball or tackled. But he had an ability to dribble past opponents that has known no equal. He did it with a mixture of exquisite balance, sleight of head, body and foot, severe control, polite invitation and an electrifying change of pace. Everybody knew what he was going to do, because his repertoire of tricks never changed, but for 33 years at the highest level he foxed opponents and colleagues alike. He made full backs all over the world feel like a child who has been invited to guess which hand the penny is in – and then discovered it was in neither. The titles and descriptions which followed this man of reserved character, middling height and slightly bowed legs along his right touchline say little about the player, but they help confirm his uniqueness: Matthews was the 'Wizard of Dribble', the 'Maestro' and the 'Ageless Wonder'.

Such was his popularity that the whole country shared his hopes and fears when he tried for a third time to help Blackpool win the Cup. Together, they had lost to Manchester United in the brilliant final of 1948 and then to Newcastle, for whom Jackie Milburn scored two memorable goals, in 1951. What Wembley did not know as Matthews lined up against Bolton Wanderers for the Coronation year final was that his selection was something of a gamble. He had pulled a muscle during training four days before and 'it made me very unhappy, very nervous', he recalled later. 'I was actually doubtful for the final and on the Saturday I had a try out, and the doctor gave me an injection, but I was still worried I might break down. I didn't – but it was always on my mind.'

The winners' medal he wanted so much seemed to be slipping from his grasp once more when Bolton took the lead after 75 seconds, led by 2–1 at half time and by 3–1 with little more than 20 minutes to go. But then, re-routing destiny, Matthews took the game by the throat. He provided the cross, high to the far post, from which Mortensen scrambled in his second goal of the afternoon and, with darting runs and bemusing centres which cut like knife-thrusts into the left side of Bolton's defence, he prepared Wembley for its finest climax. Mortensen completed his hat trick with a cannonball of a free kick with less than three minutes left – 3–3. The nation settled back with relish for an extra half-hour. But there was still Matthews, always Matthews, and, with only seconds left, he received a pass from Ernie Taylor, flickered past Bolton's left back Ralph Banks on the outside and cut the ball back for Bill Perry to score. Blackpool 4, Bolton 3 – and Matthews, his face as impassive as ever, received his precious medal from the new young Queen. Mortensen's hat trick was the key to the victory; but this will always be the 'Matthews final'.

That memorable afternoon sent the Football Association happily into its 90th birthday celebrations. Seventy nations bearing gifts were represented at a banquet at London's Dorchester Hotel, 1,700 paintings and sculptures were submitted and 150 chosen for an exhibition entitled 'Football and the Fine Arts' and England faced a Rest of Europe side selected by FIFA at Wembley. The game was right for the occasion, seriously yet sportingly contested, but, with only a minute or so to go and the Rest of Europe leading by 4–3, it seemed that this important milestone for the FA was going to be marked by England's first defeat on home soil by Continental opposition. But then England were awarded a penalty and Alf Ramsey – with an authority and coolness that was to serve England in an even more significant way in years to come – stepped forward to score with comfortable precision.

A month later, however, there was to be no last-minute reprieve. Hungary came to Wembley and defeated England with a conviction and manner which brooked no argument. The date: Wednesday, 25 November 1953. The score: England 3, Hungary 6. The defeat cast a boulder onto still waters. The Hungarians' victory should not, perhaps, have caused the surprise it did. After all they were Olympic champions, favourites to win the World Cup in Switzerland the following summer and had not lost a game for three years. Stanley Rous – by now Sir Stanley – had seen Hungary for himself and it was his suggestion that they should be invited to Wembley; and he, above all, was very clear about their quality.

Yet, while recognising that Hungary were a force to be respected, the prevailing opinion of the game's luminaries was that England at Wembley, the old masters in their fortress, now and always, would be too strong. 'Look at that little fat chap there ... we'll murder this lot,' observed a London player who would one day become a very good coach. He was pointing at Ferenc Puskas. Puskas was the Hungarians' captain and inside left, a product of the suburbs of Budapest, round and slick-haired, genial but also arrogant, a virtuoso with a left foot that should have been licensed as a lethal weapon. He was essential to the spirit as well as the grain of Hungarian football – a player, like Matthews, who stood apart. A little fat chap, perhaps. One of the definitively great players of modern football, certainly.

But England had Matthews, as well as Mortensen, Taylor and Harry Johnston of the Blackpool side which had won the Cup. Wright was there, a captain to count on, and around him was the insurance of men like Ramsey and Portsmouth's Jimmy Dickinson at left half. George Robb, the Tottenham left winger, and Taylor were winning their only cap and Ramsey, Mortensen, Johnston and Bill Eckersley, unknowingly, their last. It was not the most talented side to represent England but it was not the worst either; it had balance and resolution.

The story of the match is one of the best-known in English football: oft-told, much analysed, a tale out of a penny dreadful which took on enormous significance. Hidegkuti scored three of Hungary's six goals, including one in the first minute, Puskas got two and Bozsik one; and England replied, fitfully, through Jackie Sewell of Sheffield Wednesday, Mortensen and Ramsey from the penalty spot. Three of Hungary's goals came in a quarter of an hour in the first half, with Puskas's first the best-remembered. He dragged the ball back with the sole of his boot just as Wright launched himself into a wall-demolishing tackle; England's captain careered by like a man on his way to another engagement and Puskas coolly used his left foot to score just inside the near post.

The scoreline hurt, but the manner of the Hungarian victory wounded deeply. It touched the inner heart of English football because it confirmed, beyond excuse and smokescreen, that the country which had organised the game for the world did not understand its finer points. The 'masters' were using old text books. Charles Buchan informed his *News Chronicle* readers the next morning that England had been 'outplayed, outgeneralled, outpaced and outshot'. Geoffrey Green observed in *The Times* that England had been 'strangers in a strange world, a world of flitting red spirits'. Frank Coles recorded in the *Daily Telegraph* that the Hungarians had produced 'the most brilliant display of football ever seen in this country'.

The key to Hungary's success was their skill. Puskas, Hidegkuti, Kocsis and the dynamic Bozsik at right half formed a core of four great players, and the rest were outstanding or merely very good. Hidegkuti wore a nine on his back and was conventionally described as 'a deep-lying centre forward' but, in essence, he was a free agent with a bright mind and a cruel finish who roamed and manoeuvred and struck according to whim and opportunity. Puskas and the elegant, incisive Kocsis formed the Hungarian spearhead, but Johnston – whose bounden duty as England's number five was to hound Hungary's number nine – waited in vain for his introduction to Hidegkuti. 'I had no-one to mark,' he complained.

Fortune had dealt Hungary a precious hand, and their style and method, their understanding of space, their teamwork and their rhythm, were simply expressions of high skill. Ability, bonded by time and familiarity, was at the base of their design and symmetry and never since has Hungarian football produced such art.

But the prophets of the English game needed instant answers. There was debate, analysis and earnest soul-searching which hit even shriller notes six months later when England went to Budapest and were beaten 7–1. England's side differed in seven positions from the side beaten at Wembley, but nothing was really altered: they were overwhelmed by a Hungarian performance of lyrical quality. There were daily demands in the papers for 'something to be done', for heads to roll and revolution. 'Do we really need a panel of nine to pick a team of 11?' asked one. The FA's technical sub-committee deliberated grimly, and Walter Winterbottom patiently and realistically saw things for what they were and was at the heart of everything. English football pulled the sky down on itself. The 'Hungarian' way, it seemed, was the only way. Puskas and company were elevated to cult status.

> Walter Winterbottom is a talented and honourable man who deserves to succeed in any profession. Unfortunately, he has chosen possibly the most difficult job in England... More criticism has been hurled at this one individual than at any other five men in the football game put together... He accepts criticism from every direction with restrained equanimity. Somewhere at the end of his road may lie the glory which at times he must think he will never attain.
>
> *Jimmy Hill*, Striking for Soccer, *1961.*

Above all, however, English football seemed to accept at last that it still had something to learn. It was a step in the right direction but Sir Stanley Rous, in 'An Open Letter to John Bull' in the *FA Year Book* of 1954/5, frankly admitted that many of the English game's regulations were 'negative and prohibitive'.

> Organisational developments have usually followed events instead of shaping them and the evolution of the whole football system has been, to say the least, haphazard. At Lancaster Gate we are usually thought of as a governing body; I think we should prefer, as far as possible, to be thought of as a body that is always ready to learn.

The finals of the 1954 World Cup in Switzerland hastened this learning process. England were short of confidence after their hidings by Hungary and, while Matthews, Finney and Lofthouse were there, the development of the squad had been erratic and piecemeal. Forty players had been used in 15 internationals over the previous two seasons. The time allowed to Winterbottom to prepare his players, moreover, was patently inadequate. England reached the quarter-finals but their tournament involved just three matches. They drew with Belgium 4–4, after leading 3–1, in a game which went to extra time; they beat Switzerland 2–0 in a drab match played in melting heat; and they lost 4–2 to Uruguay, the World Cup holders, in a brilliant quarter-final in which Matthews was outstanding and in which Wright made a permanent switch from right half to centre half, a position he was to fill with distinction for the next five years.

The 1954 finals are remembered for more notable reasons than England's contribution, not least because they proved the worth of the competition. Most of all they are remembered for West Germany's triumph over Hungary in the final. Hungary were undoubtedly the best team in Switzerland and had beaten the Germans 8–3 in their qualifying group; but, in the final, with Puskas hindered by an ankle injury and Hungary clearly undermined by nervous tension, West Germany's strength and fibre earned them a 3–2 victory, and this after Hungary had scored twice in the first eight minutes. And, as in the final match of the 1950 tournament, the referee was English. Bill Ling's performance was impeccable.

Winterbottom returned home with several things clear in his mind. He wanted more time with his players and he wanted a format for building a team, instead of simply having 11 men selected for him on a loose match-by-match basis. The FA technical sub-committee met soon afterwards and its forceful conclusion was that 'a great deal more can be done towards bringing England players and teams to a high standard of performance in the next four years'. Winterbottom got his way, to a point, and it was even decided that initial team selection in future would be by the England manager and only two members of the selection committee, their choice then to be discussed and approved by the full committee. The FA's coaching scheme also moved up a gear.

English football had reached for the medicinal brandy and, a nip or two later, it was feeling more like its old self – a process helped by a couple of friendly games not long before Christmas 1954. They were played by Wolverhampton Wanderers, the League champions, and they helped launch a Cup tournament which would draw together, like fine threads, the major footballing talents, styles, ambitions, hang-ups and supporting circuses of a whole continent. It would be known as the European Cup.

Floodlights were illuminating a new future for football and, although the first Cup and League games under lights were still a year away, night matches against strong Continental clubs were a profitable fashion. Wolves relished the challenge, and their matches against Moscow Spartak and Honved of Hungary were immediately recognised as something special. It was champion stuff. Wolves beat Spartak 4–0, scoring three in the last four minutes, and English football hugged itself. But this was just muscle flexing before the main bout.

On 13 December 1954 Wolves faced a Honved side with six of the Hungarian players who had made the full might of England look like tenderfoots. The build-up was monstrously overstated and, on a raw Black Country night, Molineux was more theatre than football ground. England expected. Honved threatened to spoil the evening by scoring two early goals, with Puskas and Kocsis their inspiration, but help was at hand for Wolves. Rain started to slant across the ground, water collected on a pitch which had been liberally hose-piped before the kick-off and, in the second half, the balance of power changed dramatically. Wolves and the elements were in sweet accord. The champions' game was based on pace, stamina and simplicity; elaboration was a sin, the short pass a capital crime. Their aggression in the mud that night became obsessive, the pressure on the Honved defence was relentless and, all about them, the Molineux crowd bayed for blood.

Johnny Hancocks, with his size 5½ boots, scored Wolves' first from the penalty spot, after he himself had been crudely blocked; and, although the rapidly tiring Honved hung on until the last quarter-hour, they were then sunk by two goals in two minutes from Roy Swinbourne, who had been finding space in critical forward areas. Wolves 3, Honved 2 – hats were lost, shoes ruined in the mud, shoulder blades bruised. Heaven, for half an hour, was just a couple of hundred yards to the north of Wolverhampton's civic centre.

Stanley Cullis, down in the home dressing room, savoured every sight and sound. The Wolves manager believed in his club, his team and the long pass. 'Our players,' he once said, 'are not encouraged to parade their ability in ostentatious fashion ... every pass, if possible, should be decisive and long.' He had been a centre half of the old school, captain of Wolves at the age of 20 and of England at 22, an expert craftsman with a sensitive touch and sharp elbows, his passes measured, his intentions masked. But as a manager he was committed to driving opponents into the ground and his answer to critics who called the style 'kick and rush' could always be found in the record books: Wolves, under Cullis, won the League championship three times (1954, 1958 and 1959) and the FA Cup twice (1949 and 1960).

Cullis was a leader, a fighter and strategist, an autocrat who delivered opinion as if it was Holy Writ. And, as he relished Wolves' victory over Honved on that December evening in 1954, he pronounced again. 'There they are,' he said, pointing at his players, 'the champions of the world.' The morning papers could hardly wait. 'Hail Wolves, champions of the world now,' said one. 'Wolves can rightly claim themselves club champions of the world,' echoed another. 'The legend of Hungarian invincibility perished forever in the Molineux quagmire,' added yet another. Nobody felt obliged to point out that Honved had lost to Partizan in Belgrade only three weeks before and not everybody felt obliged to take Cullis at his word. It was, however, the moment in football's history for which Gabriel Hanot, the editor of the French daily sports paper *L'Equipe*, had been waiting.

Hanot had been both a player and team manager for France and now, in his mid 60s, he was a man of influence with a knowledge of the European game few could match. Twenty years before, he had put forward a plan for a European league, an idea which was ahead of its time, but his reply to Cullis's extravagant claim was quick and to the point. 'We must wait for Wolves to visit Budapest or Moscow before we proclaim their invincibility,' he wrote. 'There are other clubs of international prowess, such as Milan and Real Madrid, and there is a strong case for starting a European championship for clubs.'

Hanot's timing was perfect, but the birth of the European Cup was not an easy one. Hanot wanted a European league, but most countries favoured a knockout tournament. There were arguments about shape, size, organisation and method of qualification. Sir Stanley Rous, a long-standing friend of Hanot, pointed out that the competition would not get off the ground unless it was approved by all the national associations, and officially recognised by FIFA and the controlling body in Europe, UEFA. FIFA were polite but unhelpful, and UEFA, itself only a year old, seemed frightened by the idea. But Hanot persisted and invited 18 clubs – including Chelsea, who would soon be England's League champions – to an all-expenses-paid meeting in Paris on 2 April 1955. Officers and a committee were elected and a draw was even made. It was part bluff, part show of strength, but FIFA bowed to the inevitable – provided UEFA did the organising. And UEFA, try as they did, could not think of a reason for withholding their approval.

The Football League, however, could think of a reason why Chelsea should not take part in the first European Cup tournament – and it took them just 15 minutes to reach their decision. The private minutes recorded:

> Although of the opinion that they could not withhold permission, the Management Committee instructed the secretary to ask Chelsea FC to give the matter serious consideration because they thought that their playing in such a competition would not be in the best interests of the League.

The committee felt that European football was going to be a nine-day wonder and that a side which had travelled abroad in midweek would not do itself justice on the following Saturday. One member of the Management Committee was absent because of illness, Joe Mears, the chairman of Chelsea, and he agreed to the request with reluctance but without argument. The newspapers dismissed the story in brief sentences.

It needed someone with broader vision to lead English football across the Channel. Matt Busby was that man. Busby, a Scot of natural dignity and iron resolve, had been Manchester United's manager for ten years. He had fashioned United into a sporting institution and when, in 1956, he led his team to the League championship by a margin of 11 points he immediately set his sights on Europe. He went to see Sir Stanley Rous, who told him: 'Read the League rules carefully, but it's your ground and your players. As long as you meet your contractual requirements to fulfil League fixtures with your best team, there is nothing to prevent you from entering. The FA certainly has no objection.'

United informed the League that they had been invited to take part in the European Cup through the offices of the Football Association, that they had 'accepted in good faith' and that all arrangements had been made for their first tie. The League's Management Committee talked privately about 'sharp practice', but their hand was forced.

United began by overwhelming Anderlecht of Belgium (by 10–0 in the home leg), and then beat Borussia Dortmund of West Germany and Atletico Bilbao of Spain on their way to the semi-finals; but there they faced a new experience – a better team. And Real Madrid, the first holders of the European Cup and an international sweet-trolley of a side, triumphed on merit. Real won the trophy for its first five years, and at the heart of their fifth victory was a man called Puskas, a refugee and mercenary from the day Soviet tanks rumbled into Budapest in 1956.

Busby explained United's defeat with resigned honesty: 'A great, experienced team will always beat a great, inexperienced team. But our time will come.' He was not to know that little more than nine months later, still champions, still pursuing the European Cup, his brilliant young team – the 'Busby Babes' – would be destroyed in the whiteness of Munich airport.

At 3.04 on the afternoon of Thursday, 6 February 1958 their chartered Elizabethan aircraft crashed during take-off in snow and slush after a stop to refuel on their way home from a European Cup game in Belgrade. Twenty-one people were killed (two more were to die later), and among them were eight players: Roger Byrne, Geoff Bent, Eddie Colman, Mark Jones, Bill Whelan, Tommy Taylor, David Pegg and a mighty young wing half called Duncan Edwards, a First Division player at 16 and an England international at 18, who hung courageously onto life for 15 days after the crash. Among the survivors were Bobby Charlton and the indomitable Busby, who sustained serious chest, leg and foot injuries. Both still had much to contribute to the history of English football.

The Munich air crash did more than destroy a United side whose skill and artistry had won admirers far beyond the boundaries of Lancashire. It also ended

England's dream of winning the World Cup in Sweden in the summer of 1958. Winterbottom had built his side carefully: its record was impressive, its confidence high. But now, suddenly, it lacked Byrne, Taylor and Edwards who were all irreplaceable. Byrne was a left back with a will of iron, an intelligent man who played to his limits; Edwards was an attacking left half who Matt Busby, a man not given to over-statement, simply described as 'incomparable'; and Taylor was a centre forward in the classic mould of Lawton and Lofthouse.

No-one can say what the presence of this formidable trio might have meant to England in 1958, but there is no doubt that Brazil, a side of extraordinary virtuosity, deserved to be the sixth champions of the world. This was the Brazil of Garrincha ('the Little Bird'), a winger of corrosive swerve and verve, Didi and Zagallo. They had, too, a 17-year-old apprentice they called Pele.

England, in fact, were the only side Brazil failed to score against. They met in Gothenburg, for the first time in a World Cup, and England frustrated Brazil with a carefully structured defensive plan devised by Bill Nicholson, who was Walter Winterbottom's assistant and would soon be manager of Tottenham. Brazil were without Garrincha and Pele, but England's performance was brave and intelligent and there were periods in the second half when they might have scored themselves.

But England's goalless defiance of Brazil must be set in context. They were in a formidably strong group, with Brazil, the Soviet Union and a moderate Austria, and they did not win a game. They drew 2—2 with both the USSR and Austria (after twice being behind) and then lost 1—0 to the Soviets in a play-off match for a place in the quarter-finals. Thunderclaps of criticism followed. They were directed at everything from the sanity of the FA selectors to the choice of a smart hotel in Gothenburg as England's headquarters. Yet Billy Wright thought the hotel was 'superbly equipped and provided facilities for quiet and total relaxation'. He and Tom Finney, as the senior players, were also consulted on team matters — 'and I am bound to say,' he observed later, 'that I had no complaints about the selectors' choice.'

Walter Winterbottom did not escape the critical broadsides; but — without Edwards, Taylor and Byrne, and with Finney able to play only once in Sweden — he lacked players of the highest quality. Joe Mears, the chairman of the selectors, said England did not go to Sweden deliberately short of skill. Winterbottom, for all his enthusiasm and energy, was also chronically overburdened. As well as shaping and preparing England's players for World Cup battle, he was responsible for every administrative duty from arranging hotels and paying bills to booking air-tickets for members of the official party (and their wives, who reserved the right to change their minds). He even cancelled a trip to watch likely opponents because he had to arrange treatment for a selector with shingles. The FA still had much to learn.

English football – and with it the FA – moved towards a period of fundamental change. In step with the times, yet reluctantly, the FA agreed to recognise Sunday amateur football in 1960, although it would be another 14 years before a League game was played on the Sabbath. The League Cup was introduced the same year and was described as a devious ploy to undermine the sovereignty of the FA. 'Not so,' said Alan Hardaker, who became League secretary in 1957 and was an influential, controversial and respected figure for two decades. 'The FA Cup is football's Ascot, the League Cup is its equivalent of Derby Day at Epsom.'

I am the first to recognise the debt I owe to the Professional Footballers' Association, so ably represented in its negotiations during 1960/61 by my ex-Fulham chum Jimmy Hill. I recognise, too, that in supporting a demand for better wages at the top, many players lower down the ladder were risking their own future in the game. It wasn't unexpected when a number of clubs started to cut their staffs to the minimum to meet the cost of higher wages for first-team players, but what irony that Jimmy Hill should find himself one of the first to be affected when the axe fell.

Johnny Haynes of Fulham and England, the first British footballer to be paid £100 a week, in his autobiography Football Today *published shortly after the removal of the maximum wage in 1961.*

The status of the professional footballer was also changing. He had always had his special place in society, but, if he was a hero, he was, essentially, a working-class hero. The game's public loved him and gladly paid money to watch him; but he was also the victim by inheritance of an untenable system of employment. His wage was subject to a modest maximum – in 1960 it was still only £20 a week in the season and £17 in the summer – and a 'retain-and-transfer' regulation meant the contract he signed enabled his club to keep him, even against his wishes. The footballer was an artisan who was expected to know and keep his place and, if he kept his nose clean and saved his pennies, he could look forward to a pub or a corner shop once his playing days were over. But society itself was changing now, the lines of distinction between the classes were becoming blurred and, in the early 1960s, the players won their two 'freedoms'.

A strong Professional Footballers' Association made intelligent use of the media and led its members to the brink of a strike to force the removal of the maximum wage in 1961; and, two years later, George Eastham, a clever and quietly determined inside forward who played for England on 19 occasions, took a long and bitter contractual dispute with Newcastle United to the High Court. And there 'the slaves' were freed by a judge called Wilberforce. The retention regulation was deemed 'an unreasonable restraint of trade'.

The death of Arthur Drewry in March 1961 led to important changes of a different kind: Drewry, a tall and distinguished-looking man from Grimsby, had been president of the League (1949–55) before becoming chairman of the FA and president of FIFA. He was succeeded as FA chairman by Graham Doggart of Cambridge University, who had been a fine footballer himself, while, at the age of 66, Sir Stanley Rous became the third Englishman to hold the FIFA post after DB Woolfall (1906–18) and Drewry. Rous, together with Walter Winterbottom, had already made detailed plans for the FA's centenary in 1963 and even for the World Cup finals in England in 1966, and there were moves to enable him to continue as honorary secretary of the FA, as well as being president of FIFA.

> I learned to admire Stanley Rous in many ways. He had vision, he could sway men and control meetings, he was an excellent speaker who could make a point lucidly and persuasively at the dinner-table and in committee, and he was a very difficult opponent to nail down. Stanley would seem to be over a barrel in an argument, for example, but just when you would be getting ready to finish him off he would come out smoothly with the idea that you were about to suggest. If Stanley had been a politician he would very probably have become prime minister.
>
> *Alan Hardaker, secretary of the Football League 1957–79, in his autobiography* Hardaker of the League, *1977.*

There was a body of opinion within the FA, however, which believed no secretary should ever again be allowed to get himself into such a position of power and authority. Rous, after 27 years as FA secretary, was not consulted about his successor, but it was known that he favoured Winterbottom – and so did the press, who saw the England manager as an obvious choice. But the vote, by 50 votes to 20, was for Denis Follows, the FA's honorary treasurer, a Council member for 14 years and the secretary of the British Airline Pilots' Association. He was an urbane man with strong convictions, a master of detail and a skilled negotiator. Winterbottom courteously masked his disappointment, but he did not stay with the FA. He became general secretary of the Central Council of Physical Recreation and later director of the Sports Council. His contribution to British sport was exceptional: his knighthood was richly deserved. But, before all this fell into place, Winterbottom faced his fourth World Cup as England's manager.

There was even a radiant period when things went almost too well. England scored five against Northern Ireland in mid-October 1960 and then ran in nine against Luxembourg, four against Spain, five against Wales, nine against Scotland and eight against Mexico – 40 goals in six successive matches, with the mercurial Jimmy Greaves of Chelsea scoring 11 in five of them. Greaves was the knifepoint of a forward line which also had the rocky aggression of Bobby Smith of Tottenham, the authority and high strategy of Johnny Haynes of Fulham, the artful skill of Bryan Douglas of Blackburn on the right, and the classical swerve and power of Bobby Charlton, who had moved out to the left wing as Manchester United rebuilt after Munich.

They were at their best against Scotland at Wembley on 15 April 1961. England won 9–3, with Greaves scoring three, Haynes and Smith two each and Douglas and Bobby Robson of West Bromwich Albion one apiece. England were irrepressible, Scotland were confused and their goalkeeper Frank Haffey of Celtic was sure of his modest place in history. Winterbottom had been allowed to stick to one team for this period – it would have been difficult to change it – and qualification for the 1962 World Cup finals in Chile was comfortably managed at the expense of Portugal and Luxembourg.

The FA's report was obliged, however, to refer to 'a disappointing championship for England' in Chile, despite the fact that they reached the quarter-finals. England lost 2–1 to Hungary under a sullen sky, beat Argentina 3–1 with a performance of rising quality and obtained the extra point they needed to reach the last eight with a goalless draw against Bulgaria in a match of unrelieved sterility which was described as the worst of the tournament. England were back at something near their best in their quarter-final against Brazil to take the score to 1–1 at half time. But then, with the Brazilian supporters finding their own rhythm under the pine and eucalyptus trees, the world champions moved up to a higher gear and a 3–1 victory. Brazil duly retained the World Cup with a joy and conviction the rest of mankind could only envy.

The chest-beating began again. England's failure, it was said, had been one of method and morale. Haynes, England's captain, was accused of being morose off the pitch and predictable on it; and Greaves, now a Tottenham player after a few wretchedly unhappy months with AC Milan, was equally disappointing. 'Nobody could say an adoring public scattered roses in our path when we returned home,' said Jimmy Armfield of Blackpool, who, to his lasting credit, was voted the best full back in the tournament by the Chilean press.

The FA's technical sub-committee met just 12 days after the defeat by Brazil and even talked, very briefly, about the merit of combining the finest talents of England, Scotland, Wales and Ireland. Its conclusion, however, was firm: 'Under existing conditions no useful purpose would be served by considering the possibility of a Great Britain team participating in the World Cup.' It agreed instead that 'players must dedicate themselves to the task of improving personal performance . . . faster, more skilful ball control . . . accuracy under pressure . . . higher standards in shooting'. It was a sincere but familiar tune.

Tottenham Hotspur devoted more than a few seconds to the concept of a British team: they spent a large fortune on acquiring one. They garnered players from all over the UK, and the dividends on their investment were handsome. In 1961 they became the first club to complete the League championship and FA Cup 'double' in the 20th century, they retained the Cup a year later and in 1963 they won the European Cup-Winners' Cup to become the first British club to win a major European trophy. The Cup-Winners' Cup and Inter-Cities Fairs Cup (later the UEFA Cup) had been inaugurated soon after the birth of the European Cup.

Spurs were a brilliant side, full of light and shade, a team of individual distinction and collective excellence. They were captained by Danny Blanchflower of Northern Ireland, a natural leader and an intelligent improviser; he and the dynamic David Mackay of Scotland were at the heart of Spurs' formula. Blanchflower at right half and Mackay on the left . . . Irish charm and Scottish fire, one thinking the game, the other devouring it. John White of Scotland, just in front of them, was an inside forward whose nose for space and gliding movement made him as difficult to hold as a seed in the breeze. Cliff Jones of Wales was a winger with flick-knife speed and a waspish finish, a demon inside the penalty area, while Bobby Smith of England was a heavyweight of a centre forward who simply went to war, a brave and damaging figure who was sometimes underestimated. Soon, too, they would be joined by Jimmy Greaves of England, back from Italy, who was probably the greatest finisher in the history of English football. He scored 491 goals in his 14-year career – more than half of them for Tottenham. Bill Nicholson, Spurs' hugely respected manager, built his side with all the passion and insight of an artist at work on a picture.

Spurs were the stuff of dreams for a few seasons. The 1961 League title was theirs by Easter barring nasty accidents; they beat Leicester City and Burnley in their two FA Cup finals; and there were some electrifying nights on their way to the final of the 1963 Cup-Winners' Cup, in which they beat Atletico Madrid, the holders, 5–1. Two years later West Ham United won the same trophy, beating Munich 1860 2–0 at Wembley with a performance of boundless style and variety. Ron Greenwood, West Ham's manager, described the night as 'my fulfilment'.

Greenwood and Nicholson were men who both acknowledged their debt to Walter Winterbottom.

The centenary of the FA was handsomely celebrated in 1963 with a banquet, tributes and gifts, memories and visions of the future and, of course, tournaments and matches of which the highlight was a Wembley meeting between England and a Rest of the World XI selected by FIFA. Puskas was there, ten years after inspiring Hungary to their famous victory in the same stadium; so was Alfredo Di Stefano, the great Argentine forward who was the undisputed star of Real Madrid's team of stars; and so were players of the quality of Djalma Santos, who had twice helped Brazil win the World Cup, Lev Yashin, the Russian goalkeeper who was known as the 'Black Octopus', Masopust of Czechoslovakia, Kopa of France, Gento of Spain and Eusebio of Portugal.

It was probably the greatest collection of players ever drawn together, but Denis Law of Manchester United and Scotland – 'The King of Old Trafford' – shone even in this company. He scored the Rest of the World's goal and gave a performance that was arrestingly distinctive, his involvement total and his energy limitless. But England, not surprisingly perhaps, still had the edge in teamwork and determination; and goals by Terry Paine and Jimmy Greaves (two minutes from the end after a surging run by Bobby Charlton) gave them a 2–1 victory.

Royalty and heads of state, players and officials from all over the world, a full Wembley stadium and a huge television and radio audience celebrated the 100th birthday of the Football Association. And, surely, also there were the spirits of those Victorian pioneers who pulled football to its feet on 26 October 1863.

FA Cup

Year	Date	Winners		Runners-up		Venue	Attendance	Referee	Entries
1953	2 May	Blackpool	4	Bolton Wanderers	3	Wembley	100,000	M Griffiths	477
1954	1 May	West Bromwich Albion	3	Preston North End	2	Wembley	100,000	A Luty	460
1955	7 May	Newcastle United	3	Manchester City	1	Wembley	100,000	R Leafe	504
1956	5 May	Manchester City	3	Birmingham City	1	Wembley	100,000	A Bond	460
1957	4 May	Aston Villa	2	Manchester United	1	Wembley	100,000	F Coultas	438
1958	3 May	Bolton Wanderers	2	Manchester United	0	Wembley	100,000	J Sherlock	442
1959	2 May	Nottingham Forest	2	Luton Town	1	Wembley	100,000	J Clough	447
1960	7 May	Wolverhampton Wanderers	3	Blackburn Rovers	0	Wembley	100,000	K Howley	462

Year	Date	Winners	Runners-up		Venue	Attendance	Referee	Entries
1961	6 May	Tottenham Hotspur	2 Leicester City	0	Wembley	100,000	J Kelly	433
1962	5 May	Tottenham Hotspur	3 Burnley	1	Wembley	100,000	J Finney	414
1963	25 May	Manchester United	3 Leicester City	1	Wembley	100,000	K Aston	411
1964	2 May	West Ham United	3 Preston North End	2	Wembley	100,000	A Holland	400
1965	1 May	Liverpool	2 Leeds United	1*	Wembley	100,000	W Clements	395
1966	14 May	Everton	3 Sheffield Wednesday	2	Wembley	100,000	JK Taylor	403

The FA Cup

Miscellany

Most FA Cup final wins 8 – Tottenham Hotspur, 1901, 1921, 1961, 1962, 1967, 1981, 1982, 1991.

FA Cup winners three times in succession The Wanderers (1876–7–8), Blackburn Rovers (1884–5–6).

Second Division winners of FA Cup Notts County (1894), Wolverhampton Wanderers (1908), Barnsley (1912), West Bromwich Albion (1931), Sunderland (1973), Southampton (1976), West Ham United (1980).

Most individual Cup-winners' medals 5 – The Hon A F Kinnaird (Wanderers) 1873, 1877, 1878 (Old Etonians) 1879, 1882.
Charles Wollaston (Wanderers) 1872, 1873, 1876–7–8.
James Forrest (Blackburn Rovers) 1884–5–6, 1890, 1891.

Biggest win in FA Cup Preston North End 26, Hyde 0, 1st round, 1887.

Most individual goals in one season in FA Cup Alexander (Sandy) Brown – 15 for Tottenham in 1900/01.
(First player to score in every round.)

FA Cup final hat tricks Billy Townley (Blackburn Rovers v Sheffield Wednesday, 1890).
Jimmy Logan (Notts County v Bolton Wanderers, 1894).
Stan Mortensen (Blackpool v Bolton Wanderers, 1953).

Highest individual scorer in one game in FA Cup proper Ted MacDougall (Bournemouth) – 9 goals v Margate, 1st round, 1971. (Bournemouth won 11–0.)

Longest FA Cup tie 6 matches – Alvechurch v Oxford City, 4th qualifying round, 1971/2. (Alvechurch eventually won 1–0.)

Youngest player in FA Cup proper Scott Endersby (15 years 279 days) for Kettering v Tilbury, 1st round, 1977.

Oldest player in FA Cup proper Billy Meredith (49 years 8 months) for Manchester City v Newcastle United in semi-final, 1924.

Youngest player in FA Cup final Paul Allen (17 years 256 days) for West Ham United v Arsenal 1980.

Oldest player in FA Cup final Walter (Billy) Hampson (41 years 8 months) for Newcastle United v Aston Villa, 1924.

①

① The Nepstadion (the People's Stadium), Budapest, is full for England's heaviest international defeat – Hungary 7, England 1, Sunday, 23 May 1954. The stadium opened on 20 August 1953 with a capacity of 100,000. It took three years to build with 'voluntary' help, it is claimed, from 10,000 workers.

② Alf Ramsey scoring England's third goal, from the penalty spot, against Hungary at Wembley, 25 November 1953. Gyula Grosics, Hungary's goal-keeper, fails by a fingertip. Three goals at Wembley normally guaranteed England victory – but this time Hungary scored six and English football conceded, reluctantly, that it still had much to learn.

③ Hungary's fifth goal against England in the Nepstadion, Budapest, 1954 – and there were still two to come. Left to right: Josef Toth (the scorer), Gil Merrick (Birmingham), the great Ferenc Puskas (who scored twice) and Syd Owen (Luton). It was a colossal blow to the ego of English football – but Hungary's team of the early 1950s was arguably the finest European national side of all. They lost only one of 48 international matches between 1950 and the Hungarian uprising in 1956 and averaged more than four goals a game.

③

④

① The Cup belongs to Blackpool – and Stanley Matthews. The climax of the most famous FA Cup final of all, Blackpool 4, Bolton Wanderers 3, 2 May 1953. Bill Perry, right, arms outstretched, scores Blackpool's winner with less than a minute left (after Bolton had led 3–1). Matthews, who provided the centre, is on the ground, left, and Stan Mortensen, who had scored the first hat trick in an FA Cup final at Wembley, is in the centre. Mortensen's goals entitled him to be 'the man of the match', but the country's affection for Matthews, who was then 38, transcended everything. This will always be 'the Matthews final'.

② Stanley Matthews: a man alone – Blackpool 1, Huddersfield 1, Division One, 18 December 1954. Matthews was just a few weeks short of his 40th birthday and, earlier in the month, he had been England's outstanding player in a 3–1 victory over West Germany, the 1954 World Cup champions, at Wembley. Matthews had then been bemusing defences for 22 years – and his top-class career still had ten years to run.

③ Billy Wright of Wolverhampton Wanderers and England is taken for a ride after becoming the first player to win 100 international caps, England 1, Scotland 0, 11 April 1959. The transport is provided by (left to right) Peter Broadbent of Wolves, Ron Clayton of Blackburn and Don Howe of West Bromwich Albion. Wright, a modest and engaging man, won 105 caps altogether (1946–59), 90 of them as captain, first as a wing half and then as centre half. He earned his last 70 caps in successive matches and he missed only three England games in 13 years. He also captained Wolves to three League championships and victory in the 1949 FA Cup final. Wright was an uncomplicated player who did all the important things well, strong in the air and into the tackle, quick in recovery and steady and intelligent in his use of the ball. Walter Winterbottom, England's manager at the time, identified Wright as a player who made his plans work and his team-mates play better.

④ Tom Finney of Preston North End and England takes his last corner in his 569th and last first-class match on the last day of the 1959/60 season. A crowd of 30,000 gathered at Deepdale to bid him farewell, pressed forward to watch his final corner kick and then joined players and officials in singing 'Auld Lang Syne'. Few players have been more admired or respected than the 'Preston Plumber' – a modest and loyal one-club man and a forward who Bill Shankly described simply as 'the best I ever saw'. Finney was a master dribbler, a cruel finisher with either foot, a destructive tactician and a dependable tackler—a winger by inclination but versatile enough to play in any forward position. Tom Finney or Stanley Matthews? Who was the better? It was an argument which carried many a day heatedly into the small hours of the next. He won 76 caps and scored 30 goals for England (1946–58) and was the first man to be twice voted Footballer of the Year, 1954 and 1957.

①

②

③

① One hundred thousand ... and one. Jim Sanders, the West Bromwich Albion goalkeeper, cannot bear to watch Ronnie Allen take a penalty against Preston North End in the 1954 FA Cup final. 'I was praying and touching the goalpost for good luck,' he said afterwards. ' I just daren't look. Then I heard the crowd cheer and I thought "That's it".' He was right. Allen made the score 2–2 – and Frank Griffin scored a winner for West Bromwich with only three minutes of the game left.

② The 1955 FA Cup final is less than a minute old – and Jackie Milburn of Newcastle scores against Manchester City. It was the fastest goal in a Wembley final since Jack Roscamp scored in approximately 30 seconds for Blackburn against Huddersfield in 1928. Newcastle won 3–1 to take the trophy for the third time in five years (1951-2-5). Milburn – 'Wor

Jackie' – was one of the most revered of all Tyneside heroes, a buccaneer who led from the front with a dashing, tearaway, catch-me-if-you-can style: his initials, fittingly, were JET. He scored ten goals in 13 internationals, after succeeding Tommy Lawton as England's centre forward, and scored 196 goals for Newcastle in 11 seasons between World War Two and 1957. His heading ability was modest (partly because he had fibrositis) and a Milburn header was always affectionately cheered at St James's Park – but he made no mistake with his first chance in the 1955 final. It followed a corner by Len White and Milburn was left unchallenged by Roy Paul (second right in picture) who suddenly decided to mark Vic Keeble (right). Milburn was a relaxed and charming man who belonged to a rare family – the Milburns of Ashington: George Milburn (Leeds and Chesterfield), Jack Milburn

(Leeds and Bradford City), Jimmy Milburn (Leeds and Bradford Park Avenue) and Stan Milburn (Chesterfield, Leicester and Rochdale). Cissie Milburn also made her contribution: she was the mother of Jackie and Bobby Charlton.

③ Tottenham celebrate the first League and FA Cup 'double' of the 20th century, 6 May 1961. Spurs won the First Division title by eight points and beat Leicester 2–0 in the final. Left to right: Ron Henry, Bill Brown, Peter Baker, Cliff Jones, Danny Blanchflower, Terry Dyson (who scored the second goal), Les Allen (half hidden), Bobby Smith (first goal) and Maurice Norman. They were paid £20 a week (£17 in summer) and, with bonuses, they each received about £1,300 for their year's work. It was the last season for the maximum wage.

①

②

③

① Walter Winterbottom (left) – England's first team manager and FA director of coaching – a man of whom Ron Greenwood was to write: 'Many people in the game have no idea how much English football owes to Walter … his influence has reached on down through the years.' Winterbottom is talking with (left to right) Bill Foulkes of Manchester United, Billy Wright of Wolves, Nat Lofthouse of Bolton Wanderers and Don Revie of Manchester City, before the game with Northern Ireland at Windsor Park, Belfast, 2 October 1954.

② John Roderick Elliott 'Bob' Hardisty (white shirt), the best-known player in post-war amateur football, in impressive action for Bishop Auckland in the FA Amateur Cup final in front of a full house at Wembley, 13 April 1957.

Bishop Auckland, the Northern League champions, beat Wycombe Wanderers, the champions of the Isthmian League, 3–1 to win the trophy for a record third successive time. It was their tenth triumph in the tournament and their 18th final – success unapproached by any other amateur club. They were presented with a specially made replica of the trophy to mark their achievement. Hardisty symbolised Bishop Auckland's quality and spirit. He captained Great Britain's Olympic side in 1948 and was a lean and cultured wing half who played regularly with professionals during World War Two.

③ Perhaps the most talented group of players ever assembled: the Rest of the World squad which played England in the FA Centenary match, Wembley, 23 October 1963. Back row (left to right):

Ferenc Puskas (Hungary and Spain), Djalma Santos (Brazil), Svatopluk Pluskal (Czechoslovakia), Lev Yashin (USSR), Jan Popluhar (Czechoslovakia), Karl Heinz Schnellinger (West Germany), Milutin Soskic (Yugoslavia), Josef Masopust (Czechoslovakia), Luis Eyzaguirre (Chile), Jim Baxter (Scotland), Uwe Seeler (West Germany). Front row: Raymond Kopa (France), Denis Law (Scotland), Alfredo di Stefano (Argentina, Colombia and Spain), Ferreira da Silva Eusebio (Portugal), Francisco Gento (Spain). A collection beyond price – but England, led with resolution and intelligence by Jimmy Armfield of Blackpool, were the more effective 'team' and won by 2–1. Scorers: England – Terry Paine (65th minute) and Jimmy Greaves (88); Rest of World – Denis Law (83).

9

'PLAY FOR ALF'
1966

The eighth World Cup and its winning did more for English football than anything since the dawn of the Football Association, the birth of the 'little tin idol' and the rise of the Football League. The country which set football rolling could claim, at last, to be its undisputed heavyweight champion. The unimpeachable proof was a little statue of a winged seraphim, a piece of gold about the height of a milk bottle and weighing 9lb (4kg), which stood on a base of onyx. Possession of the Jules Rimet trophy – held aloft by Bobby Moore at Wembley at 5·15pm on 30 July 1966 – gave England's footballers the right to regard themselves as the best in the world for four years.

It took the Football Association nearly six years to organise the tournament and Alf Ramsey and his players six matches and 19 days to win it. The weather and the quality of the football were wildly variable; but, like a classic piece of theatre, the competition picked its way scene by scene towards a compelling climax. It was the first World Cup to receive major television coverage by way of satellite: the global audience for the 32 matches was estimated at two billion and seven out of every ten people in England followed its progress on their screens.

They saw England take a slow and sometimes bumpy road towards their championship: a goalless draw against Uruguay in a poor opening match, a modest victory over Mexico, a firm yet still unconvincing defeat of France, a narrow triumph over ten Argentines in a quarter-final which shamed the tournament, a win over Portugal in a masterpiece of a semi-final and on a Saturday afternoon of chasing sunshine and rain the most dramatic final in the history of the World Cup. England's 4–2 victory over West Germany was a compound of sustained adventure, stunning quirks of fortune and enduring controversy which ran its epic path to the last second of extra time.

For nearly three weeks, England's footballers were centre-stage. A financial freeze and weighty problems east of Suez took secondary billing. The media knew where its duty lay: television, radio and the daily prints devoted hundreds of hours and acres of space to the crusade. The thoughts of Alf were discussed in board-rooms and over back walls. Strangers who would have been hard pressed previously to spot the difference between a football and a pumpkin found common interest in the elemental shooting power of Bobby Charlton, Nobby Stiles' toothless smile, the rival claims of Geoff Hurst and Jimmy Greaves and which player had the prettiest wife or girlfriend. Football was, and is, just a game – but for the summer of 1966 it came remarkably close to being something more.

Great expectations turned to conviction as the tournament took shape, al-though there were experts and opinion-formers who retained doubts about England's chances until as late as the semi-finals. Don Revie, the manager of Leeds and the man destined to succeed Alf Ramsey, wrote in the *FA News*: 'If England win the World Cup it would be the greatest thrill of the season for me – but sadly I can-not see them doing so.' But everyone recognised that the home of the game would never have a better chance. If England could not win the World Cup in England, would they ever win it?

The faith of one man, however, never wavered – not in public at least. Alf Ramsey officially succeeded Walter Winterbottom as England's manager on 1 May 1963 and immediately declared that 'England will win the World Cup'. He said it to a journalist at Ipswich and then repeated it at a press conference in London. It was a simple statement of intent by a man not given to throwaway lines or fancy bravado. He believed England *could* win the Jules Rimet trophy but, equally importantly, he felt his pronouncement might help inject confidence into players and public alike. He thought it was a statement which had to be made. There were to be days when Ramsey undoubtedly regretted having said it, days when the phrase would be thrown back into his face, but he never looked for cover. Ramsey was appointed to lead England to World Cup victory, he said he would – and he did.

Yet Ramsey was not the FA's first choice. The post was advertised and 59 applications were received, but the six-man selection committee, headed by FA chairman Graham Doggart, were 'not satisfied the man they required was among them'. The game's leading figures were clearly waiting to be approached, on a point of pride or principle, and so the FA turned to Jimmy Adamson, Burnley's captain, an outstanding but uncapped wing half and the current Footballer of the Year. Adamson was a lanky, unflappable north-easterner, a strong and respected charac-ter who had been an FA staff coach for five years and Winterbottom's right-hand man during the 1962 World Cup in Chile. Winterbottom saw Adamson as 'an outstanding coach, a good leader and an expert at reading the game' but the Burnley captain was not a unanimous choice at the FA, where some members wanted a man with more experience. 'The England manager,' said one, 'should know his job NOW.' The issue was quickly resolved by Adamson himself. He refused the FA's invitation because 'I want to carry on as a player for a few more years . . . it is the hardest thing in the world to hang up your boots.' But he admitted later that he, too, did not think he had enough experience.

Ron Greenwood, who was coaching Arsenal and England's Under-23 team at the time, had already been informally asked by Winterbottom how he would feel about becoming England's manager. Greenwood replied: 'I would be delighted.' Winterbottom had high hopes of succeeding Sir Stanley Rous as FA secretary at that point; but Denis Follows got the job and Greenwood heard no more. Greenwood did become England's manager eventually, in 1977, and he was to admit that it was 'a blessing in disguise' that nothing came of the first approach. 'It is a job which needs experience,' he said. 'I wasn't ready for it, while Alf Ramsey certainly was.'

Ramsey had drawn his playing experience from Southampton, from Tottenham under the creative stewardship of Arthur Rowe and from England on 32 occasions. He helped Tottenham win the Second and First Division championships at the beginning of the 1950s and shared many important moments with England, some rich, some painful, including the defeats by the United States and Hungary. And, as the manager of Ipswich (1955–62), his achievements were remarkable: he levered them quickly out of the Third Division and then made such intelligent use of inhibitingly modest resources that the Suffolk club also won the Second and First Divison titles in successive seasons.

But Ramsey's ultimate achievement had its roots in his character as well as his success and experience. As a player he was a right back and a highly disciplined craftsman. There were defenders who were faster and more incisive in the tackle; but few had Ramsey's calculated understanding of the game, his intuition, his studied accuracy and his undentable temperament. He was known with ungrudging respect as 'The General'. As a club manager, too, he made the best of himself and his players. He was detached, analytical and practical. He knew what his players could do – and not do – and the staggered playing format he introduced at Ipswich consistently perplexed the best defences in the League. Ramsey stitched a collection of remnants into a quilt of quality.

Ramsey was a loyal players' man but, above all, he was his own man. He angered quickly and cooled slowly, but his strong and sombre face rarely betrayed his inner feelings. A part of him always seemed private, and attempts to trespass into these hidden corners were waspishly rejected. The style was unmistakable; and so was the man.

Doggart and his committee decided Ramsey was a man who might well be able to fashion and inspire 11 English footballers into the best team in the world. John Cobbold, Ipswich's much-loved chairman, was approached first on 1 October 1962 and readily gave the FA permission to talk with Ramsey. Doggart spent two hours with the Ipswich manager at Portman Road on 17 October and returned to Lancaster Gate to say he had 'been most impressed with Ramsey's attitude to the challenge'. A week later Ramsey, Doggart and the still-influential Winterbottom had lunch together – after which Ramsey accepted the job. The announcement, at Ramsey's request, was delayed for 24 hours.

Ramsey wanted full control over selection and the FA agreed without argument. The opinion of the country's leading club managers had been sounded a month before, at regional meetings in Manchester, York, London and Birmingham; and the FA team of Doggart, Joe Mears of Chelsea, Follows and Winterbottom reported later that 'a valuable service had been served by these small and friendly conferences'. Matt Busby, Bill Shankly and Stanley Cullis attended; and so did Don Revie, Joe Mercer and Ron Greenwood who were England managers of the future. Ramsey himself, who had not been approached by the FA at this point, was not present.

They talked about midweek internationals, England's need to train and practise together, private training sessions, get-togethers and co-operation by the clubs; and – unanimously at every meeting – it was stressed that the manager of England should have full responsibility for selecting his teams. The message was received and, on 15 October, two days before Doggart had his long talk with Ramsey, the FA's Technical Committee recommended that 'the manager should be responsible for selecting the team' ... though the Senior Selection Committee should still go 'match viewing' and 'player assessing' and should have the manager's choice 'reported to them'.

The old convention of selection by committee passed into history: selection now was by Ramsey. But there was no suggestion that Ramsey should also be the FA's director of coaching. His responsibility, the senior, Under-23 and Youth sides, was considered heavy enough; and a separate six-man committee under Doggart considered 19 applications for the coaching post (salary range £2,000–£2,250). Four candidates were shortlisted and Allen Wade, a lecturer in physical recreation at Loughborough College and a former Notts County player, was the unanimous choice. Thus it took two men to replace Winterbottom, but the jobs were changing and expanding along with the game and its demands.

England played two games between the announcement of Ramsey's appointment and his official takeover. Both were lost: France triumphed stylishly by 5–2 in a European Nations' Cup-tie in Paris and Scotland won hurtfully by 2–1 at Wembley in the Home International Championship. Ramsey's influence was marginal, but England's elimination from the Nations' Cup deprived him immediately of important competitive games. Ramsey began his job with no illusions.

Ramsey had 36 games in full charge before the opening match of the World Cup. Of these 24 were won, four lost and eight drawn: it was a record which, assessed on a League points basis, was of championship quality. But they were all classified as friendly games, because England, as host nation, did not have to run the gauntlet of qualification. Three of the four defeats were in 1964, by Scotland again and by Brazil (5–1) and Argentina (1–0) in Rio de Janeiro during a summer tournament which Ramsey summarised by saying: 'There is a big gap between "them" and "us" but it is not a gap which can't be bridged.' England still had another 21 games before the World Cup finals and, of these, they lost only one – by 3–2 to a young and experimental Austria at Wembley in October 1965.

There were peaks and troughs along the way, and the critics honed away at their knives, but a format slowly took shape. Four of the side which won the World Cup were in the first team Ramsey selected with full control: Gordon Banks (his second cap), Ray Wilson (18th), Bobby Moore (11th) and Bobby Charlton (42nd). Roger Hunt had also won one cap at this point, but the other six were first called to the colours by Ramsey himself: George Cohen in May 1964, Jack Charlton, Nobby Stiles and Alan Ball in the late spring of 1965, Geoff Hurst in February 1966 and Martin Peters in May 1966.

The defence took shape first. Banks, Cohen, Wilson, Stiles, Jack Charlton and Moore played together for the first time against Scotland on 10 April 1965. The other half of the team was much less certain in its making. Bryan Douglas, Terry Paine, Peter Thompson, Alan Hinton and John Connelly were among the wingers Ramsey examined closely; and, while Jimmy Greaves' place in the final pattern was taken for granted by most people, England's manager also looked at such providers and hit-men as Bobby Smith, George Eastham, the ever-reliable Hunt, Fred Pickering, the brilliant John Byrne, Frank Wignall, Terry Venables, Barry Bridges and a 20-year-old from Blackpool called Alan Ball.

Ball was one of the keys. He was a gnome of a man, flame-haired, combative and tireless, a player who could organise as well as attack along a touchline. He helped give Ramsey the option of playing without an orthodox winger, and the conception of 4–3–3 – basically three forwards and three midfield players in front of a defensive four – came sharply into focus in the game against Spain in Madrid on

8 December 1965. England played with furious energy yet absolute composure and Jose Villalonga, Spain's manager, said afterwards that 'England were phenomenal ... far superior'. Nine of England's World Cup-winners played in that game: only Hurst and Peters were still to come. There were back-page reservations, however, and one respected Sunday writer observed that 'young Ball' was a player who could be improved on – 'I still feel he does not have quite enough real acceleration, that he finds it too hard to shake off an opponent he has gone past, and that his play often lacks depths of imagination.'

Ramsey gave Hurst his first cap in February 1966 against West Germany at Wembley and, although England won with a goal by Stiles, it was an untidy affair which the crowd jeered and slow-handclapped. 'Listen to them moan,' said Ramsey down in the dressing room. 'But those people will be going mad if we beat West Germany by a goal in the World Cup final.' Hurst scored his first goal for England in their next game, against Scotland at Hampden Park. But, for all his perception and mobility, his powerful shooting and expertise in the air, he was still in the shadow of Greaves who was on his way back after a bout of hepatitis.

Hurst was to start the World Cup as a reserve and by then Ramsey had begun to recognise another West Ham player, Martin Peters, as a missing link. Ramsey employed Peters on the left side of the field, a player without portfolio, a free agent whose impeccable timing and understanding of space took him to key points at critical moments. He was a stealthy, thinking player who saw things others missed and a masterly technician with a sure and flexible finish. He seemed to materialise on the field only when it mattered – and his entry into the England side was the same. He won his first cap just nine weeks before the start of the World Cup finals.

Who was it who said 'Martin Peters is a player ten years ahead of his time'? And who was it who said 'This boy Peters cannot play'? The answer to both questions is Sir Alf Ramsey. Sir Alf's comment about Peters' 'futuristic' style is well known. It was a compliment to Peters' tremendous all-round ability, perception, understanding of space, perfect timing and stealthy running ... The other comment was made just after Ramsey had taken over as England's manager and three years before Peters was to play his major role in winning the World Cup. Peters played in an Under-23 international and Alf rang me afterwards. 'This boy Peters *cannot* play' he said in that clipped, emphatic way of his. 'I shouldn't worry about it, Alf ... he *can* play' I replied. The story proves that early impressions are not always right.

Ron Greenwood, manager of West Ham and then England, in his autobiography Yours Sincerely, *1984.*

England's team was almost ready for the finals: the FA certainly was. From the moment FIFA, at its Rome congress in 1960, gave England the task of staging the 1966 finals, the FA knew it was expected to surpass anything which had been achieved in organisation and presentation in the previous seven World Cup tournaments. While Ramsey had promised that England would win the World Cup, the FA had decided that England would stage the best finals yet.

Among the first priorities was an accurate assessment of requirements and a survey of stadia. Only grounds with a capacity of 50,000 or more were considered and 18 were closely inspected. Dozens of factors were involved, including the size of the pitch which, according to FIFA regulations, had to be 115 yards long and 75 yards wide. Arsenal's Highbury was eliminated because its pitch was five-and-a-half yards too short and Goodison Park was accepted only after its playing area had been expensively lengthened and widened by raising and turfing part of its running track. The ratio between seated and standing places was also important, as was space and facilities for the press, radio and television. Journalists each had to be allowed 27 inches of working space instead of the normal 18.

The eight grounds selected were Wembley and the White City (where only one game was played) in London, Villa Park in Birmingham and Sheffield Wednesday's Hillsborough in the Midlands, Everton's Goodison Park and Manchester United's Old Trafford in the north-west and Sunderland's Roker Park and Newcastle's St James's Park in the north-east. Even then a change had to be made: Ayresome Park, the home of Middlesbrough, took the place of St James's Park because Newcastle were having difficulties with the local council over the lease of the ground.

Work on the preparations hardened and quickened in 1962 and it became clear that the FA staff at Lancaster Gate, already heavily committed in the everyday running of English football at all its levels, needed to be heavily supported. So World Cup headquarters were set up in a newly erected block of eight offices at the White City where the full-time staff built up to 35.

The sudden death of Graham Doggart at the annual meeting of the FA on 7 June 1963 cast a shadow over everything. He was a Cambridge University man and a Corinthian who had won an England cap in 1924 and played first-class cricket for Middlesex. He was a man of integrity, quiet charm and patience, a strong man but also a fair one who made an important contribution to English football. He had done much to establish a harmonious relationship between the FA and the League; and his successor as FA chairman, Joe Mears of Chelsea, a pleasant and very honest man, took over at a time when English football seemed to be running on smooth rails. Mears became chairman of the FA's six-man World Cup Committee just when preparations for 1966 were moving into overdrive.

Over two million tickets were available for the 32 matches – and the subject of their prices, printing and selling was overridingly important. Ten-match 'season tickets' were priced at £25 15s for the best seats and £3 17s 6d for standing room. Five tons of paper were needed for the tickets alone and 30 tons were used for the sales brochures and application forms which had to be sent to 130 countries. The FA bore the costs and spirited efforts were made to find sponsors or advertisers – but the response of British industry and commerce was totally negative. Not one could be found. No one could see the potential. The World Cup, it was murmured, was too far away.

By March 1966 nearly £1,000,000 of tickets had been sold, of which £750,000 was tucked away at a healthy interest rate. Altogether, 1,614,677 tickets were sold for a record £1,551,099 13s 6d – a remarkable 78.44 percent of the tickets available and just a whisker short of the FA's ambitiously high target of 80 per cent.

World Cup Willie played his part in it all. He was the cartoon symbol of the World Cup, a comic little lion with a smile on his face, square shoulders and a Union Jack football shirt, which was used on everything from beer-mats and car stickers to key-rings and calendars. He became more than a successful commercial symbol, though, and for a year he was used by the newspapers to indicate the highs and lows of England's progress towards the finals: a smile today, a tear tomorrow. He seemed to reflect the World Cup hopes of the middle Swinging Sixties, but the FA resolutely refused to reveal how Willie came to be named. World Cup Willie was, in fact, the name used by the girls in the White City office to describe the World Cup's chief administrative officer, EK Willson.

Committees and sub-committees met almost daily during the year before the finals. The list of jobs and responsibilities included television and radio rights, accommodation, training facilities, advertising, merchandising, insurance, medical services, crowd discipline, transport, programmes (a million were printed), handbooks in four languages, accreditation, ball boys and mementoes . . . all took time, all caused problems and all had to be got just right. There was even a finger-clicking sub-committee – Messrs Mears, Follows and Willson – whose job was to decide which was the best World Cup tune. Their verdict: 'The World Cup Willie Song'. Nine manufacturers submitted 111 different footballs for use in the finals. One by Slazengers of Croydon was chosen and, while the order for 400 which followed was profitable, the publicity for the company was priceless.

Relatively late but welcome problems were also created by a change of mind by Harold Wilson's Government. The FA had first asked the Government to help with the improvement of grounds and provision of facilities in 1963. The approach was unsuccessful and as late as November 1964 Denis Howell, the minister responsible for sport, a League and international referee and very much a man of football, was obliged to emphasise that Government help was unlikely. But in February 1965 it was announced that funds would be available and, three months later, Howell confirmed that 'a sum not exceeding £500,000' would be available: four-fifths as a grant and a fifth as a loan.

The FA had been obliged to do its World Cup sums on the basis that no Government money was on the way but now, with just over a year to go to the finals, it was being challenged to use £500,000. Work had to be planned and carried out during a full season of League football on the six grounds outside London. In the end, £415,000 was obtained from the Government; and, with the FA lending £160,000, the work that was desirable as well as essential was completed. But it needed determination, efficiency, flexibility and good will as well as money to manage it.

Not everything went according to plan. The World Cup was even lost before it was won. The FA allowed the Jules Rimet trophy to be the centre-piece at a major stamp exhibition at Central Hall, Westminster, four months before the finals – and on 20 March 1966 it was stolen. The trophy was in its place at 11am, but by noon it was gone, a bold example of daylight robbery carried out on Mothering Sunday. In another part of the building, 200 Methodists were cheerfully singing hymns. The thief removed screws from the plate of padlocked double doors and then neatly removed the lock at the back of the glass-fronted cabinet containing the trophy. The stamps at the exhibition were worth £3,000,000, but only the World Cup, which was insured for £30,000, was taken.

The FA's embarrassment was total and the reaction of the world's press less than understanding. The story was front-page news all over the world. The FA announced that it 'deeply regretted this unfortunate incident which inevitably brings discredit to both the FA and this country'. Handsome rewards were offered and immediate steps were taken to provide a replacement. Those who knew their history glumly recalled the theft of the original FA Cup in 1895 – a trophy never recovered.

More than 100 detectives, flying squad officers and local policemen asked questions, searched gardens and lifted floorboards in derelict buildings. Then, a few days later, Joe Mears received the detachable top of the Jules Rimet trophy – about the size of an ashtray – in the post, together with a demand for money. Telephone calls followed, a rendezvous was arranged, Mears went to it in his own car and a 47-year-old dock labourer from south-east London was arrested. But the trophy was still missing.

Exactly one week after the theft, however, a 26-year-old Thames lighterman called David Corbett set out for a walk on Beulah Hill in the south-eastern London suburb of Norwood, a long and busy road with detached houses set back on both sides. He was about to put the lead on his dog, a young black and white mongrel called Pickles, when he noticed him sniffing at something under a bush near the path. 'I looked down and saw a bundle wrapped in newspaper,' Corbett said later. 'I tore part of the paper off and saw gold and the words "Brazil 1962".'

Pickles instantly became the world's top dog. He was presented with a medal by the National Canine Defence League, discussions opened for a film role at 'double the usual dog's rate' and an animal food firm presented him with a year's supply of goodies for 'his outstanding service to world football'. Mr Corbett also did very nicely ... and the next public appearance of the trophy he and Pickles had found was on the day of the World Cup final.

The battle-lines for the finals had been established at the draw at the Royal Garden Hotel in Kensington, the official headquarters of the World Cup, on 6 January 1966 and it proved to be a smooth and suspenseful first test of the FA's organisation. It also boosted ticket sales because England were clearly the favourites in the London group, the north-west was given an exciting combination of Brazil, Hungary and Portugal and the Midlands had West Germany, Argentina and Spain. The north-east alone felt aggrieved: Italy was the only country there which would bring a profitable army of supporters.

Joe Mears was centre-stage at the draw, but he did not see the World Cup finals he had worked so hard to organise and promote for three years. He died at the age of 61 while accompanying the England team on their tour of Scandinavia just before the finals began. Mears had been a member of the League's Management Committee and an FA councillor since 1948 and had developed into a legislator who was hugely respected for his kindness and generosity, as well as for his firmness and understanding of the game's complexities. The *FA News* described him as 'a big man in every sense of word'.

①

②

① A million copies were printed of the official 1966 World Cup programme. Sixty-four pages were planned, but four extra pages were added at the last moment after the death of Joe Mears, the chairman of the FA, on 1 July – ten days before the first match.

② The first British stamps featuring sportsmen in action, issued 1 June 1966. The 4d over-printed 'England Winners' was issued on 18 August: it was limited to 12 million copies and most Post Offices were sold out in hours.

① Ring of success. England at Lilleshall before the start of the 1966 World Cup finals. Clockwise order: Martin Peters, front centre, arms folded, Geoff Hurst, George Eastham, Peter Thompson, Johnny Byrne, John Connelly, Gordon Milne, Bobby Moore (half hidden), Ian Callaghan, Jack Charlton, Peter Bonetti, Gordon Banks, Ron Flowers, Bobby Charlton, Jimmy Armfield, Nobby Stiles, Les Cocker (assistant trainer), Wilf McGuinness (coach), Norman Hunter, Harold Shepherdson (trainer), Gerry Byrne, George Cohen, Ron Springett, Roger Hunt, Jimmy Greaves, Terry Paine, Alan Ball and Keith Newton.

①

②

2 Denis and friend. Denis Follows, secretary of the Football Association, with T-shirt, circa 1966. World Cup Willie also stars.

3 'That completes the draw.' The battle-lines for the 1966 World Cup finals have been established. The draw in the Palace Suite of the Royal Garden Hotel, Kensington, 6 January 1966, was the first test of the Football Association's World Cup organisation – and it went without a hitch. More than half the audience of 800 were journalists.

3

①

① Her Majesty The Queen opens the eighth World Cup finals, Wembley, 11 July 1966. HRH The Duke of Edinburgh is on the left and Sir Stanley Rous, president of FIFA, on the right. A fanfare by the trumpeters of the Household Cavalry was followed by the simultaneous unfurling of the flags of all the competing nations. They cracked open together, like the sound of a single rifle shot, with a man by every flag responding to a signal from an official on the roof of the stadium. A lollipop stick was used to keep each flag folded – until it was snapped by a sharply pulled lanyard.

So it began. Ramsey had pruned his England squad to 22 and then watched his players win their tour games in Finland, Norway, Denmark and Poland. The other countries started to arrive: a North Korean flag was raised over a Darlington hotel, the Chileans played tenpin bowling in Sunderland, the Hungarians said unkind things about British beef, the Swiss learned about the mystery of darts from Sheffield policemen and at Villa Park Juan Carlos Lorenzo, the manager of Argentina, quietly asked local reporters which way Aston Villa preferred to kick-off. Some trained a little and talked a lot: some did things the other way round. The media came too, more than 2,000 of them from 62 countries, some arriving without accreditation and without accommodation.

Her Majesty The Queen, in a pale green coat and white hat, formally opened the finals on the bright evening of 11 July 1966. The brass of the massed bands of the Coldstream, Grenadier and Irish Guards glinted in the sunshine, Middlesex schoolboys in the colours of the 16 competing nations hardly put a foot wrong and Alf Ramsey, formally clad for the opening, fidgeted with his tie.

Tradition placed the host nation in the first game and England's opponents were Uruguay, twice champions and the country which staged the first World Cup in 1930. Ramsey's team included nine of the men who were to play in the final: Greaves was predictably preferred to Hurst and, with Ramsey still inclined to play a winger, Connelly got the vote over Peters. A crowd of 87,000 paid £68,000 to be there, and they were given one of the worst games of the tournament for their money, a goalless draw fashioned by tension and Uruguayan lack of ambition. England's base was faultless and the midfield worked with drive and even style, but the attack ran into an eight- and sometimes ten-man defence which imposed itself on everything like a sticky cobweb. Uruguay's players smiled and pranced with delight at the end, while England left the field in silence. The crowd whistled, but, as Danny Blanchflower wrote afterwards, 'there isn't enough emotion at Wembley . . . there should be electricity in the air'.

Blanchflower seemed to indicate that Wembley was not a natural place for passion, that there was an element of formality about the place and a grey hint of reserve in the hopes of the crowd, but things began to change, if only slowly, as Group One took shape in England's favour. France and Mexico drew 1–1 at Wembley and then, in the unlikely setting of the White City, which was not essentially a football ground but had been used as the working headquarters of the tournament, a patently more ambitious Uruguay beat France by 2–1; which meant France's chances of qualifying were slim.

Ramsey changed his side in two places for England's second game against Mexico. Paine, another winger, and Peters came in for Connelly and Ball, so there were still nine of the team that would play in the final in the side. Mexico were a pedestrian and negative side; England beat them easily enough, with goals by Bobby Charlton and Hunt, but not well enough to convince many observers that they were potential champions. England's first goal of the tournament, however, was a pearl beyond compare, one of Charlton's finest; a goal scored from nearly 30 yards with stunning simplicity and awesome power. His cannon-shot – 'I just hit it as hard as I could in the general direction of the goal' – drilled a hole in England's mounting frustration and for the first time stirred notes of patriotism on the stadium's hillsides. Mexico and Uruguay then locked themselves up in another goalless draw which meant, barring an unlikely defeat by two goals by France, England were through to the quarter-finals.

Ramsey brought a third winger into his side, this time Ian Callaghan for Paine, but once again nine of the side that would play at Wembley were on duty. England won with two goals from Hunt, but without real authority, in a victory which put them on top of a poor group after a performance which – for the only time – dragged words of reproach from Ramsey. It was also a game that was important for other reasons. Greaves was injured, and Stiles made a savage and clumsy but unpunished tackle on Jacques Simon late in the game.

Stiles had been cautioned earlier in the match, but it was that tackle which prompted FIFA's Disciplinary Committee to request England 'to warn Stiles that if he were reported again serious action would be taken'. The fire-eating Manchester United wing half was portrayed by the media as a fearsome anti-hero, and he was a player the foreign press in particular loved to hate. Even more significantly, there were members of the FA's senior international committee who urged Ramsey to consider dropping Stiles. Ramsey stood firm: he felt his position was being undermined and – having confirmed with Stiles that the tackle was one which had simply 'gone wrong' – he refused at any cost to consider omitting a player he regarded as indispensable. Ramsey got his way.

British sports writers, accustomed to overcoming all manner of hurdles at Football League grounds, will sympathise with the Italian journalist who arrived to cover a World Cup game at Ayresome Park with his green identity pass but not a ticket for the match. He was told he could come in but would have to climb over the turnstile. The Italian looked mystified but did as he was told, hampered by a typewriter and briefcase. Once over he was promptly told he had come in the wrong entrance and would have to climb out again and enter the correct turnstile – all of 20 yards up the road.

The Guardian – 'World Cup Diary', 20 July 1966.

Outside London the tournament had rather more character and drama. Middlesbrough's Ayresome Park witnessed the biggest World Cup upset since England's own defeat by the United States in 1950 – North Korea, an unconsidered and even mysterious side of small and talented men, beat the complex might of Italy 1–0. The Koreans triumphed with nerve and verve and a historic goal by Pak Doo Ik. The north-east loved its 'Diddy men' from the other side of the world. The commentators, obliged to wrap their tongues around the names such as Im Seung Hwi and Sim Zoong Sun, had their reservations. The USSR and North Korea qualified and Italy retired in shame after deciding, wisely, that they would arrive home 'at an unannounced hour between midnight and dawn and at an unannounced airport'.

The tournament lost another of its leviathans when Brazil failed to survive the strongest group of all in the north-west. They arrived as the champions of 1958 and 1962, unbeaten in any World Cup game since 1954, and heralded as a force of high skill and experience, a product of meticulous preparation. Above all, they had the finest footballer in the world: although Pele was in his prime at 25, this was not to be his summer. He scored in Brazil's 2–0 victory over Bulgaria, missed a beautiful game against Hungary (who won 3–1) because of injury and was then brutally and systematically kicked by Portugal (who also won 3–1) at Goodison Park. Pele vowed grimly never to play World Cup football again, but, in truth, Brazil were dethroned because too many of their players were past their best. Hungary and Portugal qualified and, more predictably, they were joined in the quarter-finals by West Germany and Argentina who were both unbeaten in the Midland group.

Argentina had won few friends. They were gifted and inventive, but they were better remembered in Birmingham and Sheffield for their provocation and meanness. They were, however, to be England's next opponents at Wembley and the build-up to their quarter-final was short and nervous. Ramsey made two more changes. Hurst was the obvious replacement for Greaves, who had four stitches in a gash on his left shin, and Ball came back for Callaghan. The last pieces of the puzzle had fallen into place. There were to be no more orthodox wingers and – although not even Ramsey knew it at that point – no more changes. Circumstances as well as judgment shaped the side which won the World Cup.

Ball was to say that Argentina were the one team good enough to have stopped England winning the World Cup: 'They had so much talent they could have given any side trouble if they had just concentrated on playing football.' Argentina chose, instead, to stain their quarter-final against England by kicking, body-checking, punching, arguing, shirt-pulling, spitting and play-acting – or, as FIFA's Disciplinary Committee saw it, they 'brought the game into grave disrepute by their flagrant breaches of the Laws and disregard for discipline and good order'.

Argentina also played some composed and impressive football but, on a day of sunshine and shirt-sleeves, one sending-off and one goal settled everything. Antonio Rattin, Argentina's captain and orchestrator, was at the heart of all that was wrong about the afternoon, a tall, forbidding and arrogant figure who seemed bent on hijacking control of the game. His name went into the book of the referee, Rudolf Kreitlin of West Germany, and then, as yet another Argentine, Luis Artime, was being cautioned, Rattin mouthed one oath too many. Rattin was to claim that he was only asking for an interpreter but Kreitlin, a small and officious man with a shining bald head, decided Argentina's captain would have to go if the game was to continue.

Rattin disagreed, profoundly, and for nearly eight minutes there was chaos. Kreitlin, whistle in mouth, left arm pointing towards the dressing room, was dwarfed by Argentine players who seemed to be shouting that if Rattin went, they would follow. Argentine officials joined in and so did Harry Cavan of Northern Ireland, FIFA's nominated official for the match, and Ken Aston, the large and experienced head of the Referees' Committee. Police hovered in the background and the crowd sang 'Why are we waiting?'.

Order shakily prevailed in the end and Rattin went, firing abuse at all within earshot, which left ten men barring England's path to the semi-finals. The home side still did not find it easy, and there were moments of lost concentration which might have cost them dearly; but 13 minutes from the end West Ham found the answer. Peters delicately made room for himself on the left and his high, measured centre was glanced home, near post to right corner, by the head of Hurst.

Ramsey and FIFA now had words to say. 'We have still to play our best football,' said England's manager in a television interview. 'It will come against the right type of opposition, a team who come to play football and not act as animals.' It was a remark which was colourfully embroidered all round the world and which FIFA, in a letter to Lancaster Gate, described as 'unfortunate . . . and against good international relations in football'.

But FIFA directed their sharpest arrows at Argentina for their wild conduct after the game as well as during it. 'The attack on the referee after the game . . . was particularly regrettable,' said their official report. 'The referee would have been justified in bringing a charge against certain players for assault.' Argentina were fined and warned that they would be barred from the next World Cup unless their behaviour improved. Rattin and two other players were suspended for several matches.

One other moment during that angry afternoon caused a stir in the crowd. It was the scoreboard's news of the latest position in the quarter-final at Goodison Park: 'Portugal 0, North Korea 3'. Would England, if they won, be playing Pak

Doo Ik and the rest of the Korean unpronounceables in the semi-finals? It was the stuff of fiction; but the storyline was ruined by a dark and lithe destroyer called Eusebio, one of the world's outstanding forwards, who scored four (including two penalties) to give the composed Portuguese victory by 5–3. In the other quarter-finals West Germany firmly beat Uruguay, who had two players sent off, 4–0 at Hillsborough; and at Roker Park, in front of a crowd of under 27,000, the USSR punished Hungary for defensive charity by winning 2–1. The semi-finals belonged to Europe.

Letters by the sackful were now arriving at Lancaster Gate and Hendon Hall, England's hotel in north London, many of them containing precise instructions on how to play and win. The players were checked and weighed daily – 'like prize breeding pigs' said one. There was much television and some cinema, with Ramsey always at his ease with a Western; and there was cricket for light relief. Friendships hardened, with the three goalkeepers, Gordon Banks, Ron Springett and Peter Bonetti, going everywhere and doing everything together. They were known as 'the Marx brothers'. And there was, too, a daily allowance of £2 for each player – agreed by the FA on the understanding that 'it should not, in any way, be considered as a precedent'.

Goodison Park believed it was going to get England's semi-final against Portugal, and even the FA understood this to be true at one point, but FIFA's small-print was clear: the choice of ground for the semi-finals would be made after the quarter-finals had been completed – and it was a majority decision by FIFA's organising committee, taken for financial reasons, that England should stay at Wembley. It was, however, a decision which strengthened a conviction among some South American and European countries that there was a conspiracy afoot in England's favour. There were claims that referees had been biased and even bribed, and one Argentine radio station reported as fact that England's players had been drugged. Dr Alan Bass, the England doctor, a popular and respected man, was in charge of the tournament's anti-doping measures.

To rub salt into the city of Liverpool's wounded dignity, the semi-final at Goodison was a poor one – West Germany beating the USSR 2–1 after the Soviets had had one player sent off and another crippled before half time. The score at Wembley the following night was also 2–1, but there the resemblance ended. The manner of England's victory over Portugal, and the richness and honesty of the game itself, was a joy to watch and a triumph for the competition. It was enough to morally re-arm football after the seedy events of the preceding week.

Much of the credit belonged to Portugal. They may have caused grievous bodily harm to Pele at Goodison Park but here at Wembley, despite the heavy tension of the occasion, they expressed their skill and traced their patterns without an evil thought in their minds. They did not commit a single foul until the 57th minute. It was, in essence, a contest between Portugal's brilliant forwards and England's dreadnought defence – and Moore and company not only survived but provided the platform for Bobby Charlton to score one in each half, the first simple, the second spectacular.

It was enough for England, but not quite the end of Portugal and, with eight minutes left, they obliged Banks to pick the ball out of his net for the first time in the competition. It was a penalty conceded by the other Charlton for a handling offence; and as Eusebio, the European Footballer of the Year, prepared to take it Jack Charlton noticed a white-coated attendant on the big scoreboard behind the goal. He was jumping up and down and waving his arms in an attempt to distract Eusebio. His ploy did not work – but Charlton thought 'What a good supporter'. Portugal's decision to play an open game was not a quixotic gesture. They decided their skill was a match for England's and the key to victory. But there were to be warm Portuguese handshakes for Bobby Charlton; and Portugal, with Eusebio contributing a penalty, his ninth goal of the tournament, beat the USSR 2–1 to earn the right to call themselves the third best team in the world.

The country was now waiting for the answer to one question: would Greaves, arguably the greatest finisher in the history of English football, be recalled for the final? Greaves was fit and desperate to play; and Hurst, while waiting for Ramsey's decision, took to walking around the shops in Hendon with the excuse that he needed toothpaste or shampoo. 'My room ended up looking like a salesman's sample-bag,' he remembers. But Hurst should not have worried. He had scored against Argentina, made the second goal against Portugal and his endless and intelligent running had given the side a new dimension. He was the most hittable of target-men. 'I could find him with a pass in the dark,' Ball was to say. Ramsey announced an unchanged team on the morning of the final, and Greaves accepted the biggest disappointment of his wonderful career with as much dignity as he could muster.

Ramsey had designed his team, with a little trial and error, to do a job. He believed in his players who, by now, were household figures. Banks of England: what better name for a goalkeeper who was a master of his trade? Cohen and Wilson, the full backs, were as complementary as bacon and eggs. Cohen, a solid and perky Londoner, thundered along the right and Wilson, smaller, neater and very much a man of the north, twinkled up the left. The marriage of captain Moore and Jack Charlton in central defence might also have been made in heaven. Moore, fair-haired and open-faced, was a stylist who gave dignity to the simplest chore as he covered and provided; and big Jack, guardsman tall and constructed in equal parts of leg and neck was a natural destroyer.

Stiles was the little warrior in midfield, unlikely looking with his absent teeth, knobbly knees and receding hair, but a marker and a ball-winner who was loved or hated. Peters, alongside and in front, perceptively exploited space and weaknesses; and the other Charlton, young brother Bobby, with his surging pace and murderous shooting, was one of the handsomest sights in football. Ball, up and down the right, was a force of nature who demanded everything from himself and everybody else. Hunt contributed aggression, strength, honesty and selflessness, his qualities ruefully recognised by opponents but not always appreciated by the terraces, while Hurst chipped in handsomely with his unorthodox mobility, driving power and relish for the big occasion.

'It's going to be the biggest day of your lives and you are going to win,' Ramsey told them on the eve of the final. 'Goodnight gentlemen.'

Helmut Schoen, the wise and dignified manager of West Germany, probably said something similar at their headquarters at Welwyn Garden City. Their progress to the final had been erratic, and the record books insisted they had never beaten England, but in the elegant Franz Beckenbauer they had an outstanding young player who was to become one of football's great figures, and around him there was a well organised blend of robust experience, athletic talent and durable character.

Wembley was ready, its best bib and tucker in place, and so were the England supporters. They had started the tournament cautiously, half-believingly, but had begun to forge a link with their team in the game against Argentina and then filled the old stadium with such rolling fervour during the semi-final against Portugal that the players were to say they felt like joining in.

But, on an afternoon when the game and the weather were in close harmony — elation and sorrow, sunshine and rain — the first real roar of triumph was unmistakably German. Wilson made his first culpable mistake of the tournament and the blond Helmut Haller, with a right footed shot past Banks' right hand, scored from a dozen yards. England were a goal down for the first time in the tournament, but just six minutes later West Ham provided an equaliser. Moore floated and dipped a 35-yard free kick into the German penalty area where Hurst read it perfectly, timed his run irresistibly and used his head deftly to send the ball inside the right post.

England, with Moore implacable and Bobby Charlton restlessly creative, were in control for another quarter of an hour; West Germany's turn to threaten came either side of half time; and then, for 25 minutes or so, the game balanced and settled. But now Ball had begun to make an indelible mark on the afternoon and, with 13 minutes left, the Blackpool man forced a corner and took it himself. The ball was driven by Hurst into a thicket of defenders and from there, stopped but not cleared, it spun compliantly towards Peters and Jack Charlton; and it was Peters who found a thinly protected net.

Two goals to one to England, and Hunt and Bobby Charlton between them had a chance to add a third, but Hunt miscued his pass and Charlton, unbalanced, was wide. The Germans attacked again, for the last time, and Gottfried Dienst of Switzerland, the referee, gave them a free kick ten yards outside the English penalty area. Emmerich took it and there was an English appeal for hands but, with Moore's arm still raised and Wilson a part-second late with his lunging block, the ball fell for Weber to score firmly at the right post. Should the free kick have been given against England? The film of the game indicates that Jack Charlton was obstructed. Did Karl Heinz Schnellinger handle the ball? The evidence suggests it was accidental. The one certain thing was that a World Cup final was rolling into extra time for the first time since 1934.

The interval was brief, the exhaustion mutual, but Ramsey said to his players: 'You've won it once . . . now you must win it again' – or words to that effect. 'You think you're tired . . . look at them.'

Ramsey's appeal tapped hidden reserves and Ball, above all, was an inspiration, a fusion of passion and horsepower. The more energy he used, the more he found. And, in the 100th minute of the final, it was Ball on the right who moved busily onto a pass from Stiles. He cut the ball inside and Hurst's powerful shot from eight yards struck the underside of the crossbar. The ball dropped vertically – and exactly where it landed will never be known. It remains one of the great controversies of the World Cup.

Referee Dienst himself was in no position to see if the ball had crossed the line, so he consulted his linesman Tofik Bakhramov, a tall and greying Russian, who was 15 yards down the touchline but whose view was unobstructed. The seconds were long and tense as they talked, but then Dienst turned and pointed dramatically to the middle.

All manner of evidence and argument has been used to 'prove' which side of the line the ball bounced. Films and photographs have been studied, the position of the ball's shadow has been analysed and all related angles meticulously compared. Much, too, has been made of the reaction of Hunt, who was only five yards from the line. Hunt's natural instinct, if in doubt, would have been to chase the rebound – but he turned, instead, with arm raised in triumph.

The controversy endures, but the goal stood; and had the score remained 3–2 the incident might have ended diplomatic relations between the two countries. With referee Dienst counting away the last seconds, however, Hurst chose to make history of another kind. Moore chested the ball down inside his own penalty area. 'There were West Germans all around him and I wanted to scream at him "Clout it for ------- sake!",' remembers Hurst. 'But then he had it beautifully under control, I saw him glance up and I made the little gesture with my arm that seasons of playing together would tell him I was ready for a pass.' The pass came, 35 yards long, measured to the inch, and Hurst took it just over the halfway line. He thundered towards the German goal and – in his own words again – 'just belted it'. His shot completed the first hat trick in a World Cup final and gave England victory by 4–2, a comfortable step beyond all reservation and controversy.

Jack Charlton sank to his knees, head in hands, Bobby Charlton shed a tear, Wilson slapped his hands on the grass and Stiles, with gappy smile and fallen socks, did his famous little jig. There was a lump in Wembley's throat as Bobby Moore – who was to be named as the tournament's outstanding player – received the World Cup from the Queen. And Ramsey, soon to be knighted, sat impassively at the moment of his fulfilment.

The celebrations continued with a Government reception and an FA banquet and went on to see in the dawn. Half the people in the capital seemed to be in Kensington High Street as the players appeared on the glass and concrete balcony of the Royal Garden Hotel, and the other half seemed bent on climbing Nelson's Column.

There were to be reservations and protests, of course. The football was often pedestrian, and the refereeing was erratic. There were complaints that the gap between games was too short and that FIFA's Disciplinary Committee was both prejudiced and inconsistent. Phrases such as 'incredible partisanship' and 'robbery consummated' drifted back from South America, where there were deep suspicions of the light traffic – Argentina's obstruction apart – on England's road to the final. Never before, it was stressed, had a host country been allowed to play all its games on one ground. *Cronica*, an evening newspaper in Buenos Aires, depicted World Cup Willie in skull-and-crossbones clothing with a patch over one eye and a wooden leg.

The tournament threw cold light on all the World Cup problems faced by FIFA and caused by differences in temperament, expression, style, interpretation, custom and monetary reward. Some of the criticism was justified; but some smacked of disappointment and self-pity. Neutral opinion, on the whole, saw the tournament as efficiently organised, profitable, relaxed and well won.

Under the headline 'They win wars and cups' *Il Messaggero* in Rome said that 'somehow the English always win at the last moment … from this day is not the name of England to be pronounced with renewed respect.'

Harold Shepherdson and Les Cocker, England's two highly respected trainers, had used a little phrase of their own when talking to players during that long summer month in 1966.

'Play for Alf.'

England

Miscellany

Most capped players 125 – Peter Shilton (Leicester City, Stoke City, Nottingham Forest, Southampton, Derby County), 1970–90.
108 – Bobby Moore (West Ham United), 1962–73.
106 – Bobby Charlton (Manchester United), 1958–70.
105 – Billy Wright (Wolverhampton Wanderers), 1946–59.
Leading scorer 49 – Bobby Charlton.
Biggest win Ireland 0, England 13, 18 February 1882, Belfast.
First defeat by foreign opposition Spain 4, England 3, 15 May 1929, Madrid.
First home defeat by foreign opposition England 0, Eire 2, 21 September 1949, Goodison Park. (Nine of the Irish side played in the Football League.)
Most consecutive internationals 70 – Billy Wright (Wolverhampton Wanderers), 3 October 1951–28 May 1959.
Fastest hat-trick for England 3 goals in 3½ minutes – Willie Hall

(Tottenham Hotspur) against Ireland, 16 November 1938, Manchester.
(England won 7–0 and Hall scored five.)
Division Three players to win 'full' caps since war Tommy Lawton (Notts County, 1947), Reg Matthews (Coventry City, 1956), Johnny Byrne (Crystal Palace, 1961), Peter Taylor (Crystal Palace, 1976), Steve Bull (Wolverhampton Wanderers, 1989). England caps for Third Division players before the war were more common.
Oldest England player Stanley Matthews of Blackpool (42 years 104 days) v Denmark, 15 May 1957, Copenhagen.
Oldest 'first' cap Leslie Compton of Arsenal (38 years 65 days) v Wales, 15 November 1950, Sunderland.
Youngest player for England Duncan Edwards of Manchester United (18 years 183 days) v Scotland, 2 April 1955, Wembley.

①

②

① Oriental interlude. Brian Clough and son Nigel, who was then 14 years old, before Nottingham Forest's World Club Championship final with Nacional of Uruguay in Tokyo, February 1981. It was the first one-match decider between the champions of Europe and South America – and Nacional won 1–0. Brian played his first game for England in 1959 and Nigel won his first cap in 1989.

② Shirts, boots, a trophy and a smile. Bob Paisley of Liverpool, the most successful manager in the history of English football. In nine seasons (1974–83) he led the Merseyside club to six League championships, three European Cups, three League Cups, one UEFA Cup and five Charity Shields. Pictured in the Anfield boot-room with the League championship trophy.

①

②

③

① 'A little bit of the hand of God ... a little of the head of Maradona.'

Diego Maradona's description of his controversial first goal for Argentina against England in the Aztec Stadium, Mexico City, in the quarter-finals of the 1986 World Cup finals. Peter Shilton's legal fist is a foot short. Final score: Maradona 2, England 1.

② Viv Anderson of Nottingham Forest becomes the first black player to represent England, against Czechoslovakia at Wembley, 29 November 1978. Anderson, a tall and authoritative full back, later played for Arsenal and Manchester United and won 30 caps in an international career which lasted ten years. Also in picture: left to right – Dave Watson (Manchester City), Tony Woodcock (Nottingham Forest), Peter Barnes (Manchester City) and Tony Currie (Leeds United).

③ John Barnes (number 11) scores his first international goal – and England are on their way to their first victory over Brazil in the Maracana Stadium, Rio de Janeiro, 10 June 1984. Barnes, aged 20, ran nearly half the length of the pitch before calmly wrong-footing the Brazilian goalkeeper Roberto Costa. Mark Hateley headed England's second goal and moved from Portsmouth to AC Milan for around £900,000 that same summer. Barnes joined Liverpool from Watford for a similar fee in June 1987.

① The spring of 1989. Anfield – seven days after the Hillsborough disaster.

ACTION IMAGES

①

①

① Rising power. North Korea beat Italy 1–0 at Middlesbrough in the north-east group – a shock almost, but not quite, comparable to England's one-goal defeat by the United States in 1950. The Americans were a sketchily con-ditioned patchwork side; the North Koreans had prepared rigorously for three years. Pak Doo Ik scored the Koreans' winner and Ayresome Park adopted them as their own. North Korea confirmed their ability, remarkably, by taking a three-goal lead against Portu-gal in their quarter-final at Goodison Park – but were then overcome by the power of Eusebio. Portugal 5 (Eusebio 4), North Korea 3.

①

① Eusebio – known as the 'European Pele' – consoles the authentic Pele during the Group Three match between Portugal and Brazil at Goodison Park. Pele was injured after half an hour and, his right knee heavily bandaged, was a passenger for the rest of the game. Eusebio scored twice in Portugal's 3–1 victory. The referee is George McCabe of England.

② Rudolf Kreitlein of West Germany orders off Antonio Rattin (left), the captain of Argentina, during the quarter-final against England at Wembley. Most of the Argentine side joined in the protest, the game was delayed for nearly eight minutes and the crowd sang 'Why are we waiting?'. England won 1–0 – and Rattin was suspended for Argentina's next four matches.

③ Eusebio of Benfica and Portugal – alias the 'Black Panther' and the 'European Pele' – sheds a tear after the 2–1 defeat by England in a memorable semi-final. Eusebio, a forward of dramatic skill and pace, finished as the tournament's leading scorer with nine goals. In his autobiography, *My Name is Eusebio* (1967), he wrote: 'I wept convulsively, just like a child suffering the first great disappointment of his life.' He also quoted the *Daily Sketch* (whose thoughts may have gained a little in translation) as saying: 'These proud princes of Portugal, who have brought their intelligence to the magic of football, died like the knights of antiquity: fighting to the last breath.'

②

③

The jury deliberates: thousands of eyes ... and a flash of handily placed photographers. Was the ball over the line? Geoff Hurst's controversial goal in extra time in the 1966 World Cup final. The ball hit the crossbar and then dropped vertically.

④ Roger Hunt (21), with the best view in the stadium, begins to raise his arms in triumph.

⑤ The referee Gottfried Dienst decides to consult his linesman Tofik Bakhramov. Bobby Charlton (9), Hurst and Martin Peters (16) lend their weight to the argument and, long seconds later, a goal is given.

⑥ No picture has conclusively proved the decision right or wrong ... not even the picture from the film *Goal! World Cup 1966*. Bakhramov is at the bottom.

①

②

③

④

① 'I just belted it' – Geoff Hurst launches himself into history by completing the first hat trick in the final of a World Cup. England are seconds away from being World champions – and Kenneth Wolstenholme, commentating on BBC Television, is saying: 'There are people on the pitch. They think it's all over' ... and as Hurst scores ... 'It is now!'

② 'I wanted to laugh and cry at the same time' – Jack Charlton after the last whistle of the eighth World Cup finals. Geoff Hurst (10) and Martin Peters, having delivered England's final four goals on behalf of West Ham, are still in step.

③ The party is under way. England's World Cup winners on the balcony of the Royal Garden Hotel overlooking Kensington High Street. 'It is your day,' Alf Ramsey told them after the match. 'Enjoy it.'

④ Alf Ramsey, manager of England, and Harold Wilson, Prime Minister of the same parish, debate higher tactics at the Government reception which followed the 1966 triumph. The man in the middle is well qualified: Denis Howell, Minister for Sport, was a highly respected Football League referee.

10
PROGRESS
1967–77

English football's self-esteem was never higher than in the jaunty years which followed the winning of the World Cup. The Jules Rimet trophy was locked away in a Paddington bank, many of the 'missing millions' returned to the terraces and Manchester United became the first English club to win the European Cup. Liverpool and Leeds United drew themselves up to their full sovereign height, Manchester City began to relish the finest years in their history and two Third Division clubs, Queen's Park Rangers and Swindon Town, had the audacity to win the League Cup at Wembley. Alf Ramsey, for his part, looked forward to the 1970 World Cup finals in the heat and altitude of Mexico. 'England can win again and that is not sales talk,' he said. 'It is something I genuinely believe. If we are not successful the responsibility is mine.'

There was sunlight on the surface; but there were threatening currents below. The game had always had its sinners and scamps but in the mid-1960s they took on a new and sharply defined identity. The age of the football hooligan had arrived, a problem that was to cost the sport and society dearly. The number of cautions, censures, suspensions and fines handed out to players by the FA. Disciplinary Committee increased by more than 20 percent. 'Quite appalling,' said the FA. 'Everyone associated with the game will feel a sense of shame and anxiety.' Profit and loss was another painful matter. The popular cost of admission had crept up to five shillings, but if income was growing so were players' wages (up by 120 percent since the abolition of the maximum wage in 1961) and other expenses. Just over half the clubs in the First Division balanced their books, but the majority were obliged to ignore Mr Micawber's dearest principle. The result, of course, was mainly misery.

An important, if not rapturously applauded, analysis of the game was provided by the Chester Report in 1968 – the findings of a Government enquiry 'into the state of Association Football at all levels including the organisation, management, finance and administration'. The probing team properly consisted of 11 men, captained by Norman Chester, Warden of Nuffield College, Oxford, and included Bill Slater, once an elegant centre half for Wolves and England, and international referee Mervyn Griffiths.

The committee's task was weighty. Each week around a million men and boys, belonging to nearly 31,000 clubs and 12,000 schools, played the game; and another million watched it. A major game on television could count on an audience of between seven and ten million viewers. But Slater, Griffiths and the industrialists, politicians, academics and lawyers who made up the rest of Chester's side tackled their job with enthusiasm. The Committee held the first of its 36 meetings during the World Cup finals in 1966, received evidence from 65 organisations and individuals and took two years to prepare its report, which ran to 133 pages and included 36 recommendations.

The report recommended that the League should be increased to five divisions, the top three national and smaller with four-up and four-down promotion and relegation to raise interest and leave room for European and international football. It suggested, where suitable and profitable, that clubs should amalgamate, share grounds, move to new areas or co-operate with local authorities in building multi-purpose community sports complexes. It wondered if clubs should have smaller staffs with more part-time players. It championed the need for better facilities for the public and for professional football on Sundays. It recommended that every contract between a club and player should be for a fixed period, with freedom of choice for both at its end. It recognised that many amateurs were being paid and recommended a new class of player – the semi-professional. It also, above all, urged the Government to raise £1,000,000 a year from a levy on Pools betting for the development of British football as a whole.

There were also salient words for the Football Association. The Chester Report recommended that Council members should retire at 70 – 'otherwise there is a danger of remoteness, of a game for young men being administered wholly by old men'. It questioned if a Council of more than 80 members could be an effective policy-making body and recommended a smaller committee for central policy and planning. It urged that the FA should make greater use of experts on their committees and that rules prohibiting former or current players from administering the game should be abolished. It also suggested that the FA should contribute more from its income – 'greatly increased since 1966' – to the County Associations and more extensive coaching facilities.

Lancaster Gate's reply came in the next edition of the *FA News*. 'It is not expected,' said an editorial, 'that a body of this kind [the Chester Committee] can fully understand the ramifications of the complex Football Association ... it is not surprising, therefore, that the FA does not accept some of the criticisms.' A decision to form an Executive Committee had already been taken at the FA's summer meeting; and, added the editorial, the distribution of funds after their 'shot in the arm' from the World Cup was not a matter for hasty decision but for long-term planning.

History is judging many of Chester's findings with a kindly eye and the FA, despite its reservations, was quick to acknowledge that his report deserved serious study. A sum of £200,000 was earmarked for the County Associations but, by this time, the FA had been blitzed from all quarters for failing to distribute its World Cup profits of £435,000. There was a hungry glint in the eye of the taxman. But, as the FA said in its next journal: 'It is true that the Football Association with its diversity of interests does not appear to move very fast. That does not mean it is not moving at all. Far from it. Much goes on behind the scenes which cannot be revealed for fear that premature disclosure of information may spoil, or indeed make impossible, a worthwhile project.'

The 'worthwhile project' in this case was a claim that, for tax purposes, the World Cup was a 'special case' and not part of an ordinary year's work. The tax inspector finally agreed and, on top of the £200,000 set aside for the County Associations, he allowed another £140,000 to be used for the development and expansion of the game. But, as Dr Andrew Stephen of Sheffield Wednesday, a shrewd and discerning Scot who had become chairman of the FA during the season which followed the World Cup, told fellow councillors: 'More should have been made of professional advice.'

It took the 1966 squad even longer to win their game with the Inland Revenue. All 22 players had received a bonus of £1,000 and, two-and-a-half years after the World Cup, they were each sent a tax demand for more than £300. The matter dragged on to a High Court hearing in 1972, where Mr Justice Brightman agreed with a submission on behalf of the players that the bonus was 'a once-and-for-all payment and a testimonial to mark a prime event in the football history of this country'. Even so, Pickles and his owner got more for finding the World Cup than England's players did for winning it.

Different, perhaps even deeper, chords of emotion were to be struck at Wembley on Wednesday, 29 May 1968. Celtic, a year before, had become the first British club to win the European Cup; but, when Manchester United faced Benfica of Portugal in the 13th final of the tournament of champions, they had more on their minds than another line in the record books. They were remembering the Busby Babes, and there was a tangible feeling that those who had perished at Munich ten years before were somewhere there in the shadows of that May evening. Matt Busby, though, made one thing clear: 'You are professionals first and last. You are playing for the present, not the past.'

Bill Foulkes and Bobby Charlton, two other Munich survivors, were at the heart of a United side of character and ambition, an astutely balanced mixture of wise craftsmen and rare talent. Denis Law of Scotland was prevented by cartilage trouble from playing in the final, but George Best of Northern Ireland, a symbol of the 1960s, and Charlton of England were too much for Benfica. United won 4–1 in a game that went to extra time (1–1 after 90 minutes), with Charlton scoring their first and last goals and Best their second.

Best, with his dark and modish good looks, was sport's most eligible bachelor, misunderstood by some, understood only too well by others, who often worked hard into the night promoting his pop-idol image. There were those who saw him as the brazen standard-bearer of a declining society but, at his peak between 1964 and 1970, he excited crowds as no other player did. Matt Busby was to say that Best was gifted with more ability than he had seen in any other player – and unique in the *number* of his gifts. There was an element of fantasy in his finishing and dribbling, but there was also fire and tenacity to give point to his talent. Space and time were luxuries he did not appear to need. His Wembley goal against Benfica was brilliant and just one of many.

The so-called naturals of the game are not so natural nowadays and there are not so many of them either. What there are need spotting early, nursing carefully and protecting totally from the idiotic ego involvement of some teachers, parents and coaches who use these kids to satisfy their own frustrated ambitions. We don't respect football talent in the way we respect and protect a talented young artist, mathematician or musician. When it comes to sport, and particularly to football, talent is abused and exploited.

Allen Wade, FA Director of Coaching, 1977.

It was Bobby Charlton, however, who made the sharpest and most memorable mark on the night. He scored his first goal, unusually, with his head and his second, handsomely, with a turn on his left foot and a whipped flick with his right. It was Charlton, as United's captain, who led his team up to the Royal Box and it was

Charlton, bodily and emotionally drained, who slowly followed his team and their giant trophy to the four corners of Wembley on their lap of honour. It was a night of tribute and fulfilment – 'the most wonderful thing in my life,' said Busby.

These were lustrous years, too, for Manchester City under the joint stewardship of Joe Mercer and Malcolm Allison – Mercer, wise, liberal and a popular figurehead; Allison, a brilliant coach, innovative, outspoken and sometimes outrageous. City won the League championship in 1968, just before United's European triumph at Wembley, and followed up with the FA Cup in 1969 and – the first double of its kind – the European Cup-Winners' Cup and the League Cup in 1970.

Yet the sun was not shining just for the grand and ugly city of Manchester and its two football clubs. How could it be with managers of such quality and diverse character as Bill Shankly, Don Revie, Bertie Mee, Bill Nicholson and Brian Clough in charge of clubs of high ambition? Shankly of Liverpool was all Scot and all Scouse, part granite and part candyfloss, a complex man but also a man of disarming simplicity, a strutting, gravel-voiced little Napoleon, with a wit that could delight or humble to order. He turned a game of shifting values into a faith and created the modern Liverpool. They won the League championship in 1964, the FA Cup for the first time in 1965 and the championship again in 1966 – the new foundations of a club that over the next quarter of a century was to become the most successful in the history of English football.

Shankly knew his team would always have at least one peer, however, as long as Don Revie was manager of Leeds United. Revie, like Shankly, started from scratch and he transformed a club that was on the brink of relegation to the Third Division into one of post-war football's most efficient units; a mean machine to begin with, but later a side of rich expression and range. He was a man of the north-east, a bear of a figure, who spoke about being a 'professional' as if it was the most important word in the English language. He was generous in many ways yet coldly single-minded, practical yet superstitious, a man of broad vision yet obsessed by detail, a winner – but also a loser. Leeds won the League championship in 1969 and 1974, the League Cup and the European Fairs Cup (later the UEFA Cup) in 1968, the Fairs Cup again in 1971 and the FA Cup in 1972; but they also lost six other finals. They were in at the death for 17 major prizes . . . and won six. But they were failures only by their own towering standards.

Leeds and Liverpool both went close to completing the League and FA Cup 'double', but it was Arsenal who managed it in 1971, a feat then equalled only by Bill Nicholson's Tottenham, across the rooftops of north London, in the 20th century. And, in many ways, Arsenal's achievement was the more remarkable. Tottenham won both trophies in 1961 because they had, outstandingly, the best side. Arsenal's triumph, with a team few considered exciting, was one of dauntless character and solid organisation. They kept going over a heartless course.

Arsenal were seven points behind Leeds at one stage, but needed to win their last League game – at White Hart Lane of all places – to take the title. Yorkshire fretted ('I would hate to see my players pipped on the post again,' said Revie) and north London divided ('Arsenal are the last people we want to win the championship,' said Tottenham's captain Alan Mullery). More than 51,000 squeezed into White Hart Lane and nearly as many were locked out for a derby date that has rarely been equalled for importance or confusion. The game itself was taut and edgy and either side might have won; but Arsenal got there with a goal by Ray Kennedy, a header that went in off the underside of the bar, just three minutes from the end. Arsenal's fans danced jubilantly on their neighbours' grass and scaled up the front of the main stand like pirates in search of loot. Arsenal's manager Bertie Mee lost his tie and cuff-links; but he, above all, was a winner. He had been the club's trainer, a first-class physiotherapist, and had moved into the manager's chair with some reservations. He was softly spoken, sensitive and a careful dresser but, slowly and firmly, he proved himself an expert at man-management and a shrewd judge of talent and character. 'I do my best for my players and they do their best for me,' he would say.

Mee and his players still had one duty left after their famous victory at Tottenham – a Cup final with Liverpool five days later. They won that too, their belief in themselves hardened by their success in the League. But it was not easy – a game against Shankly's Liverpool never was. Two stubborn defences steered the game into extra time but, after Steve Heighway had put Liverpool ahead and Merseyside had filled Wembley with its victory anthems, Arsenal scored through Eddie Kelly and 20-year-old Charlie George – and Frank McLintock, Arsenal's captain and inspiration, bounded up the 39 steps to the Royal Box as if he suspected someone was going to run off with the Cup.

A year later Arsenal were back at Wembley again, their fifth final of one kind or another in five years and their eighth FA Cup final, but the Cup is nothing if not democratic, and this time the old trophy was held aloft by a club that had never won it before . . . Leeds United. The game also celebrated the 100th birthday of the FA Cup, and it was properly marked by song, flag and ceremony at the stadium and a banquet at the Royal Garden Hotel where the guests included representatives of nine of the clubs which took part in the first tournament of all.

But the postscript to the season was still to come. Just 48 hours after the final there was an evening of League drama which has no parallel. Leeds, requiring only a draw to complete the 'double' themselves, lost at Wolverhampton; Liverpool, who could have taken the title with a decent win, drew with a defiant Arsenal at High-bury; and Derby County, who had completed their programme and gone to Majorca for a holiday, heard from afar that they were League champions for the first time in their history. Derby finished with 58 points, Leeds, Liverpool and Manchester City all had 57.

There was some sympathy for Leeds, who had been ordered by the FA to play their first eight matches away from home following crowd trouble. Bill Shankly, on Liverpool's behalf, claimed that a late 'goal' by John Toshack should not have been disallowed for offside. But Derby were honest champions and Brian Clough, their manager, accepted the praise as nothing more than his due.

> Referees have the most difficult job in the world. They've got to make split-second decisions and don't have the chance to sit back and ponder on what they should do. I fear that at times we managers feel referees should be absolutely perfect for 90 minutes; and that everything has got to be dead right every second of the game. Yet we can't get this as managers. We don't always pick the right team; carry out the right training method and book the right hotels. Players don't put every pass right, and coaches don't always bring youngsters through as they should. So we're wrong in expecting referees to be perfect when we're not perfect ourselves.
>
> *Don Revie in* World Soccer Referee, *1976, the autobiography of Jack Taylor of England who refereed the 1974 World Cup final between West Germany and Holland.*

Clough and his partner Peter Taylor had joined Derby in 1967, after a shop-floor apprenticeship at Hartlepool, and begun a long career of building very good football teams. Clough's style was different, some said gently eccentric, others said seriously mad, but all had to accept that it worked. He was regularly analysed and duly identified as a Victorian radical, an immoderate maverick, a tilter at windmills, an involved obsessive, a Rolls-Royce Communist, a turbulent tyro – and, by Taylor, who knew him rather well, as 'a chap who suffers from terrible insecurity: you'll never see him alone'. Most of all, perhaps, Clough was to be a manager who wanted things done properly. The wrapping was sometimes bizarre, his words and opinions provocatively extreme, but he had standards. He rarely compromised.

Yet no manager carried a heavier sack than Sir Alf Ramsey. His success in 1966 increased the burden of expectation as he picked his way towards England's defence of the World Cup in Mexico. But there was little pressure to begin with, as

Ramsey set his mid-term sights on the European Championship finals in 1968 for which the Home International tournament was used as a qualifying group. Scotland immediately ruffled England's hair by winning 3–2 at Wembley in April 1967, after Jack Charlton had been reduced to a limping passenger for most of the game; and when Celtic won the European Cup by beating Inter-Milan in Lisbon five weeks later there was at least one country that believed Glasgow was the heart of the universe.

Scotland lost to Northern Ireland in Belfast, however, and it was England who qualified for the quarter-finals in which they beat Spain twice, with a Bobby Charlton goal in the first leg at Wembley and by 2–1 in front of a cruel crowd in the Bernabeu Stadium in Madrid. But then, in their semi-final against an underestimated Yugoslavia in Florence, England lost a bitter game by a late goal to nil, and also Alan Mullery, who was sent off for retaliation a minute from the end – the first England player to be sent off in an international. Honour and tempers were restored when England beat the Soviet Union 2–0 in Rome in the play-off for third place; and Ramsey's players returned home with no more than a dent in their crown.

Ramsey had always made it clear that his first priority was the World Cup and the make-up of the side he considered his best was changed by form and circumstance during the build-up to Mexico. Cohen, because of injury, and Wilson dropped out of the international scene, Jack Charlton was ageing, Hunt moved into his 30s and on to Bolton Wanderers, Mullery succeeded Stiles and Greaves asked not to be included in any squad if he was unlikely to be in the team – which did not impress Ramsey. But in 19 games between the European finals and the start of the World Cup finals England lost only once; and that was in Rio de Janeiro, where Brazil scored twice in the last ten minutes to win by 2–1, during an exploratory summer tour of Mexico and South America in 1969.

The draw in January 1970 put England into a group with Brazil, Rumania and Czechoslovakia, which was considered tough but negotiable, and the party which left for Mexico was described by Neil Phillips of Middlesbrough, England's doctor, as 'high in morale and character'. Harold Shepherdson, who had been England's trainer for more than 120 matches, said that 'if we play as well as we've prepared we'll skate the World Cup'. But Mexico and its neighbours still had one or two tricks left.

There were immediate problems in Mexico with customs and accommodation, and the Mexican press – which had been incensed by Ramsey's coldness towards them a year before – did their ingenious and daily best to discredit England. They did not have to wait long for a story that made headlines, not only in Mexico but all over the world.

England devoted two weeks to acclimatisation in Mexico and then headed for competitive tests in Colombia and Ecuador. These were won, firmly and reassuringly, but the big story was provided by a shop-girl called Clara Padilla, who worked in a small jewellery boutique in the Tequendama Hotel where England were staying in the Colombian capital of Bogotá. She claimed that, only two hours after booking in, Bobby Moore had stolen an emerald and diamond bracelet worth £600. England's captain denied the allegation and, after making a statement to the police, it was assumed the matter was over. But, at the end of the short tour while on the way back from Ecuador to Mexico, England's plane put down at Bogotá again – and Moore was accused of theft once more. A 'witness' had conveniently been discovered, Moore was detained and the world champions had to leave without their captain. Dr Andrew Stephen, the FA chairman, and Denis Follows, the secretary, also stayed behind.

For four days there were questions, elaborate investigations, hearings and even a stagy reconstruction in front of an army of reporters and cameramen. Inconsistencies in the evidence of the shopowner and his assistant became apparent, and it also emerged that other visiting celebrities had been accused of theft by the same modest establishment and that some had hastily paid for silence. It was more theatre than justice and Moore, to his eternal credit, saw it through with unruffled dignity. He was released on various vague conditions and returned to Mexico to a hero's welcome and an outstanding World Cup.

England were based in Guadalajara, Mexico's second largest city, colonial in style and 400 miles to the north-west of the capital. Their central hotel was the Hilton, tall and modern with a walled pool at the rear, where they were regularly subjected to disturbances, part Mexican, part Brazilian, before games – especially the one against Brazil. The music and honking horns filtered up to the players' level and some changed rooms in vain pursuit of sleep. All is 'fair' in love, war and the World Cup.

Six of the 1966 team played in England's first game against Rumania. Banks and Moore had the strong orthodoxy of Everton's Brian Labone at centre half and Keith Newton, again of Everton, and Terry Cooper of Leeds as their quick and enterprising full backs; Mullery, a dauntless all-rounder, had taken Stiles' place in midfield alongside Ball, Bobby Charlton and Peters; and Hurst's hunting partner in front was the dynamic little Francis Lee of Manchester City. Rumania were defensive, England were patient and a second-half goal by Hurst gave them a victory they deserved.

England's game against Brazil was given a Broadway build-up: the meeting of champions, the old world against the new, the *real* final. It was not a matter of life or death for either side, because two nations from each group could qualify for the quarter-finals, but it was self-evident that both sides cared desperately about winning. It was a match of sustained and enthralling quality that England could well have won but went Brazil's way thanks to a goal sweetly devised by Pele and scored by Jairzinho. Yet the game is remembered more for a goal that Brazil nearly scored than the one they did.

The game was only ten minutes old when Pele, the world's finest player, confronted Banks, the world's best goalkeeper. Pele was ten feet from the far post for a centre from the right by Jairzinho and forehead met ball with exquisite timing and thuggish power. The ball sped sharply and downwards for a reserved place just inside the post. Banks, meanwhile, was a foot or two off his line and within arm's length of the near post; but he turned and plunged like a diving swallow to his right. His right hand made contact inches from the line, the ball looped to safety and fevered rows of commentators swallowed the word 'goal'. Banks simply got to his feet and brushed himself down.

England needed only to draw with Czechoslovakia, who had already lost to Rumania and Brazil, to reach the quarter-finals. Ramsey drafted in four reserves to help conserve energy; and a penalty early in the second half by one of them, Allan Clarke of Leeds (winning his first cap), gave England a dour victory which satisfied no-one.

The performance led to general pessimism about England's chances of winning their quarter-final against West Germany, especially as their second place behind Brazil in the group meant they now had to travel to industrial Leon 6,000 feet above sea level in the semi-desert heart of Mexico. The players themselves did not share the doubts. They had played so well against Brazil that they could see a hard but straight road to Mexico City and the final – and a second meeting, perhaps, with Pele and company.

The difference between success and failure can be very small, but it is always important and the story of how England lost to West Germany after leading 2–0 has been chewed over so often that not one of its central characters would appear to be blameless. South American hostiles – even, for some reason, the CIA – have been darkly accused of 'fixing' Gordon Banks before the game. Banks himself is still not certain it was simply fickle fate. But, whatever the cause and despite the vigilance of Dr Phillips, England's goalkeeper was smitten by violent stomach pains just before the party left for Leon. Ramsey named him in his strongest side and Banks even attended the team meeting on the morning of the match; but more nausea followed, he pulled out of the game and Peter Bonetti of Chelsea – 'the Cat' – took his place with no time to prepare himself mentally for a match of paramount importance.

For more than an hour, none of this seemed to matter. England scored twice, through Mullery and Peters, and the overall quality of their performance, their sturdy control in midfield and their flexibility in pushing men forward to join Hurst and Lee in front, seemed to be a complete justification of Ramsey's strategy. England slowed the game down, bent on making the Germans chase the ball in heat now approaching 100 degrees, while on the touchline the wonderfully fit Colin Bell of Manchester City prepared to take the place of Bobby Charlton who was winning his 106th cap – one more than Billy Wright's record. England were, in most minds, through to the semi-finals. Then it all went wrong.

Franz Beckenbauer pushed forward for West Germany and was manoeuvred by Mullery into shooting from an angle that Bonetti had covered; but the Chelsea goalkeeper's reaction was late and the ball passed under him on its way into the net. Two-one ... and there were just over 20 minutes left. Bell went on and Bobby Charlton withdrew to save his legs for the semi-final just three days later. No-one guessed that Charlton was, in fact, leaving an international field for the last time in his distinguished career.

Bell raised England's tempo again, pushing forward with fresh lungs and powerful stride, and the Germans suddenly found they had a little more room. Ramsey's answer was to send on Norman Hunter of Leeds, a left-sided defender with a famously destructive tackle, to shore things up on the left where the explosive place of Jurgen Grabowski, a substitute himself, had been undermining Cooper. Hunter could have replaced Newton, who was injured, but Ramsey pulled off Peters. The balance and range of England's midfield was now different and, before Hunter had time to make his mark, Germany equalised through Uwe Seeler. He strained to reach a cross from the right and, although he was off-balance and his contact untidy, his header sent the ball looping wearily over the head of Bonetti who was in no-man's land.

Two-two and extra time – but there the 1966 script was thrown away. England had their chances: Hurst, Lee, Mullery and Labone all went near, but this only strengthened the feeling that everything was going Germany's way. Five minutes into the second period of extra time Grabowski centred from the right, Johannes Lohr at the far post headed inside and Gerd Muller – sensing that Labone would not reach it – moved into space away from the England centre half and found himself with the ball, at comfortable volley height, only three yards out. Muller was a killer in front of goal, one of the finest the European game has produced, and he did not miss. He finished as the tournament's top-scorer with ten goals.

England's players left the pitch looking as if they could not believe they had lost. There were blank expressions, and even a few tears, as shirts were exchanged.

Ramsey congratulated Helmut Schoen with dignity but, as he tried to comfort his players, his face showed no more emotion than it had done at the moment of victory four years before. It was no consolation that Brazil, who were to win the World Cup for a third time, gloriously, were to say that England had given them their hardest game.

The inquests grumbled on for weeks. Would Banks of England have saved the day? Should Hurst and Lee have been left to battle alone in front under a blazing Mexican sun? Should Ramsey have played a winger, especially as it was a winger, Grabowski, who had turned the game for West Germany? Were Ramsey's substitutions the key to it all? Should Hunter have come on earlier to counter Grabowski? Should Bell have started instead of Bobby Charlton? Why was Peters and not the injured Newton pulled off? Who can be sure of the answers? All that is certain about England's performance is that they played admirably for an hour and scored twice. It could be that the reason for their defeat was a causeless combination of individual blunders and bad luck. It could be that for the second hour West Germany raised their game to a higher level than England's.

There were no reproaches at the Football Association. Ramsey reported that England's players had done everything he had asked and, given the same challenge again, he would pick the same players and play the same way. His position in the late summer of 1970 was still strong. No-one knew that it would be 12 years before England next played in the finals of a World Cup.

①

②

③

① Gordon Banks (right) hands over his job as Leicester City's goalkeeper to a promising lad called Peter Shilton, March 1967. Banks of England – described by Ron Greenwood as 'a goalkeeper with everything: impossible to better' – joined Stoke City and won 73 caps before an eye injury sustained in a car crash in 1972 ended his career while still at the top of his profession. Shilton, unlike Banks, did not earn a World Cup-winners' medal – but he did play 125 times for England (a world record) in a career with Leicester, Stoke, Nottingham Forest, Southampton and Derby County which lasted 25 years. Shilton also played more first-class matches – around 1,300 – than any other footballer in the history of the British game.

② Cup – and son of cup. Manchester United have beaten Benfica 4–1 after extra time in the final of the European Cup at Wembley, 29 May 1968 – and, left to right, Pat Crerand of Scotland, George Best of Northern Ireland and Matt Busby have the silver to prove it. United, ten years after the Munich disaster, were the first English club to win the cup for champions.

③ The end of England's defence of the World Cup. Gerd Muller bludgeons West Germany's third and winning goal – after England had led 2–0 – five minutes into the second period of extra time of their quarter-final in the 1970 World Cup finals. Peter Bonetti of Chelsea was a late replacement as England's goalkeeper for Gordon Banks, who had suddenly been attacked by a Mexican speciality – violent stomach trouble. Muller finished as the tournament's leading scorer with ten goals.

①

②

③

① Ray Crawford of Colchester United sits down to score his second goal against Leeds United in the fifth round of the FA Cup in 1971 – and the Fourth Division club are on their way to one of the most remarkable giantkilling feats in the history of the tournament. Colchester were 75th in the League and 100–1 for the Cup, the side cost £15,000 to build and, with seven players over 30, were known as 'Granddad's Army'. Leeds, managed by Don Revie and with nine internationals, were well-backed favourites to win the League championship, FA Cup and UEFA Cup. But a full house of 16,000 at Layer Road saw Crawford, who had played twice for England nine years earlier, score twice before half time and Dave Simmons add a third shortly afterwards – and Leeds, despite a spirited fight, were beaten 3–2. Dick Graham, Colchester's manager, an honest and perceptive sergeant-major of a man, recalled later: 'On the morning of the match I went down to the waterfront at nearby Holland-on-Sea, and sat down on a bench for a few moments to myself. It was beautiful, just like a summer day, with blue sky and a calm sea. And as I looked out I knew, beyond all

shadow of doubt, that we were going to beat Leeds. I can't tell you why – I just did. It wasn't wishful thinking. It was total conviction. I knew we were going to win.' In the picture, Leeds goalkeeper Gary Sprake of Wales hesitates, and Jack Charlton of England watches.

② The draw for the FA Cup: one of the tournament's simplest and most dramatic rituals. All clubs are equal as numbered boxwood balls are drawn, two at a time, from a blue velvet bag. Luck is everything: for the big clubs it promises Wembley, for the small it may mean survival and for the smallest it can offer national celebrity. Until the mid-1930s, the draw was made in private. The door of the Council Chamber was locked and only officers of the FA were present. Details of the draw were then taken to another room and, again behind a locked door, read to the press. On 16 December 1935, however, the third-round draw was broadcast by BBC Radio for the first time – and FA secretary Stanley Rous was requested 'to ensure that the bag is shaken for a few seconds to produce a distinctive and suitable sound'. Picture (left to right):

Ted Croker (FA secretary), Sydney Needham (FA Cup Committee), Steve Clark (FA Competitions Department) and Professor Sir Harold Thompson (FA chairman).

③ Smiles to fill Wembley. Sunderland have just beaten Leeds United 1–0 to become the first Second Division club to win the FA Cup for 42 years – and Bob Stokoe, Sunderland's manager, embraces his goalkeeper Jim Montgomery, 5 May 1973. Ian Porterfield scored the goal in the 31st minute, but Montgomery gave Wembley one of its favourite goalkeeping memories when he made a brilliant double-save with 20 minutes left. He pushed away a header by Trevor Cherry and got to the ball again, diverting it to safety via the underside of the crossbar, when Peter Lorimer blasted in a second shot from close range. The tall and angular Stokoe, mackintosh billowing, raced jubilantly across the pitch to Montgomery after the final whistle – another indelible memory for Wearside.

①

②

(3)

(4)

① David Webb (number six) heads Chelsea's winning goal in extra time of their FA Cup final replay against Leeds United at Old Trafford, 29 April 1970. Chelsea were behind three times (twice in their first game at Wembley which was drawn 2–2) before they won the replay 2–1 – and the Cup for the first time in their history. It was the first time a Wembley final had been drawn; the replay, in fact, was the first for 58 years.

② The Centenary final of the FA Cup: a day of sunshine and memories, 6 May 1972. Bertie Mee of Arsenal and Don Revie of Leeds United lead out their sides at Wembley. Arsenal were the Cup-holders and League champions but Leeds won the trophy for the first time with a second-half goal by Allan Clarke. At the head of the procession is the familiar figure of Nigel 'Dickie' Bird who led finalists towards the Royal Box for 30 years. Dickie, a warm, friendly and diplomatic man, joined the FA staff in 1939 and was deputy secretary of the Association when he retired after nearly 50 years' service at Lancaster Gate.

③ All roads lead to Tow Law.

④ Penthouse view: FA Cup fourth round replay, Upton Park, 14 February 1972. An official crowd of 42,271 – and another crowd that was unofficial, uncounted and unidentified – watch West Ham United beat Hereford United of the Southern League with a hat trick by Geoff Hurst. Hereford had beaten another First Division club, Newcastle United, by 2–1 in a third round replay at Edgar Street – and they were national heroes. Hereford's reward was election to the Football League.

①

①

②

① The 'Parliament' of football: the full FA Council enjoy September sunshine outside 16, Lancaster Gate, 1989.

② The first FA Cup semi-final to be played at Wembley: Arsenal 1, Tottenham Hotspur 3, Sunday, 14 April 1991. The stadium was chosen for 'safety and convenience', but the FA ruled the semi-final should not have the ceremony of a final – so the teams are led out by mascots instead of managers. The two north London clubs were to complete a new 'double'. Arsenal won the League championship (for the second time in three seasons) and Tottenham won the FA Cup. There was also a 'double' for the referee, Ray Lewis of Great Bookham, Surrey – two Wembley games in eight days. The following Sunday he refereed the League (Rumbelows) Cup final between Sheffield Wednesday and Manchester United (1–0).

①

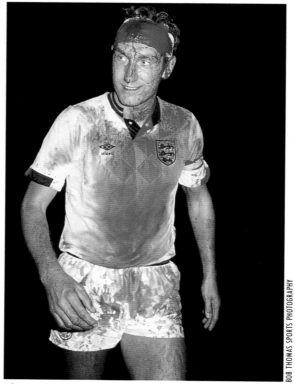

②

③

① Welcome home. Enough people to fill Wembley came from all over the country to Luton to greet England's return from the World Cup finals in Italy, Sunday, 8 July 1990. Bobby Robson and Gary Lineker were missing: they were at the Rome final between West Germany and Argentina (1–0) to receive England's Fair Play trophy.

② 'For as concerning football playing, I protest unto you it may rather be called a friendlie kind of fight, than a play or recreation; a bloodie and murthering practise, than a fellowly sport or pastime.' Philip Stubbes, *The Anatomie of Abuses*, 1583.

Terry Butcher, forehead stitched, bandaged and bloodied, leaves the pitch at the Rasunda Stadium in Stockholm, 6 September 1989. Butcher was England's captain for the night and a goalless draw with Sweden made qualification for the 1990 World Cup almost certain.

③ David Platt scoring his first goal for England in the last seconds of extra time against Belgium in Bologna in the 1990 World Cup finals. It was a goal which Platt, who had come on as a substitute, is unlikely to better: his surge forward was perfectly timed, Paul Gascoigne's free kick floated over his right shoulder and the ball was hooked in on the volley. But England's 1–0 victory was as much about character and the will to win as it was about skill and technique.

① Rising elegance: Arsenal Ladies against Millwall Lionesses in the 1991 Mycil Women's FA Cup semi-final at Watford. The Lionesses won 2–1 and went on to beat Doncaster Belles 1–0 in the final at Tranmere Rovers' Prenton Park. Women's factory teams in Lancashire played for charity in World War One, but it was not until after the 1966 World Cup that women's football became popular. The Women's FA was formed in 1969 and was soon recognised by the FA, UEFA and FIFA. More than 300 clubs now belong to the Women's FA which has full county status with the Football Association. England won the Mundialito – the Little World Cup – in 1985 and 1988.

② Malaysian welcome for England in Kuala Lumpur during their summer tour of 1991. Australia, New Zealand (twice) and Malaysia were all beaten in a round trip of 25,000 miles – with Gary Lineker scoring all of England's goals in their 4–2 victory over Malaysia. Lineker was then only four goals behind Bobby Charlton (49 goals) in England's list of scorers. New Zealand and Malaysia were new opponents and increased the number of countries England have met at full international level to 54.

②

① Martin Buchan (right) of Manchester United and Kevin Keegan of Liverpool tangle in the 1977 FA Cup final. United won by 2–1 – and Buchan became the only player to have captained Scottish and English FA Cup-winning sides: Aberdeen in 1970 and Manchester United in 1977. Keegan joined Hamburg 12 days later for £500,000 ... after helping Liverpool win the League championship and, for the first time, the European Cup. Keegan won 63 caps for England, Buchan 34 for Scotland.

② 'I'm a people's man. Only the people matter. You could call me a humanist' – Bill Shankly, the spirit of Anfield: folk hero, incorrigible romantic, humourist ... and humanist. Dauntless wing half for Carlisle, Preston North End (FA Cup winner 1938) and Scotland, and manager of Carlisle,

Grimsby, Workington, Huddersfield and Liverpool (1959–74).

③ Emlyn Hughes holds the Charity Shield for Liverpool in 1974 – the first time the trophy was competed for at Wembley. Liverpool had beaten Leeds United by 6–5 in a penalty shoot-out after a 1–1 draw. The Charity Shield was first played for in 1908 by Manchester United and Queen's Park Rangers and later, at various venues, it offered such encounters as Professionals against Amateurs and even a World Cup XI against an FA Canadian touring side (4–2, 1950). The initiative of Ted Croker, in his first year as FA secretary, moved the event to Wembley – and, as a curtain-raiser to every season, this fixture between the League champions and FA Cup winners has become very popular. Since 1974 it has raised around £3,000,000 for charity.

③

West Germany again proved too much for England in the quarter-finals of the next European Championship. A virtuoso performance from the blond, mane-haired Gunther Netzer and two late goals gave them a 3–1 victory at Wembley in April 1972; and all that England could manage in the second leg in Berlin a fortnight later was a goalless draw with a team designed to save face rather than tilt at the near impossible. Germany complained about England's 'brutal methods' and Ramsey said he was 'satisfied and proud'. His self-assurance was like a suit of armour.

The pain of that failure, however, was nothing compared with the ramifications of England's match with Poland at Wembley on 17 October 1973. It was a game which England had to win if they were to qualify for the World Cup finals in West Germany the following summer. They had drawn at home with Wales and lost 2–0 to Poland in Chorzow (where Alan Ball was sent off) and the criticism directed at England's manager found an even sharper edge. Ramsey's attitude to the media continued to be unrelentingly cold and often hostile. At a press conference which followed the defeat in Chorzow a young Polish reporter asked: 'We are charming surprised that we win, but we do not understand why, what reasons?' Ramsey replied: 'You are employed as a writer and you ask me a question like that? Poland scored two goals and England didn't score any. That's why.'

The critical frost became heavier as the home game against Poland approached, not even softened by a seven-goal victory over Austria at Wembley just three weeks before, but at least their task was clear: England needed to win, while a draw would do for Poland. Ball was suspended and Ramsey named the side which had demolished Austria, with Hunter again preferred to Moore, who was nearing the end of his international career. Only Peters remained of the 1966 side and he was captain.

Wembley was full and thunderously committed; and what it saw was a game in which England exerted massive pressure on the Polish defence, earned 26 corners to their opponents' two, hit post and bar, were given the bonus of a penalty from which Clarke scored and were faced by a goalkeeper that Brian Clough, in his role as a television expert, called a 'clown'. At the end of it all, however, the Wembley scoreboard was brightly firm about the result: England 1, Poland 1. Poland had scored first through Domarski in the 57th minute after a palpable error by Hunter in front of the Royal Box had allowed Lato to make the opening; and although Clarke's penalty levelled the score only six minutes later England found the 'clown' too much for them. Jan Tomaszewski, the Polish goalkeeper, chose that night for the most remarkable performance of his controversial career. He stopped England with fist and fingertip, foot, leg, chest and most other recruitable parts of his long and awkward looking frame. Some of his saves were brilliant, some bizarre, some lucky. Clough's 'clown' was unbeatable – and England were out of the World Cup. 'The gods were against you,' Ramsey told his players.

All daggers were now unsheathed. Ramsey's 'sins' were meticulously listed: he was accused of everything from tactical suicide to contempt of the public. His style and selections, his 'wingless wonders' and his inflexible convictions were said to have damaged the shape and morale of English football. Critics who had openly admired him now crossed to the other side of the floor. It seemed the only question was not *if* but *when* he would go.

The FA International Committee's first instinct and action was to back Ramsey. It was minuted on Guy Fawkes' Day that 'Sir Alfred Ramsey has the unanimous support and confidence of the members of the senior committee'. On 4 February, the committee approved a request from Ramsey that he should be permitted to watch the World Cup finals. But the media pressure grew and on 14 February – St Valentine's Day – a sub-committee was formed 'to consider our future policy in respect of the promotion of international football'. The sub-committee met on 7 March and 1 April and it was clear from the start of the first meeting that Sir Andrew Stephen, the chairman of the FA, believed it was time to change the England manager. Sir Alf, he said, wanted a new contract and an increase in salary; but Ramsey was 53 and Stephen wondered if he would still be the right man for the job in four or five years' time. Professor Sir Harold Thompson, vice-chairman of the FA, was adamant that Ramsey should go.

Dick Wragg, the affable, pipe-smoking chairman of the International Committee, urged that 'no snap judgment' should be made, but it is minuted that on 8 April Sir Andrew 'gave a detailed resumé of the discussions which had taken place and informed the Executive Committee that the special committee had unanimously agreed that the engagement of Sir Alfred Ramsey as team manager be terminated and that a new manager be appointed as soon as possible'. The recommendation was 'unanimously approved' by the Executive Committee. Sir Andrew and Ted Croker told Sir Alf a few days later that his services were no longer required and, at another meeting of the Future of Football Committee on 21 April, he asked that the announcement should be delayed until 1 May. He was on holiday when the FA recorded 'its deep appreciation for all that Sir Alf has accomplished and the debt owed to him by English football for his unbending loyalty and dedication and the high level of integrity he has brought to world football'.

Some of Ramsey's fiercest critics, perversely, condemned the FA for sacking him, others found fault with the timing of his dismissal and a group of MPs put down a motion inviting the House of Commons to record its appreciation of his services. Croker, in his annual report, said 'the financial implications resulting therefrom [England's World Cup defeat] over the next two or three years could be considerable'. Alan Hardaker, the secretary of the Football League, wrote:

> The financial loss to the FA caused by England at higher levels could not be ignored. Profits from this source are now so important to the health of the FA, and its contribution to the game at all levels, that our national body has become rather like a football club. It is a business in which profit and loss are closely related to victory and defeat. National team-managers ask for and get full control and therefore, if and when they fail, they are held responsible. It is one of the professional game's little rules and, in the end, it defeated even Alf Ramsey.

Hardaker brought down the full might of the press on himself before the Poland game when he said that if England lost 'it will be a terrible thing for about six weeks and then everybody will forget it'. 'A Head in the Sand' raged the *Daily Mirror*. It was Hardaker, too, who once announced: 'There is now a state of war between the League and the Football Association.' The reason was a disagreement over television fees in 1972, although discord between the two authorities was nothing new. In 1965, the 92 clubs of the League even resigned from the FA, which wanted club chairmen to guarantee that no illegal payments were being made by any of their employees. The chairmen decided they would not carry the buck for something over which they had no control. The break lasted for 48 hours before the FA announced that the order was intended for amateur clubs. In 1968 there was a row about players' registrations; in 1970 there was friction about discipline, which led to broader arguments and some militant Midland clubs talking again about a breakaway; and ongoing quarrels about money reached new heights in 1973 when FA and League meetings began to be described as 'war cabinets'. Some clubs wanted to boycott the FA Cup, others said that the FA should pay for the privilege of having League clubs in its tournament.

For the most part, however, common sense and tradition prevailed: the arguments stopped short of damaging a structure which had stood the test of time. Sometimes, after a good row, the two bodies would seem closer than ever. Denis Follows commented in a private letter to Alan Hardaker:

> It is a strange thing, but I feel the present disputes seem to be bringing us personally much closer together. If both you and I accept that we are acting as agents for our respective employers then I think individually we can ride the storm . . . I may not agree with your methods but I accept that what is done is done with the best interests of your employers at

heart. I may disagree fundamentally on certain principles but I do not assume that I necessarily am right.

Denis Follows retired in 1973, later to become chairman of the British Olympic Association and to be knighted in 1978, and his place was taken by the tall and personable Ted Croker, who brought different experience and a new approach to the post. He had played for Charlton Athletic, served with the RAF during World War Two and the Korean War, survived a plane crash in the Pennines and had become a very successful businessman. He had something to learn about the FA's committee structure, but he inherited a staff of 56 with a wealth of experience among its senior members. He saw things with a fresh and perceptive eye, and one of the first things he did was to make it simpler for the man in the street to buy a ticket for England games. 'The FA telephone number was ex-directory,' he was to say 'and trying to get tickets was as hard as trying to get into MI5.'

It was Croker who received a telephone call from Don Revie not long after Ramsey's departure. The Leeds manager said he was interested in the England job and would like an opportunity to talk about it. He did not want to apply in the normal way but was prepared to put his name forward. The search stopped there. Jimmy Bloomfield of Leicester City, Gordon Jago of Queen's Park Rangers and Gordon Milne of Coventry City were among those who had been considered, while the popular Joe Mercer had agreed to become caretaker manager for the Home International Championship and the summer tour of 1974. He went to Lancaster Gate to discuss the details and was asked by the receptionist if he had an appointment. 'Yes, for seven matches,' said Joe. And under his relaxed but knowing control England lost only once.

Mercer did not want the job full time and, in any case, Revie's credentials were surpassingly impressive: he had been voted Manager of the Year three times and was the architect of one of the finest sides in the history of English football. Sir Andrew Stephen, Dick Wragg and Ted Croker went to see him at Elland Road and, in a short meeting, Revie impressed them as a man who knew the system, understood his responsibilities and did not want to make sweeping changes. Leeds demanded a fortune for Revie's handsome contract but changed their minds 24 hours later.

One man saw things slightly differently. Alan Hardaker rang Croker to ask if news of the appointment was true and, when told it was, said simply: 'You must be off your heads.' Alf Ramsey had not always been given the help he needed from club managers and Hardaker, who let little escape him, wrote later: 'Revie as England manager was a classic case of poacher turning gamekeeper.'

Don Revie struck me as being outwardly less of a strong personality than Alf Ramsey. He was quiet and methodical and put his view over in typically Yorkshire forthright manner without being demonstrative. The basis of his appeal was patriotism. We were going to do it for the fans and the country and it came as no surprise when he adopted 'Land of Hope and Glory' as England's anthem. We had our own tune within the camp, 'It's a Grand Old Team to Play for'. Revie tried to create the togetherness he had built up at Leeds. He was desperate to succeed and passionately wanted the England team to be back as Number One in the world. In the end, and this was possibly why he failed, he tried too hard.

Trevor Brooking of West Ham and England in his autobiography Trevor Brooking, *1981.*

Revie immediately asked for the postponement of League matches involving England players on the Saturday before major competitive internationals and claimed, soon afterwards, that the League had promised it would happen. Hardaker accused Revie of jumping the gun and a picture emerged of two men who would find co-operation painfully difficult. But Hardaker quickly came up with a plan: instead of postponing matches, and causing fixture congestion later on, he proposed that games should be brought forward to midweek dates which would be left clear. Many supporters complained bitterly, but Revie said that people would have to decide what was more important to them, their club or their country.

Revie was full of ideas and optimism. More than 80 players, probables and possibles, were summoned to a get-together in Manchester at which England's new manager ran through his battle-plans and pointed the way to a bright new future. He told them they were responsible for the game's image and should coach schoolboys for nothing. He announced new bonuses as well: £200 for a win, £100 for a draw. And, starting with his first match, a European Championship qualifier against Czechoslovakia, Revie had the Wembley crowd bellowing 'Land of Hope and Glory'. England won 3–0 and 90,000 went home convinced they had witnessed a new dawn.

West Germany were beaten 2–0 in the 100th full international at Wembley, with Alan Hudson in stunning form in midfield; Cyprus bowed to the muscular aggression of Malcolm Macdonald who scored five; and England won the British championship by running in another five against Scotland. England were unbeaten in their first season under their new manager, and Revie reflected his happiness with life in general by saying that footballers should 'go down on their hands and knees every night and thank God they are doing something which they love and being well paid for it at the same time'.

Soon after the start of the following season, on Revie's instigation, the FA agreed to give England's players £5,000 each if they won the European Championship and handsome bonuses for reaching the quarter-finals and beyond. 'Money, money, money!' raged Alan Hardaker. 'Football is a short career,' replied Revie.

No bonuses were paid. England, after a 24-hour postponement because of fog, were beaten 2–1 by Czechoslovakia in Bratislava – the first defeat under Revie – and were then held to a 1–1 draw by Portugal in Lisbon. The international class of some of England's players was rudely questioned; and Czechoslovakia qualified for the 1976 finals, an exhilarating tournament from which they emerged as European champions.

Revie, patently, was discovering there was more to the guardian role of England manager than he had imagined. Moulding an established group of beholden British internationals into a successful club side was one thing . . . building an effective international side with other managers' players, little time for preparation and the weight of a nation on his shoulders, was quite another.

He was criticised for his defensive caution and his lack of continuity in selection. He used 52 players in his 29 games, during which he awarded 29 new caps and only once fielded an unchanged side. He was criticised by players, too, for his famous dossiers which analysed opponents' strengths and weaknesses in heavy detail – and which he recommended as bedtime reading.

England won 14 of the 29 games under Revie and of the seven defeats the one which undermined confidence most was Italy's 2–0 triumph in a World Cup qualifying game in Rome in November 1976. England's side showed six changes, while Italy included seven Juventus players. It was not much of a contest. 'We are all very disappointed,' said Revie. 'Now we have to rely on Finland taking at least one point off the Italians and we must beat them at Wembley.' England did indeed beat Italy, but Finland were spanked twice by Italy and so England failed again to reach the finals of the World Cup. And by then England had a new manager.

Revie's stewardship ended with secrecy and bitterness. England's summer tour in 1977 was to Brazil, Argentina and Uruguay, but they left without their manager: it was said he was going to watch the World Cup game between Finland and Italy in Helsinki. Revie missed a goalless draw in Rio de Janeiro, in which Liverpool goalkeeper Ray Clemence was outstanding, but rejoined the party for two more drawn games in Buenos Aires and Montevideo. It was the first time England had avoided defeat on a full South American tour and there was evidence of new confidence and hope on the relaxed journey home.

A month later the truth was revealed by Jeff Powell in the *Daily Mail*, a renowned journalistic coup, under the headline 'Revie quits over aggro'. Revie explained:

> I sat down with my wife one night and we agreed the job was no longer worth all the aggravation. It was bringing too much heartache to those nearest to us. Nearly everyone in the country seems to want me out. So I am giving them what they want. I know people will accuse me of running away . . . but the situation has become impossible.

There was knowing speculation that Revie would join Manchester United, who were without a manager; but the truth, revealed by Powell again the following morning, was infinitely more dramatic. Revie was to become 'football supremo' of the United Arab Emirates with a four-year contract worth £340,000 tax-free. He had, moreover, negotiated the deal in Dubai while he was supposed to have been in Helsinki.

The FA hierarchy was aggrieved, disappointed and – according to one senior figure – 'shattered'; but they were not wholly and totally surprised. When Revie rejoined the England party, after his secret trip to the Persian Gulf, he asked Dick Wragg, the chairman of the International Committee, for a talk 'somewhere quiet'. And, in Wragg's bedroom, Revie said he believed the FA were going to dismiss him and 'to save trouble' he was willing to resign, provided his contract was paid up. This would amount to £50,000 for its two remaining years and he also wanted another £5,000, which was then the upper tax-free limit for a golden handshake. Wragg said his future had not even been discussed and later Peter Swales, the chairman of Manchester City, also tried to persuade him to stay. Croker asked Revie if he had another job to go to and the reply was a firm 'No'. It was assumed Revie would change his mind.

The *Daily Mail*'s revelations, however, were confirmed by Revie's formal letter of resignation and the FA, after a four-hour meeting, issued a statement 'deploring the action of Don Revie' and threatening action for breach of contract. He was duly charged by the FA with setting a bad example, acting deceitfully, debasing his official position, making statements to the press which were not in accord with his contract, negotiating a new post when his full attention should have been given to the national team's success and damaging the image of football and the FA.

Revie's solicitors said they did not accept that the FA had any jurisdiction over him and he would not be attending the hearing. The FA commission announced that Revie would be 'suspended from any involvement with football under the FA' until he did appear. A year later, Revie said he would answer the charges and, represented by Gilbert Gray QC, at a hearing just a week before Christmas in 1978, he spoke of frustration, hostility, criticism and pressure. He also denied that he had worn a heavy disguise to go to Dubai. 'The only thing I had was sunglasses,' he said.

The verdict of the commission was that Revie should be banned for ten years from involvement in English football from the date of his departure to the United Arab Emirates in July 1977. It was the heaviest penalty ever imposed by the FA. A year later, however, Revie successfully asked the High Court to revoke his ban. Mr Justice Cantley said Revie had 'published and presented to the public a sensational and notorious example of disloyalty, breach of duty, discourtesy and selfishness' and also spoke of the 'commercially advantageous bargain' he had made with the *Daily Mail*. But, he added, while Professor Sir Harold Thompson, the chairman of the FA, was 'an honourable man' he should not have presided over the tribunal which banned Revie. Reasonable persons would think there was a real likelihood of bias on his part – 'however hard he tried to be fair, as I am sure he did'. The letter of the law was obeyed. The FA's legal and professional fees in 1979 came to £79,377.

Harold Thompson had become chairman of the FA in 1976 in succession to Andrew Stephen. He was a complex, persuasive and forceful man, the son of a Yorkshire colliery manager; and he was knighted in 1968 for his work as an international scientist. He was a Fellow of the Royal Society and president of the Great Britain-China Society – and a man who loved his football. He played at centre half for Oxford University in the late 1920s and founded Pegasus which brilliantly brought the best of Oxford and Cambridge together after World War Two. 'Tommy' and controversy were travelling companions. Sir Harold was a product and champion of the amateur game but, somewhat surprisingly, he had a realistic appreciation of professional football's problems. In 1972 he was a party – with mixed feelings – to the decision that all footballers, paid or unpaid, should be known simply as 'players'. He had regrets about the passing of the FA Amateur Cup, first won by the Old Carthusians in 1894 and twice by his own Pegasus, but the case to end something the FA could not control – 'shamateurism' – was overwhelming.

The historic decision by the FA Council also meant the end of amateur internationals and a realignment of thousands of amateur and part-time professional clubs. The game formally went open in 1974, strengthened the FA Challenge Trophy (introduced in 1969 for the major professional and semi-professional clubs outside the League) and led to the birth of the FA Challenge Vase in place of the Amateur Cup. Denis Follows, who had fought 'shamateurism' tooth and nail for more than a decade, said simply: 'My headache has gone. It has passed on to the tax man.'

FA Cup

Year	Date	Winners		Runners-up		Venue	Attendance	Referee	Entries
1967	20 May	Tottenham Hotspur	2	Chelsea	1	Wembley	100,000	K Dagnall	406
1968	18 May	West Bromwich Albion	1	Everton	0*	Wembley	100,000	L Callaghan	429
1969	26 April	Manchester City	1	Leicester City	0	Wembley	100,000	G McCabe	438
1970	11 April	Chelsea	2	Leeds United	2*	Wembley	100,000	E Jennings	451
Replay	29 April	Chelsea	2	Leeds United	1*	Old Trafford	62,078	E Jennings	
1971	8 May	Arsenal	2	Liverpool	1	Wembley	100,000	N Burtenshaw	464
1972	6 May	Leeds United	1	Arsenal	0	Wembley	100,000	DW Smith	471
1973	5 May	Sunderland	1	Leeds United	0	Wembley	100,000	K Burns	471
1974	4 May	Liverpool	3	Newcastle United	0	Wembley	100,000	GC Kew	468
1975	3 May	West Ham United	2	Fulham	0	Wembley	100,000	P Partridge	453
1976	1 May	Southampton	1	Manchester United	0	Wembley	100,000	C Thomas	441
1977	21 May	Manchester United	2	Liverpool	1	Wembley	100,000	R Matthewson	454

①

②

① Malcolm Macdonald of Newcastle heading one of his five goals against Cyprus in a European Championship qualifying game at Wembley, 16 April 1975. The electric scoreboard, at the end of the game, read: 'SuperMac 5, Cyprus 0'. Only three other England players – all before World War Two – have managed five goals in a full international: Oliver Vaughton (against Ireland in Belfast, 1882), Steve Bloomer (against Wales at Cardiff, 1896) and Willie Hall (against Ireland at Old Trafford, 1938). Hall (right) scored his first three in $3\frac{1}{2}$ minutes – England's fastest hat trick.

② Ted MacDougall of Bournemouth and Boscombe Athletic who scored nine goals against Margate of the Southern League (beaten 11–0) in the FA Cup first round proper, 20 November 1971 – a record for the tournament. MacDougall scored 47 goals in season 1971/2 and later played for half a dozen clubs, including Manchester United, Norwich and Southampton, and also won seven caps for Scotland.

①

②

③

④

① ''Ere, 'ere … I think I can see straight through.' Joe Mercer of Coventry (left) during his short spell as caretaker manager of England in 1974, and trainer Les Cocker of Leeds United. Mercer, a highly respected and loveable man, took over between the departure of Alf Ramsey and the appointment of Don Revie – and lost only one of seven matches.

② 4 July 1974: Donald George Revie of Leeds United becomes the third full-time manager of England. Left to right: Revie, Ted Croker (secretary of the FA), Sir Andrew Stephen (chairman) and Dick Wragg (chairman of the International Committee). Revie's career at this point had been successful and distinctive. As a player he was stylish and thoughtful, capped by England on six occasions, Footballer of the Year in 1955 and best remembered for his role as a deep-lying centre forward (in tactically less flexible times) for Manchester City when they won the FA Cup in 1956. As the manager of Leeds (from 1961) he was hugely 'professional', competitive, single-minded and addicted to detail: he transformed a club on the brink of relegation to the Third Division into one renowned throughout Europe. But as the manager of England he was defeated by the myriad frustrations of the post and the higher challenge of international football and, after three years, he suddenly and gracelessly resigned and took a handsomely paid job in the United Arab Emirates. He was suspended from domestic football for ten years by the FA for 'bringing the game into disrepute', but later successfully challenged the ban in the High Court. As a man he was misunderstood by many, and understood only too well by a few, but he was essentially a friendly and caring man, devoted to his family, his profession and golf. He died of the rare motor neurone disease, aged 61, on 26 May 1989.

③ Football showing its age. Left: Scottish Football Association's Centenary match – Scotland 0, England 5. Centre: FA Cup Centenary final – Arsenal 0, Leeds United 1. Right: England's 100th full international at Wembley – England 2, West Germany 0.

④ Scottish supporters 'celebrating' Scotland's 2–1 victory over England at Wembley, 4 June 1977. The bar was broken, while parts of both goals, as well as turf from the pitch, were taken away as souvenirs. It was the first major invasion of the Wembley pitch and led to the erection of fences at the foot of the terraces.

St onley Row

"... *I still derive a tremendous amount of enjoyment and pride from the way things I have worked on are developing.*

"*I don't want to look back instead of looking forward, but I do hope football never becomes anything other than a game.*"

Sir Stanley Rous 1984

①

②

① Sir Stanley Rous, one of the most influential administrators in the history of football. He was secretary of the FA for 27 years and president of FIFA for nearly 13 years – an ambassador and a visionary who maintained a delicate balance between the powers of Europe and South America and aided and guided the emerging countries of the Third World. What he could not do – and in the end it cost him his FIFA post in 1974 – was check the rising influence within the game of money and politics. His days began with a cold bath and he watched about a hundred matches a season. The FA organised a 90th birthday dinner for Sir Stanley in 1985, a celebration attended by guests from six continents. He died a year later and a Service of Thanksgiving was held in Westminster Abbey.

② The FA Challenge Trophy – competed for by the cream of English football's non-League clubs. The Trophy is silver, nearly 30 inches tall and weighs over 20 pounds. It was presented to the Football Association in 1905 by Sir Ernest Cochrane, a member of the English Bar, with an office in New York, who envisaged an international tournament involving England, Canada and America to promote Association Football in North America – an idea that was still-born. The Trophy was first competed for in season 1969/70 by non-League clubs which employed professionals, but was broadened when the FA Amateur Cup was wound up in 1974. Around 200 clubs compete for the Trophy each season – and the final is held at Wembley.

11

SUCCESS ...
AND STRESS
1978–84

'We've a bit of a situation,' said Professor Sir Harold Thompson, as the country earnestly debated the manner and morality of Don Revie's departure. 'The image of the game is all wrong. Everyone is being roasted, including myself and the rest of the International Committee, and we don't like it. We need a firm, stable hand immediately and we're wondering if you would take over as caretaker-manager of England for a while.'

The invitation was to Ron Greenwood and it was made to the accompaniment of hammer and saw in the basement of the Park Court Hotel just a few yards from the FA's headquarters in Lancaster Gate. Thompson and Greenwood had gone there for 'a chat away from it all', failed to find a quiet room and finished up below stairs where they were immediately joined by a gang of workmen. 'It was a bit silly,' Greenwood was to remember, 'but we decided to stay put.'

Greenwood was 55 years old, and it occurred to him that he was being called to the colours mainly because he was available. Season 1977/8 was about to start and the FA would not have been popular had they stolen a manager from a club at that stage. 'We are going to advertise the job, so no promises. See what you can do,' said Sir Harold. Greenwood said he would be delighted, and the formal announcement of his appointment declared he would 'act as team manager for the next three internationals until December next'.

Greenwood, however, was much more than a stop-gap: his character and managerial career might have been designed with the England job in mind. He was a kind and highly principled Lancastrian who had played his first football in clogs in a village near Burnley, but he had spent most of his professional career in the game in London. He had been an above-average player, a dependable centre half who won a

'B' cap for England and a League championship medal with Chelsea. He was an innovative coach with Arsenal and then, as West Ham United's manager for 16 years, he made his mark as a man who saw football as an exciting challenge, championing open, attractive play and studying the international game. He was one of the many coaches whose eyes were opened by Walter Winterbottom and one of the few, too, who had seen the 1953 Hungarians as living proof that football can be a lovely art as well as a muscular science.

He led West Ham to triumph in the FA Cup and the European Cup-Winners' Cup, while three of his players, Moore, Peters and Hurst, led England to victory in the World Cup. He also managed England's Youth and Under-23 sides. In 1974 Greenwood became general manager at West Ham, handing over control of the team to John Lyall, a decision he soon regretted because it divorced him from the aspects of the game he cared most about – daily and creative contact with players and the challenge of competition. Greenwood became increasingly depressed during the next two or three years and the invitation from the FA came when, in his own words, 'my spirit – and the game's – was low . . . but I felt the fire rising in me again and I saw my task quite clearly: I was going to help restore faith and dignity in our game and prove to the world we could play a bit.'

He was as good as his word. He acted as England's caretaker-manager for the last three games of 1977 and then, with a strong sense of purpose, held the post for another four-and-a-half years. In that time, England reached the finals of the European Championship and the World Cup and Greenwood retired with dignity in the summer of 1982. Many felt it was a pity he had not been given the job earlier in his career.

The English game was feeling sorry for itself when Greenwood took over. Morale was low and hooliganism was a spreading sore. Overdrafts were growing and many clubs were sending up distress signals. Television was becoming a thorny issue and players were threatening industrial action to support their case for freedom of contract, which they won in the spring of 1978. The role of the agent and accountant took on a new importance in the game.

Hooliganism was the major issue: it had become an integral part of the football scene during the previous 15 years or so and was the most serious problem faced by the professional game in England in its long and furrowed history. There had always been a degree of violence in football, emotional outbursts for the most part, caused by anger or frustration with the way the game was being played or controlled. But the new disorder was different. It had less to do with emotion than violence and vandalism for its own sake. It was a social illness which was probably given its first expression by the travelling fans of Everton and Liverpool in the late 1950s. The majority of games were trouble-free, but during the 1960s the number of disturbances – and the media and public consciousness of the problem – steadily increased. Evidence of a general malaise persisted: vandals who had nothing to do with football wrecked telephone kiosks and smashed train compartments; seaside resorts were the scene of mods-and-rockers-style gang fights and inner-city riots at Toxteth, St Paul's, Moss Side and Brixton took their place in history.

The 'football hooligan', however, was now clearly identifiable. His chosen theatre was the football ground which provided a perfect climate and cloak for his ugliness. There was fighting on the terraces, obscene chanting, coin- and missile-throwing and pitch invasions. The timing and area of the villainy varied and spread. It took place before and after matches in large areas around grounds and even in nearby towns: there was damage to buses, trains, shops and property. Spontaneous confrontations between rival fans developed stage by stage into calculated gang warfare in which co-ordination and strategy played a part. The National Front and other extreme right-wing groups entered the scene in search of recruits. Inevitably, too, the hooligan followed England and its clubs abroad.

The men who ran football were not law enforcement officers, but the problem was in their goal area. Professor Sir Harold Thompson attributed the problem to 'unsettled social conditions, the bad health of the nation and a lack of teaching of values, virtues and discipline'. The Government blamed football's authorities for failing to take firm measures and its players for not setting a good example. The media blamed everybody and used the language of war to shock its public and give the hooligan an identity he cherished.

The Football Association and the League set up their own committees and contributed weightily to the working party of Denis Howell when he was Minister for Sport. There were discussions with the Magistrates' Association which led to stiffer sentences. There were meetings of club chairmen and conferences for anyone with anything to contribute. And there were enquiries: the Harrington Report (1968), the Lang Report (1969) and the Wheatley Report, which followed the 1971 Ibrox disaster in which 66 people died during the New Year derby between Glasgow Rangers and Celtic. This led to the stringent Safety of Sports Grounds Act of 1975 which cut ground capacities and required major stadia to be licensed.

Crowd safety and control were in close step: the face and mood of the game changed. Visiting supporters were escorted to and from grounds like columns of prisoners. Fences and cages were erected. Fans were searched and segregated. Closed-circuit television was introduced. The sale of alcohol was limited and the distribution of tickets was carefully monitored, with the FA establishing its own

Travel Club to control the movement of England supporters abroad. The police contributed enormous manpower, advice, evolving strategy and advance intelligence. But the cost of policing football (£2,000,000 in 1981) was a heavy drain on finances at a time when most clubs were struggling desperately to make ends meet.

The League was operating at a loss of more than £5,000,000 a season in the early 1980s, with players' wages swallowing around 60 percent of all match receipts. Pools, television and, belatedly, sponsorship made good most of this loss and the Football Grounds Improvement Trust, with money contributed by the Pool Promoters' Association from its spot-the-ball competition, made grants of up to 75 percent for safety work and improvements. The cost of bringing grounds up to standard rose annually, but club directors were in no position to protest. The threat of hooliganism was already cutting attendances and a general fear about safety would have accelerated the decline.

On the field, as it happened, English football got its hands on the European Cup and refused to let go. Liverpool won the trophy in 1977, beating Borussia Moenchengladbach 3–1 in Rome – the first of six successive seasons in which the magnificent Champions' Cup finished in an English showcase: Liverpool again, Nottingham Forest twice, Liverpool once more and then Aston Villa. Along the way there were sour rumbles in some Continental papers. English football was even berated for its lack of soul; but its effectiveness and resolution were beyond censure.

Nottingham Forest was now run by Brian Clough and Peter Taylor, who had left Derby in late 1973 after their relationship with some of the club's directors had become openly hostile. They took charge together at Brighton, but then Clough moved on alone to Leeds to succeed Don Revie – an astonishing appointment because Clough had been a persistent and caustic critic of the Elland Road club. He found a split board, an uneasy back room, resentful fans and rebellious players; and he lasted just 44 days. Nottingham Forest brought Clough and Taylor together again, however, and the most successful period in the club's history began with promotion from Divison Two in 1977. The League championship and the League Cup followed in 1978, the European Cup and League Cup again in 1979 and the European Cup once more in 1980. Clough and Herbert Chapman are still the only managers who have guided two clubs to the championship.

But, as Ron Greenwood contemplated his three games as England's caretaker-manager in August 1977, he knew exactly where to begin. Liverpool were outstandingly the most successful club, their experience of Europe was unmatched, the backbone of the side was English and they played football Greenwood admired. They were controlled now by Bob Paisley, who had served the club as player, reserve-team trainer, first-team trainer, first-team coach, assistant manager and, with mild protest, as manager after Bill Shankly had surprisingly retired in 1974. Paisley, a round and avuncular Durham man, knew he was being asked to replace the irreplaceable, but he managed it without a break in step because he understood the Liverpool way of doing things better than anyone. He bought the best players available and stuck them together with patience, style, loyalty, confidence and simplicity. The continuity was perfect, and Liverpool kept on winning. Paisley became the most successful manager in the history of English football: in his nine seasons as manager (1974–83) Liverpool won the League championship six times, the European Cup three times, the League Cup three times and the UEFA Cup.

> If I told people that the secret of Liverpool's success is a dip in the Mersey three times a week, I not only reckon they'd believe me but I think our river would be full of footballers from all over the country.
>
> *Ronnie Moran, Liverpool's trainer, 1980.*

Greenwood began his England stewardship by going to Anfield and, in a long and honest talk with Paisley and his players, discovered as much about himself as he did about them. He decided he could do worse than impose Liverpool's proven method and confidence on the England side, thus giving it an instant identity. He picked six Anfield men and Kevin Keegan (who had just moved from Liverpool to SV Hamburg) for his first game, a friendly against Switzerland at Wembley, but against opponents who were clever and cautious the result was a goalless draw. Five Liverpool players were also in Greenwood's second team, for a World Cup qualifier in Luxembourg, but, although they won, they only scored twice – not enough in a group in which Italy were in pole position. Italy, moreover, were England's opponents at Wembley for Greenwood's third game.

Greenwood now decided to trust his instincts and changed his pattern. He gave first caps to two wingers, the busy and intelligent Steve Coppell of Manchester United on the right and Peter Barnes of Manchester City, fast, elusive and a potential match-winner, on the left. Bob Latchford of Everton, a strong and aggressive goalscorer who was bang in form, also came in for his first international. Keegan was just behind them and two stylish London players, Trevor Brooking of West Ham and Ray Wilkins of Chelsea, were in midfield. And there were three Liverpool men in defence: Emlyn Hughes, who was captain, goalkeeper Ray Clemence and Phil Neal. 'A basic shape,' said Greenwood, 'but simple jigsaw puzzles can still produce splendid pictures.'

England won 2–0 in front of a delighted 90,000 crowd: Brooking made the first goal for Keegan, while Keegan made the second for Brooking. It was a bright and measured performance and, despite ridiculous murmurs that Italy had not tried too hard, it was a clean and deserved victory which gave the English game an important shot in the arm. But it was not quite enough to send England to the 1978 World Cup finals in Argentina. Italy beat Luxembourg 3–0 in Rome in their last qualifying game – and pipped England by a goal difference of just three. Italy went on to beat the host country in the first stage of the finals but the last word, resoundingly, was Argentina's.

The FA now had to choose a man to take England towards the 1980 European Championship finals in Italy. A shortlist of five was agreed on without much argument: Greenwood, of course, Brian Clough, Lawrie McMenemy of Southampton, Bobby Robson of Ipswich and the FA's director of coaching Allen Wade. Robson and McMenemy were personable, experienced and articulate men of the north-east who had done a marvellous job with modest clubs.

They were invited to Lancaster Gate on 4 December 1977 and, in relaxed interviews which each lasted about 45 minutes, talked with persuasion and enthusiasm. Clough, who had been overwhelmingly voted as the people's choice by readers of the *Daily Mirror*, had never seen eye to eye with Professor Sir Harold Thompson but, during his interview, he and the FA's chairman were pointedly cordial to each other. It was agreed that Clough's interview was excellent, but there was a broad feeling that the controversial Nottingham Forest manager was not the man for the job. The right kind of experience, it was decided, was the key factor and Greenwood – with his long connection with the FA and the memory of the victory over Italy still vividly fresh – was the firm choice.

Greenwood's first priority was to build a support team of managers and coaches. 'This will give us continuity, something we've never had before,' he stressed before and during his interview. 'We will be able to make assessments and the International Committee won't have to make any more one-off, on-the-spot choices as it did with Don Revie and myself. It should have been done years ago.'

Bobby Robson and Don Howe, who had been Arsenal's coach during their 'double' year, were given control of England's 'B' side. The talents and experience of Dave Sexton, Terry Venables and Howard Wilkinson were brought together for the Under-21s. Brian Clough and Peter Taylor were confirmed as heads of the Youth team with John Cartwright, a former West Ham player and a gifted teacher, as full-time coach. 'I'll crawl all the way to Lancaster Gate just to be involved,' Clough had told Greenwood. But Clough's involvement with Nottingham Forest, who were on their way to winning the championship, meant he had little time for the other responsibilities. His England connection was highly publicised, unsettling – and brief.

Greenwood's side took shape as it qualified for the 1980 European finals by dropping only one point in a group completed by Bulgaria, Denmark, Northern Ireland and the Republic of Ireland. Eight players took part in six or more of the eight qualifying ties, with Kevin Keegan and Trevor Brooking at the heart of everything.

Keegan had six resounding years at Liverpool before moving to Hamburg in 1977 and, in Greenwood's opinion, he was 'the most modern of modern footballers … a rare and brilliant little chap'. He was a balanced, muscular player with a quick mind and twinkling feet, as difficult to hold as a bar of wet soap, and a leader of character and courage who shaped and influenced games. And with his dark, trendily cut hair, fashionable clothes and easy conversation he was, perhaps, the first player to turn his job into a big business. He had a thick portfolio of contracts to promote leisurewear, sports goods, toiletries and other commodities, several companies registered in tax havens and he was in constant and profitable demand by television and newspapers. But his priorities were always right. He was, above all, a professional footballer.

Brooking was a player Greenwood knew better than anybody because their careers had developed together at West Ham. Brooking was a tall and elegant conductor of the game, a midfield player of natural authority and broad range who was adventurous but not reckless, an artist who happily accepted responsibility. He was popular, unfailingly courteous and utterly unflappable; and he, too, was a successful businessman. 'Keegan and Brooking: what a pair they were,' Greenwood wrote later. 'They cooked up goals for England that suggested telepathy.'

England won 20 and lost only three of the 29 games under Greenwood before the start of the European finals. They had the best qualifying record in the tournament and there were notable victories in friendlies against Spain, 2–0 in Barcelona, and Argentina, the world champions, 3–1 at Wembley. One Spanish paper suggested Spain's players should be given a grant to go to England to learn what the game was all about; and the win over Diego Maradona and Argentina was stylishly achieved in front of the managers of all the other European finalists.

Prime Minister Mrs Margaret Thatcher invited the squad to a reception at 10 Downing Street and this seemed to reflect the hopes and interest of the country. Greenwood was convinced England were going to do well, even though an Achilles' tendon injury robbed him of the greyhound speed and stinging finish of Trevor Francis on whom Brian Clough had bestowed a permanent line in the record book. Clough and Nottingham Forest paid Birmingham the first British transfer fee to breach the million-pound mark for Francis in February 1979.

In the event, the 1980 finals of the European Championship proved to be a leaden disappointment for England and the game as a whole. The tournament was smothered by negative thinking and undermined by poor crowds. It lacked outstanding players and even the smallest pinch of fantasy. The Italians themselves were interested only in their own team and, along with the rest of Europe, wailed about everything else in front of their television sets. The finals were in step with the times and emphasised the harm that football was doing to itself.

The format of the 12-day tournament was simple: the eight nations were split into two groups of four with the winner of each qualifying for the final. England's group was completed by Belgium, who were competitive and durable; Italy, who were gifted and technically excellent but burdened by expectation; and Spain, who were useful but, as England had proved in Barcelona, also vulnerable.

A good start against Belgium in the Comunale Stadium in Turin was important; and England did not manage it. Ray Wilkins, who had moved from Chelsea to Manchester United, sprang the Belgian offside trap to score a goal of rare quality and Tony Woodcock, a bright and mobile striker who played a major part in Nottingham Forest's success before moving to FC Cologne, had what seemed to be a perfectly good goal disallowed. Belgium soon equalised through Jan Ceulemans, however, and it was then that the game – and the tournament – began to go wrong for England.

Nearly 6,000 members of the FA Travel Club were at the game and, before the kick-off, they and the England team warmly acknowledged each other. But many others bought tickets at the ground, segregation was poor or non-existent and alcohol was available. Italian fans taunted the English, seats were jumped on and fierce fighting started on the terrace behind England's goal. The Italian police wasted no time on gentle admonition. They moved in with batons and, faced by resistance, they fired tear-gas canisters into the general area of the trouble. Yellow and grey smoke slowly began to spread and drift. Ray Clemence of Liverpool, England's goalkeeper, rubbed his eyes and indicated to the England bench that he was in trouble. Greenwood quickly moved over to the match adjudicator and asked him to signal to the referee to stop the game. The referee, a West German, seemed confused as he approached Greenwood who immediately asked: 'What's going to happen if a goal is put past our goalkeeper because he can't see?' 'It would count,' said the official. 'In that case,' said Greenwood, 'don't you think you should stop the game until the gas has cleared?' The stoppage was for five minutes; and when the game resumed it had clearly lost much of its impetus.

Sir Harold Thompson called the trouble-makers 'moronic louts and saboteurs', but also said he had been approached after the game by groups of England fans with tears of remorse and disgust in their eyes. More than 70 fans needed hospital treatment. Mrs Thatcher, who was in Italy on Common Market business, described the riot as 'a disgraceful embarrassment'. UEFA fined the FA £8,000, a surprisingly modest sum, and there were suggestions in the Italian press that England should be thrown out of the tournament. The FA's own report, later, was less dramatic but stressed that diligent control of tickets at their end counted for nothing if they were also readily available at grounds on match-days. There was a reference to over-reaction by the Italian police and the need was stressed again for some Government initiative on the problem.

Greenwood was concerned there would be repercussions during England's confrontation with Italy in the same stadium three days later; but this time the crowd was 60,000 – four times the gate for the Belgium game – and there was little room for anything except noise. There were also dark rumours that any England fans who were arrested could count on a permanent address in the deepest of local dungeons.

England's manager decided to play Gary Birtles, a choice which surprised even his players because the young Nottingham Forest forward's experience of international football amounted to just ten minutes as a substitute at the end of the friendly against Argentina. But Birtles had helped Forest win the European Cup twice and Woodcock was an old hunting partner. Greenwood knew he was taking a gamble, but he also felt the element of surprise might work in England's favour. Birtles was strong in the air, deceptively quick and clever at holding the ball until support arrived, qualities which Manchester United also appreciated because, four months later, they paid £1,250,000 for him. It was not Birtles' or England's day, though, and a late and finely designed goal by Marco Tardelli gave an abrasive Italy their victory. England beat Spain 2–1, with goals by Brooking and Woodcock, in Naples in their third game; but that same evening Belgium held Italy to a goalless draw to earn a place in the final in Rome ... a good final, and the best match of the tournament, which a rising West Germany won 2–1.

'You have nothing to be ashamed about,' Greenwood told his players. England missed the sharpness of Francis, however, and Keegan was not at his best after a gruelling season with Hamburg. Chances were missed, especially in the game against Italy, and England lacked the penetration to make an impact on a short, high-pressure tournament which was coldly ruled by caution. The calmly authoritative Wilkins finished it with high credit and Kenny Sansom, then of Crystal Palace but soon to join Arsenal in another million-pound transfer, established himself at left back with skill and enterprise.

①

②

③

① 'We joined the police to go up in the world ... so why are we on an escalator going down?' The 39 steps up to the Royal Box at Wembley were waiting for Everton, who beat Watford 2–0 in the 1984 FA Cup final.

② Dangerous character. One small desperado under close surveillance at the Clock End at Highbury while Arsenal play Liverpool, 10 September 1983. In season 1983/4 the cost of policing football was 9½ percent of game receipts.

③ England fans scatter as gas cannisters fired by Italian police explode on the terraces of the Comunale Stadium in Turin during England's game with Belgium in the European Championship finals, 12 June 1980. The game was stopped for five minutes and drawn 1–1. Sir Harold Thompson, chairman of the FA, called the English trouble-makers 'moronic louts and saboteurs' and UEFA fined the FA £8,000.

① The management. Ron Greenwood (England manager 1977–82) and his 'team' of managers and coaches. Back row (left to right): Don Howe (full England and England 'B'), Bobby Robson (England 'B'), Howard Wilkinson (Under-21), Dave Sexton (Under-21), Ted Croker (FA secretary), Alan Odell (International secretary). Front row: Terry Venables (Under-21), Ken Burton (Youth), Ron Greenwood, Bill Taylor (full), Geoff Hurst (full).

② Room for a view. Aston Villa are on their way to their first League championship for 71 years – and hundreds of fans take a narrow and variegated view of Villa's game with Ipswich, 14 April 1981. A crowd of nearly 48,000 inside the ground saw Aston Villa lose 2–1 to Bobby Robson's Ipswich. But Villa had the last word: Ipswich were runners-up.

The road to the European finals had been smooth and straight, but the finals themselves were an overexposed indictment of the modern game. However, Greenwood made it clear from the start that his real target was the 1982 World Cup finals. England got there in the end, but their route to Spain was by way of a steep and narrow path along the edge of a cliff, a journey of so many twists and pot-holes that Greenwood himself barely survived.

England were in a qualifying group of five – two to qualify – along with Rumania, Hungary, Switzerland and Norway. Things began well enough with a 4–0 victory over Norway at Wembley on 10 September 1980; but only one of the next eight games was won, the worst run in England's international history, and Greenwood found himself bitterly assailed on all sides. Spain, Brazil and Scotland won at Wembley and, more importantly, England seemed to be heading for early and humiliating elimination from the World Cup. They lost 2–1 to Rumania in Bucharest, were hard-pressed to beat Switzerland by the same score at Wembley and were then held to a goalless draw in the return fixture with Rumania. Five points had been earned from four games, and their prospects of reaching the finals in Spain looked tissue-thin. Ahead of them, moreover, were qualifying games in Switzerland and Hungary. Greenwood recalled:

> I was hurt and I had a feeling of shame. I felt I had let the country down. Even ordinary conversation was difficult and I could sense people looking at me as if I had committed some crime. We had been badly hit by injuries but they were still my teams, playing my way, which had been failing. 'For God's sake, Ron, pack up' advised the headline in one paper … but I convinced myself anything was possible. I knew I had to believe if others were going to.

Greenwood's honest conviction was to be sorely tested before things got better: the visit to Basle, the first stage of England's short summer tour of 1981, was both shameful and embarrassing. England's followers caused widespread damage and trouble, and England's footballers lost to Switzerland for the first time in 34 years. The civil and sporting authorities of Basle were hopelessly unprepared for the worst of England's camp followers, with their grubby T-shirts (some proclaiming 'Battle of Turin') and their dirty Union Jacks. They sprawled and drank in the squares of the city, and then carried their fighting and wrecking into the stadium itself. The Swiss police planned to have 30 men at the game and, after an earnest appeal by the FA, reluctantly raised the number to 80, but they admitted afterwards that the behaviour of the England fans was 'outside our experience and beyond our control'.

England's 2–1 defeat, with the Swiss scoring twice in little more than a minute midway through the first half, seemed to Greenwood to be the last straw. England had taken only five points from the first five of their eight qualifying games – and within minutes of the end of the Swiss game he decided to retire. It was a decision totally out of character for a man of such pride and determination but it expressed, exactly, the pressures of his job.

Greenwood kept it to himself for a couple of days and then told Dick Wragg and Ted Croker: 'It's time for a change. I'm going to retire ... not resign, just retire. But I'll tell you one thing: we'll win our next game in Hungary. I'll make sure of that. This will be our ticket to the World Cup finals, but then I'll step aside and this will give you a chance to bring in someone new in good time for Spain.' Wragg and Croker attempted to change his mind, but Greenwood was adamant. They even discussed financial arrangements. Wragg was about to return to England for the FA's summer meeting and it was decided he would meet the party when it arrived at Luton, after the Hungary game, and then make a formal announcement. No-one else was told.

Greenwood's feeling about the game against Hungary in the Nep Stadium in Budapest proved right. His determination communicated itself to the players and there was a special intensity in the way they trained. Greenwood spent most of his spare time in his room in England's hotel beside the Danube and then announced the most experienced side he could – a side which gave him an impressive 3–1 victory; and again Brooking and Keegan were at the heart of it. Brooking scored twice, his second struck with such power that the ball lodged behind a stanchion, and Keegan added another from the penalty spot.

The victory, Greenwood would say later, was 'one of the great moments of my life', but it did not change his mind about retiring. His press conference afterwards was his shortest: 'I'd like to thank you for your support over the years. Our win was a good one, well deserved, and it's given me great pleasure personally to beat the Hungarians. I don't want to answer any questions. Thank you.' It was a final statement and a mighty story. No-one spotted it.

Greenwood decided to tell the players about his retirement on the flight home. Twenty minutes from Luton he quietly pulled a curtain to separate the England party at the front of the plane from the rest of the passengers. 'I'd like to thank you all,' he said, 'but I've decided the moment is right for me to retire. I'm telling you now because Mr Wragg's waiting at the airport to make the announcement. It's my own decision ... there's been no pressure. We've seven points out of 12 and, with Norway away and Hungary at home to come, the new chap will have a chance. And it goes without saying I wish you all the best of luck.'

There was a long silence followed by commotion and a huddled conference. Then came the protests: 'You're out of order ... think it over.' The players left Greenwood alone for a few minutes and then returned to try to persuade him to stay on. The appeals continued across the tarmac and into the luggage area at Luton, and it was there that Greenwood relented. He decided that if the players wanted him to stay that much, then it would be right to change his mind. Dick Wragg was told – 'I was going to try and talk you out of it anyway,' he said – and Greenwood conducted his last press conference of the tour without dropping a hint that he had been so near to retiring to his home in Brighton.

Everybody kept quiet about it – a remarkable feat. The detailed story did not surface until Greenwood related it himself in his autobiography, *Yours Sincerely*, which was published in 1984. But if Greenwood had been allowed to go, it would have given the FA a major problem and might well have created a situation similar to the very one which Greenwood had been hired to ease after the departure of Don Revie. Confidence and the image of the game would have been painfully bruised again. In any case there were still some nasty hairpin bends to come. England's seventh qualifying game was in Oslo on 9 September 1981 and, as they had never scored fewer than four goals against Norway, home or away, the game was viewed with a forgiveable degree of confidence.

Greenwood made changes from the side which beat Hungary: Trevor Francis came in for Steve Coppell; Russell Osman of Ipswich was preferred to Dave Watson, whose time as the pillar of England's defence was running out; and Glenn Hoddle took the place of Trevor Brooking, who was not match-fit. Hoddle was a beautiful player, a tall, willow-slim and effortlessly elegant Londoner who controlled and delivered the ball as if it was a personal friend. Even opposition crowds applauded him at his best and a clamorous section of the press saw him as the definitive key to success. He scored a fine goal and made an instant impression in his first international, against Bulgaria in late 1979, but Greenwood had early reservations about him: he was unsure about Hoddle's fitness and involvement, and felt he did not shape a side but needed a side shaped around him.

Hoddle was, however, a member of England's squad for the 1980 European finals, winning Greenwood's vote for one of the last places over a different kind of midfield player, Bryan Robson of West Bromwich Albion. Robson did not have Hoddle's sublime talent, but he was certainly skilful; and to this he added passion, courage, perpetual involvement, vision and enough other qualities to persuade some sensible judges that he was near to perfection as a midfield player. A month after the game against Norway he was sold to Manchester United for a British record fee of £1,500,000. Hoddle and Robson were together in England's midfield in Oslo and, with Keegan and Francis in front of them, England were not short of promise.

England even took an early lead in the Ullevaal Stadium, Robson scoring his first international goal. But from that point on they were frog-marched towards a defeat that was to be compared with the American upset in 1950. Norway scored twice in the quarter-hour before half time and, with their fans giving them thunderous support around a small, cramping pitch, they resisted the best and worst of England for the rest of the game. Norway 2, England 1 . . . and there was nowhere to hide. 'Our game hit the sky just because we were playing England,' said Tor Fossen, Norway's manager. 'That's the price you pay for fame.'

The sky, having been hit by Norway, then fell on Greenwood and his players. Greenwood said he was made to feel like Public Enemy Number One, and Keegan and his team were described as mercenaries who cared more about their bank manager than their football manager. Politicians joined the queue of carpet-beaters, but that is never surprising. There were others who should have known better. Greenwood said simply: 'My team failed as players, not as human beings.'

> We are the best in the world. We have beaten England. Lord Nelson . . . Lord Beaverbrook . . . Sir Winston Churchill . . . Sir Anthony Eden . . . Clement Attlee . . . Henry Cooper . . . Lady Diana. We have beaten them all. Maggie Thatcher, can you hear me? Maggie Thatcher, your boys took a helluva beating. Norway have beaten England at football!
>
> *Borge Lillelien, Norwegian radio commentator, at the end of his broadcast on Norway's first victory over England, 2–1, in a World Cup qualifying game in Oslo in 1981.*

England had seven points from seven games and only their home game against Hungary to come. They were on top of the group, but Hungary, Rumania and Switzerland all had enough games in hand to overtake them. And it was then, with the sky at its lowest and darkest, that England found light. Switzerland, improbably, won in Rumania, lost emphatically in Hungary to ruin their own chances and then drew their return with Rumania in Berne. Hungary had therefore qualified before their game at Wembley just a week later on 18 November 1981 – and a draw was all England needed to join them in Spain.

Memories of the defeat by Norway went out through the back door. All tickets were quickly sold and, with the League having cleared the Saturday before the international of all games involving England's players, the squad was able to sweat and plot together for five days. The publicity suggested that Armageddon rather than a game of football lay ahead. 'We have been given a kiss of life,' Greenwood told his players. 'Let's show everyone what we're made of.' But their best, on a rainy night in the old stadium, was not required. Hungary, having qualified, played without conviction and a goal in the 16th minute by the effective Paul Mariner of Ipswich, after Trevor Brooking had mishit a shot, was enough. England had beaten Hungary twice and, with help from Switzerland, they had reached the finals of a World Cup for the first time since 1970. The booming sound of 92,000 people singing 'You'll Never Walk Alone' followed them down to their dressing room – a welcome thought, reflected Greenwood, for players who sometimes *had* walked alone.

England's success pleased and relieved no-one more than Bert Millichip, who had just succeeded Harold Thompson as chairman of the Football Association. Sincere, sympathetic and softly-spoken, Millichip brought to the job a wide experience of the game and a sturdy determination to nurse it back to full health. He had been a good cricketer and footballer, playing for West Bromwich Albion as an amateur, and at the time he took over at Lancaster Gate he had been a director and then chairman of the Hawthorns club for 18 years. Like many of his early predecessors, he was a solicitor, the senior partner in a family firm, and had chaired or sat on all the FA's major committees. Millichip's experience of the game abroad was also wide and would expand still further with UEFA and FIFA. He knew his task was going to be demanding; but he had no inkling that he was about to lead English football through the most difficult and tormented decade in its history.

The Cup, however, was in good shape. It had just been won and lost for the 100th time, although Tottenham were taken to a replay before they got the better of Manchester City. The celebrations began with a banquet, attended by 600 guests at the Royal Garden Hotel, with HRH The Duke of Kent, the president of the Football Association, in the chair. Football people from every county and nearly 30 countries were present – and so, too, were some of the grand old men of the game. Among them was Jack Swann, who played for Huddersfield when they lost to Aston Villa at Stamford Bridge in the first final after World War One in 1920. Villa won in extra time after Billy Kirton and Huddersfield's centre half Tom Wilson had jumped together for a corner. Jack Howcroft, the referee, insisted the ball went into the net off Kirton's head – and the record books had never argued. 'But that wasn't the way of it,' said Swann, 61 years later, as the Cup prepared for its 100th final. 'I was right there, defending, and it was an own goal by Wilson'.

Swann, who was nearly 89, was discovered by David Barber, the FA's publications manager, having a lunchtime drink in an ex-servicemen's club in Hendon not far from Wembley. Barber, in fact, spent the best part of a month tracking down every living Cup final captain; and 30 of them were at the banquet and also at the final, where they were introduced to a warmly responsive crowd. At the game with Swann was Dick Pym, also 88, who had been Bolton's goalkeeper against West Ham in Wembley's first final – the 'White Horse' final – in 1923.

The 1970s produced some memorable finals. Bob Stokoe's Sunderland (1973) and Lawrie McMenemy's Southampton (1976) won the Cup for the Second Division; and Arsenal, having begun the decade by completing the 'double', ended it by beating Manchester United 3–2 by way of one of the tournament's most remarkable climaxes. Arsenal led 2–0 with only four minutes of the 1979 final left, United equalised with goals in the 86th and 88th minutes, and then Alan Sunderland snatched Arsenal's winner in the last 60 seconds. 'Has there ever been a final like this!' wondered the *Sunday Express*.

The 1980s, however, began with another triumph for the Second Division – West Ham beating Arsenal with a rare headed goal by Trevor Brooking. It was Arsenal's third successive final, but it was also the third time in eight years that a Division Two club had won the trophy. The only things that can be taken for granted about the Cup are its democracy and its uncertainty.

Something out of the ordinary was required for the 100th final in 1981 and Tottenham and Manchester City managed it. It was only the tenth final to finish as a draw and, for the first time, a replay was staged at Wembley; and the Cup, as always, chose its heroes and anti-heroes with a sense of drama. The first game was drawn 1–1 and the Cup delegated the oldest man on the pitch to score both goals. Thirty-three-year-old Tommy Hutchison, Manchester City's angular Scottish international forward, put his club ahead with a spectacular header and then gave Spurs their equaliser by deflecting a shot from Hoddle into his own net. Wembley was again full for the replay five days later, and the hero of an even better game was equally unlikely – Ricardo Villa of Argentina.

Villa joined Spurs in July 1978 along with Osvaldo Ardiles, a slight, neat midfield player, quick as a finger-snap in thought and movement, a high-stepping, combative, endlessly inventive stylist who had been at the heart of Argentina's World Cup-winning side. They cost around £700,000 together, and it was a remarkable coup which was welcomed by the game as a whole but cautiously questioned by Cliff Lloyd, the loyal and long-serving secretary of the Professional Footballers' Association, who said: 'We would not stand for a big influx of Argentines'. Spurs were perfectly content with their pair. Ardiles adapted himself to the English game quickly and smoothly; and Villa, a swarthy and powerful forward, justified himself memorably in the replay of the 1981 final.

The bearded Villa was substituted in the first game and, head bowed, shoulders rounded, he trudged back to the dressing room and – for all he knew – out of the history of the FA Cup. He was not to know that the replay would be the crowning point of his career. Villa scored the first and last goals in a game of quality and rising drama which Spurs won 3–2. His winner, by happy consensus, was one of Wembley's finest: he spun past three defenders before scoring with calculated ease – a perfect flourish for the 100th final.

Spurs won the Cup again the following season, beating Queen's Park Rangers in yet another replay, but this time there was no Ardiles or Villa. England and Argentina were involved in another kind of conflict over the future of the Falklands; and Ardiles and Villa, inevitably, were a target for hostility. Ardiles even joined the French club Paris St Germain for a spell.

①

②

① Captains on parade for the 100th FA Cup final, 9 May 1981. Thirty Cup-winning captains were at Wembley to help celebrate a very special day in the history of English football.

Left to right: Dave Mackay (Tottenham, 1967), Danny Blanchflower (Tottenham, 1961 and 1962), Dick Pym (Bolton, 1923, 1926, 1929, aged 88, not captain but one of the oldest surviving finalists), Pat Rice (Arsenal, 1979), Peter Rodrigues (Southampton, 1976), Bobby Kerr (Sunderland, 1973), Graham Williams (West Bromwich, 1968), Ron Yeats (Liverpool, 1965), Noel Cantwell (Manchester United, 1963), Jack Burkitt (Nottingham Forest, 1959), Johnny Dixon (Aston Villa, 1957), Jimmy Scoular (Newcastle, 1955), Joe Mercer (Arsenal, 1950), Johnny Carey (Manchester United, 1948), Tom Smith (Preston North End, 1938), Ronnie Starling (Sheffield Wednesday, 1935).

Opposite, left to right: Tom Parker (Arsenal, 1930), Jack Swann (Huddersfield, 1920, aged 88, not captain but played in first final after World War One), Raich Carter (Sunderland, 1937), Don Welsh (Charlton, 1947), Billy Wright (Wolves, 1949), Joe Harvey (Newcastle, 1951 and 1952), Len Millard (West Bromwich, 1954), Nat Lofthouse (Bolton, 1958), Bill Slater (Wolves, 1960), Bobby Moore (West Ham, 1964), Brian Labone (Everton, 1966), Frank McLintock (Arsenal,

③

1971), Emlyn Hughes (Liverpool, 1974), Mick Mills (Ipswich, 1978), Roy Paul (Manchester City, 1956), Tony Book (Manchester City, 1969).

② The start of the road to Wembley: Whitehawk of the Sussex County League versus Horndean (Hampshire), FA Cup preliminary round, 3 September 1983. It takes nearly nine months, 13 rounds (including the final) and around 600 matches to produce a winner from the 500 or so clubs which enter the FA Cup

each season. An army of optimists from every nook and cranny of the country take part in the preliminary round and four qualifying rounds; 20 survivors join the Third and Fourth Divisions of the Football League in the first round proper; and the First and Second Division clubs enter the lists at the time of the third round proper. The secret of the undentable popularity of the tournament, its essence and its charm, lies in its democracy. Whitehawk, having beaten Horndean, then beat Whitstable Town

and Walton and Hersham before losing to Tooting and Mitcham United in the third qualifying round. Had Whitehawk continued to win they would have met Dartford, Millwall, Swindon, Carlisle, Blackburn Rovers, Southampton, Sheffield Wednesday and Everton before overcoming Watford in the final.

③ Alan Sunderland, reclining on right elbow, scores Arsenal's winner in one of the most dramatic climaxes of any FA Cup final. 12 May 1979: Arsenal 3, Manchester United 2. Arsenal were leading 2–0 with four minutes left, but goals from Gordon McQueen (86th minute) and Sammy McIlroy (88th) equalised for United; and, with 50 seconds left, Graham Rix (top left) centred to the far post where Sunderland beat Arthur Albiston (number three) to give Arsenal the Cup for the fifth time.

①

②

① Trevor Brooking, about to sit down, heads West Ham's winner against Arsenal in the 1980 FA Cup final. Brooking seems to be well marked and Arsenal's line is manned efficiently – but the ball still finds the net. It was the third time in eight seasons that a Second Division club had won the Cup.

② Elton John, pop superstar and chairman of Watford, greets his players before the 1984 FA Cup final against Everton. Watford were an anonymous Fourth Division club when he took over in May 1976 – but, with Graham Taylor (who was to take charge of England's team 14 years later) as his manager, he saw Watford rise to the First Division in the next six years. They then finished runners-up in Division One in 1983 and reached the Cup final a year later. Everton, however, were unimpressed: they beat Watford 2–0 ... and Elton John shed a tear in the Royal Box.

③

④

③ Ron Greenwood beside the smooth water of the Danube in Budapest before England's World Cup qualifying match with Hungary, 6 June 1981. His smile gives no hint of his sudden decision to retire immediately after the game. But England won 3–1 to put themselves back on the road to the 1982 World Cup finals – and, after an emotional appeal by England's players on the flight home, Greenwood changed his mind. England lost only one of their next 13 games before Greenwood retired with dignity after the finals in Spain.

④ Outlook: poor. John Lukic of Leeds United looks for survivors during an FA Cup fourth round second replay against Arsenal at Highbury, 9 February 1983. Arsenal won 2–1 and were impressed by Lukic: they bought him for around £50,000 the following summer and, seven years later, sold him back to Leeds for £1,000,000.

There was much anguished debate before the 1982 World Cup finals about whether England, Scotland and Northern Ireland should take part in a tournament with Argentina. Ron Greenwood said: 'If people are being shot and the Government does not want us to play then we do as it asks.' Neil Macfarlane, the Minister for Sport, immediately said the decision would be left to the FA. Ted Croker made it clear, after informal discussion at Lancaster Gate, that he thought the British teams should go to Spain, although he had private reservations about playing Argentina themselves. He also believed that countries at war taking part in international sporting competition should be allowed, if they chose, to withdraw without penalty. FIFA did not agree: it announced that the FAs of the Home Countries would be fined £4,400 each if they withdrew. The Falklands War went Britain's way, the World Cup finals drew nearer and England, it was accepted, were going to take part in football's most prestigious tournament for the first time since 1970 . . . a bigger carnival than ever, because the number of finalists had been increased from 16 to 24.

There were other problems, of course. The draw in Madrid six months before, a poorly organised affair, had put England into the northern group in Spain along with France, Czechoslovakia and Kuwait. England's base was the industrial port of Bilbao and there were real but unfounded fears that ETA, the aggressive Basque separatist organisation, might use the high profile occasion to further their cause. More justified was the fear that the worst of England's followers would cause problems again. The FA had by now appointed a security officer, Leslie Walker, a distinguished former Metropolitan Police commander, and his expertise was to become increasingly important in the fight against hooliganism. His knowledge and thoroughness helped the police in Bilbao prepare for the worst – which never happened. The behaviour of the English fans was always acceptable; apart that is, from one attempt to take a donkey into a bar.

It would have needed a small army, in any case, to puncture the security of England's hotel, Los Tamarises, about eight miles from the city centre. It backed onto a cliff, faced a beach and armed police were on guard around the clock. Months before the finals a photographer discovered a dead dog on the beach, which, like most resort beaches, was left to itself in winter, and his pictures were used in many papers to suggest that England would be living on top of a Mediterranean rubbish dump. By the time England arrived the beach had been given its annual wash and brush-up and was looking like a 'wish you were here' scene on a postcard.

England arrived in Bilbao with a run of seven unbeaten games behind them including victory, with a goal by Paul Mariner, in the 100th international against Scotland. Keegan and Brooking, however, were both unfit. Keegan, who had by now moved from Hamburg to Southampton following some masterly management by

Lawrie McMenemy, had back trouble and Brooking had a groin injury.

Greenwood was in no doubt about the team he intended playing against France in the tall and straight-backed San Mames Stadium – known locally as the 'cathedral' – but first he had to announce a long-awaited decision. Ray Clemence and Peter Shilton had been sharing the England goalkeeper's job – 'an unusual but practical solution to the problem of having two of the best in the world,' recalled Greenwood later. 'It was no problem for them: it was others who saw it first as a problem.' But Greenwood told the two rivals that if and when England reached the World Cup finals he would make a choice and, in the end, he preferred the mighty authority of Shilton to the more naturally gifted Clemence, who had moved from Liverpool to Tottenham at the start of the previous season.

Shilton took his place behind a defence that consisted of two Ipswich players, Mick Mills as captain and Terry Butcher as its towering central column, Liverpool's Phil Thompson who provided balance and cover and Kenny Sansom at left back. Sansom, in turn, played behind another Arsenal man, Graham Rix, whose left foot was capable of picking most locks; and the midfield was completed by three Manchester United players: Bryan Robson, Ray Wilkins and Steve Coppell. At the sharp end was Trevor Francis (who had moved on to Manchester City in another million-pound deal), with his wounding pace and Paul Mariner, with four goals in his three previous internationals. Three clubs contributed eight players: it was a side with unity and shape.

England's first game in the finals of a World Cup for 12 years was on 16 June 1982 – the day after the end of the Falklands War – and they wore red for a kick-off in oven-hot heat. Twenty-seven seconds later they were a goal in front. Wilkins and Coppell earned an immediate throw-in on the right, Coppell's long heave was nudged back by Butcher at the near post and Robson, timing his run into the French area beautifully, fell to his right to adjust his balance and line for a left-foot volley. It was the fastest goal in World Cup final history and won him an imposing gold watch. France responded intelligently: they had players of the quality of Michel Platini, one of European football's outstanding artists, Alain Giresse and Gerard Soler, who equalised with the only goal Shilton conceded in the finals. But Greenwood made a significant adjustment at half time, giving Rix a deeper role which allowed Robson to make more of his telling forward runs, and this swung the game in England's favour again. Robson headed his second goal from a pass by Francis and, with France tiring in the heat, Mariner added a third.

Weight-loss was considerable, Mariner shedding 11 pounds, and this emphasised the importance of England winning the group which would give them the right in the second phase – again a mini-league – to kick off at a later and cooler time. An unchanged team beat Czechoslovakia 2–0, with goals from Francis and Mariner, but Robson strained his groin and was replaced by Hoddle for the third game, against Kuwait – a disappointing affair won with a first-half goal by Francis.

Brazil was the only other nation to win all three first-round matches and, as England moved on to Madrid for matches against West Germany and Spain, Greenwood still hoped Keegan and Brooking would have a part to play. Brian Roper, West Ham's consultant surgeon, had flown out for a day – under the alias of 'Mr Smith' – to treat Brooking's deep-seated groin injury; and Keegan, at his own request, had gone to Hamburg to see a specialist in whom he had faith. Keegan, extraordinarily, drove the 250 daunting miles from Bilbao to Madrid by himself at night in a small, borrowed car. He flew to north Germany to see his specialist and returned without anyone spotting him. 'I feel better, boss … definitely,' he told Greenwood. The confidence of the England party was reflected in discussions about the protocol of inviting a member of the Royal Family and perhaps, too, the Prime Minister to the final. West Germany and Spain were not underestimated, but Italy, Brazil and Argentina were all in Barcelona – and England could see a path to the top.

West Germany, the European champions, had won few friends or admirers in the first round. They lost 2–1 to Algeria – a classic upset – and beat Austria 1–0 in a game that was shamefully devoid of ambition. They were acidly criticised, even by their own media, but it meant West Germany and Austria both qualified for the second round … a damning indictment of the tournament's format. Jupp Derwall, West Germany's manager, then dropped Pierre Littbarski, the exciting little Cologne winger, for the game against England and it was apparent their sights were not set very high. Greenwood sent out the team which beat France and Czechoslovakia, but it failed to find any sort of key to the Germans' tight man-to-man marking and the outcome was a goalless draw – a poor and distant relation to the encounters of 1966 and 1970.

Everything depended on the final two games of the group, Spain's matches with West Germany and England, and Greenwood and his players found the tide and the wind against them. The time for manoeuvring was past and West Germany, needing to win, brought back Littbarski. He scored and the Germans beat Spain by 2–1. England had earlier assumed that if they beat Spain by the same score as West Germany they would qualify for the semi-finals. It was a reasonable interpretation of a rule which said that if two nations finished the second round level on points and goals 'the team having the better classification at the end of the matches of the first round will be qualified'. England and West Germany both topped their groups in round one – but England won all three of their games and the Germans lost one.

England also had a better goal difference. FIFA, however, insisted that 'classification' meant only position – so England and West Germany were level – and that if there was still nothing between them at the end of the second round the issue would be decided by a draw. The England camp seethed: a 'bad day for the World Cup,' said Professor Sir Harold Thompson. An appeal was made, but FIFA stuck to their interpretation, which meant England had to beat Spain at least 2–0 or 3–2.

England knew exactly what they had to do, however, against a Spanish team that was already out of the tournament, a team that had lost to Northern Ireland in the first round. Woodcock took the place of Coppell, who was unfit, and there were two new substitutes: Keegan and Brooking. Greenwood would have liked to play them from the start but they were still not perfectly fit and would not have lasted a full game. 'You're my two trumps,' said England's manager. 'I'll send you on if things aren't going well.'

Spain chose the game for their most resolute and spirited performance of the tournament, fired by pride in front of a crowd of 75,000, and, with 27 minutes left, the Bernabeu Stadium still waited for a goal. It was time for 'Kev and Trev' – Greenwood's only gamble of the tournament – and they went within a split whisker of winning the game. Keegan was on the spot for a centre by Robson and Brooking worked himself into an equally fine position to score. And both missed. Keegan has never been able to explain how or why he headed wide of an empty net and Brooking allowed Luis Arconada, Spain's captain and goalkeeper, to make a fine save because 'the ball ran away from me at the last minute'. Spain 0, England 0. England were unbeaten after five games in which they had conceded only one goal ... and they were out. A fit Keegan and Brooking might have made all the difference; and, even without them, England's side was a good one. But it lacked a cutting edge and too many honest chances were missed. Paulo Rossi would probably have done as much for England as he did for Italy.

By the time Italy beat West Germany by 3–1 in the final, with the help of Rossi's sixth goal of the tournament, England had a new manager. Ron Greenwood had retired just as he said he would, his job well and honourably done, and Bobby Robson had a five-year contract. This time there was no shortlist. Robson, one of the five candidates interviewed after Revie's departure and after that a senior member of Greenwood's coaching team, was the unanimous choice of Bert Millichip and his small selection committee.

The procedure was formal and, after Ted Croker had asked Ipswich chairman Patrick Cobbold for permission to talk to his manager, Robson attended meetings at Lancaster Gate and the Chiltern Hotel at Luton not long before the start of the 1982 World Cup finals. The FA told Robson they wanted him to be the national coach as well as England's team manager, just as Walter Winterbottom had been after World War Two. The double responsibility was a heavy one, with the coaching work less publicised but hardly less demanding. 'I like the sound of the job,' said Robson; and then, when told of the salary the FA had in mind, he added '... but I don't like your terms.' The FA were surprised at the size of Robson's salary at Ipswich, but when he met the selection committee again, during the second phase of the World Cup finals in Madrid, an offer was made which he found acceptable. A press conference was called, but it confirmed rather than revealed the news of Robson's appointment. He had long been identified as England's sixth manager.

Robson's record at Ipswich, a club of modest resources but warm heart and generous spirit, had been exceptional. Their consistency during most of his 13 years at Portman Road was bettered only by Liverpool; they were rarely out of the top six in Division One, winners of the FA Cup in 1978, championship runners-up and UEFA winners in 1981 and second in the League again in 1982. More than a dozen full international players came out of the club's much-admired youth scheme, while in the transfer market Robson bought wisely and prudently and sold profitably. He managed with dash and a sure touch – much as he played at wing half for Fulham, West Bromwich Albion and, on 20 occasions, for England. Other clubs liked his managerial style: Everton, Manchester United, Derby (after Brian Clough), Leeds (after Don Revie), Sunderland, Bilbao and Barcelona all made him offers. Ipswich, for their part, gave him the first ten-year contract in League history and, as Patrick Cobbold told him: 'The only way you'll leave this club with our blessing is to become manager of England.'

It did not take Robson long, however, to discover that his new job was outside all his previous experience. After 13 years of success with Ipswich, it took him just 13 games to fail with England. Exactly one year after taking over – a year in which only two games were lost – he found himself being thumped painfully on the head by the nation's newspapers. One even went to the expense and trouble of producing 'Robson Out' lapel badges. Robson had moved straight into the qualifying competition for the 1984 European Championship finals in France. England's group was completed by Hungary, Greece, Luxembourg and Denmark – and it was Robson's misfortune that Denmark were developing the best team in their history with a covey of talent that only France, perhaps, could match in Europe. Denmark, with its deep amateur roots, had never beaten England; but their team of the 1980s was one of adventure, charm and penthouse quality.

Robson's first game was in Copenhagen and he invited – and duly received – criticism by not selecting Keegan, who had just moved on to Newcastle. Robson felt Greenwood's captain had passed his peak ... Keegan disagreed angrily and said he never wanted to play for his country again. His international career deserved a better end. England, nonetheless, drew 2–2, with Denmark snatching an equaliser in the last minute through Jesper Olsen, a slight and elusive winger who would later join Manchester United. But the match belonged largely to Denmark – and to Peter Shilton who was mulishly brilliant.

Greece dug in at Wembley to earn a point, after losing 3–0 in Salonika; but, with nine goals against Luxembourg and two more against Hungary in other home games, it seemed England were making honest progress towards the finals. Then Denmark came to London and provided Robson with what he was to call 'the blackest day of my career'. Denmark did not play well, but they won by a disputed penalty scored by Allan Simonsen, who had spent the previous season with Charlton Athletic – and at the end Robson was jeered and whistled at until he was out of sight. Robson accepted he had made a mistake in exaggerating the quality of the Danes to his players, which he believed affected their confidence, but in the next few days he learned much about his job and the human race. The best of the press were aggressive and the worst bitterly offensive; and when he watched a game at Villa Park the following Saturday he was greeted by a force-ten storm of boos from the crowd. The abuse cut into his private life. His family, too, were involved. Robson cared deeply, passionately, about his job but there was one morning, he was to recall, when he looked into his shaving mirror and thought '... after all it is only football'.

The defeat by Denmark duly cost England a place in the European finals. England won 3–0 in Hungary, with a balanced and spirited performance, and scored four in Luxembourg where the fans again caused serious trouble. They had won five and drawn two of their eight qualifying games, scoring 23 goals and conceding only three, but Denmark finished with one point more. The depression became deeper as England lost to France in Paris, to Wales in Wrexham and to the Soviet Union at Wembley, where Robson was spat at, had beer thrown over him and again had the crowd chanting for his head.

Robson insists, however, that at no stage did he consider resigning – even when Barcelona approached him, determinedly and persuasively, for a third time. Instead, he recommended Terry Venables and Barcelona, after initial reservation, hired the young Queen's Park Rangers manager. Barcelona won the Spanish championship the following season for the first time in 11 years. Robson, for his part, was assured by Dick Wragg that he had the full support of the FA.

Ahead of England was a summer tour of Brazil, Uruguay and Chile, and there were media suggestions that it should be scrapped. Form was poor, the squad was weakened by injury and a variety of other more frustrating reasons – why risk humiliation? Robson put on a bold face, however, and included three young forwards,

Mark Hateley of Portsmouth in the centre, with Mark Chamberlain of Stoke and John Barnes of Watford outside him, in his side for the game against Brazil in Rio de Janeiro. It was a gambler's decision and there seemed little reason to suppose that Robson's choice would become the first England side to beat Brazil in the monstrous Maracana Stadium.

Peter Shilton and his defence held tight at the start, Bryan Robson and Ray Wilkins began to deal the right cards in midfield and a minute before half time Barnes started a run just inside the Brazilian half which did not finish until he rolled the ball into the net. He avoided defenders rather than beat them. He discovered a path without obstacles. The Brazilians did not recognise what was happening until he was almost underneath their crossbar. Barnes then wrong-footed their goal-keeper Roberto Costa on to his backside – and placed the ball past his left hand.

It was a goal that the Cariocas of Rio might have expected from one of their own; but never, ever, from an Englishman. Not that Barnes was a product of England's cobbled streets and back-to-backs. He was born in Kingston, Jamaica, a natural athlete and a sumptuously gifted footballer, a winger with a feathery touch and a cutting change of pace and direction. He was often accused of being inconsistent, a charge which was to follow him to Liverpool in 1987 and around the pitches of the world with England; but the style is the man and Barnes, a relaxed and unaffected character, will one day hear the final trumpet call – and still finish his book.

Barnes' goal in Rio, his first for England, impressed a worldwide television audience; and one or two people in Italy took special notice when Hateley also scored his first for his country, a header at the far post from a centre by Barnes midway through the second half, to give England a 2–0 victory. AC Milan could hardly wait to pay £915,000 for the tall Second Division forward. That famous victory also gave Robson the break he needed. England lost 2–0 to Uruguay in Montevideo, were held to a goalless draw by Chile in Santiago and were infuriated by a handful of England followers, who, as the tour progressed, introduced a racist line into their songs and comments. But the victory over Brazil stood apart. It gave a new pride to England's players and new hope to Robson. 'It's taken a big weight off my shoulders,' he said in interviews afterwards. 'It's a fresh start.'

Robson's other responsibilities received little publicity, but as national coach he found himself immediately involved in a major development that was the result of many years of planning – and dreaming – at Lancaster Gate. Its culmination was the opening by the Duke of Kent of the Football Association GM National School at Lilleshall Hall in Shropshire on 4 September 1984. The first decision to open a national centre was taken in 1969, at around the time the FA began to look at sponsorship with a kindly eye, and Annesley Hall, with 128 acres in Nottingham-shire, was bought three years later. Several plans at various costs were prepared, the most expensive involving a new hall, and the chosen estimate was for a million pounds with an opening in 1977. Costs escalated (to £4,000,000 by 1975) and other sites at Birmingham, Coventry and St Albans were considered. Annesley Hall itself was sold for £110,000 in 1977. The initiative lost some of its impetus and was 'temporarily suspended' – but a Sports Centre Trust was established into which the FA continued to pay a substantial covenant.

The Sports Council's Lilleshall Hall National Sports Centre – a 20-minute drive from the M6 and a place where most of English football's leading coaches had attended courses – was seen as a better bet. The FA put £500,000 of its Trust funds into building a new residential block, which opened in April 1981. The Sports Council contributed nearly £2,000,000 for pitches, facilities and lecture halls.

English football had a permanent training facility at last, and the FA continued to invest heavily in its coaching programme. In 1982, £425,000 was spent on educational activities; and when Bobby Robson joined the FA that year, he was asked immediately to provide 'a blueprint for the pursuit of excellence in football'. The cream of the country's young talent was not being groomed early enough or well enough. The standard of coaching and facilities was declining at many schools, where other sports and activities competed for youngsters' interest and time. There were fundamental differences of opinion about the age at which boys should have their first contact with professional clubs. The English Schools' Football Association was not in line with the thinking in many of the leading football nations in Europe. The ladder from the England Under-15 team up to the full international level needed strengthening. New thrust and a new platform were required.

There was no simple and immediate solution to all the problems, but the FA tackled them from different directions. The National School at Lilleshall, backed by a four-year contract with powerful sponsors, General Motors, was described by Ted Croker as 'one of the most important developments for English football for many, many years'. Twenty-five of the country's best 14-year-olds, chosen from a list of recommendations from scouts all over the country, began a two-year residential course. They were expertly coached at football at Lilleshall and formally educated at nearby Idsall School. Each September, too, there was an intake of 15 new boys.

Robson and Charles Hughes, the assistant national coach, committed themselves to getting the concept right. Hughes had joined the FA staff in 1964, managed England's amateur team and would later become the FA's director of coaching and education. His conviction that controlled direct football was more effective than possession football placed him at the heart of a fierce and long-running ideo-logical debate on how the game should be played. His critics called him a 'professor of kick and rush' and a 'Messiah of the long ball'. Hughes argued, and provided analysis to champion his case, that nearly 90 percent of all goals came from move-ments involving five passes or less. 'The facts are irrefutable, the evidence over-whelming,' he insisted. The game's hardy professionals are deeply suspicious of statistics; but debate is always healthy.

There were also mixed feelings about the National School, with some club managers and the English Schools' Football Association among those with reser-vations. There were fears that boys would be poached as well as coached; and there was talk, too, of 'conveyor belt' footballers. The names of many good youngsters did not reach the FA. Dave Sexton, the National School's technical director, was a calm and humorous man and a highly accomplished coach who had managed such clubs as Chelsea and Manchester United and been in charge of the England side which won the UEFA Under-21 championship in 1982 and 1984. The principal of the school was Denis Saunders, who had taught at Malvern College for 30 years, half of them as a housemaster, and been an outstanding amateur footballer with Pegasus, captaining them to success in the FA Amateur Cup finals of 1951 and 1953. The National School was in good hands. The boys' development was carefully monitored, demands on them were controlled and their experience was broadened by representative football. Many, since, have moved smoothly into League football, while others have not fulfilled their promise. There could be no guarantees; but the big majority left Lilleshall as better players and better people.

The next stage of the FA's 'blueprint' was the setting up of more than a hun-dred licensed Centres of Excellence for promising youngsters between the ages of 11 and 14, many of them at professional clubs, and also non-residential Soccer Fun-weeks for boys and girls aged between eight and 13 at sports centres all over the country. Qualified coaches ran them, and stars of the game made guest appear-ances. Potential was harnessed and directed, and for the younger people the message was clear: football is fun.

The Home International Championship had by now died an almost natural death; and one of the reasons was that it ceased to be fun. It lost its public appeal apart from the game between England and Scotland and, in the opinion of many, it was just a relic of the past and a wearisome chore. Scotland were the first winners in 1884 and Northern Ireland the last exactly 100 years later. It was the first tourna-ment of its kind and for many years was the only form of international expression for the Home Countries. Its history is studded with memorable games and, in the 1950s, it was even used as a qualifying group for the World Cup. The championship's decline and fall, however, was in step with the times. The rise of European football helped push it to the back of the season as an eight-day tournament in 1968/9. The bi-annual invasion of London by Scotland's followers became increasingly turbulent. Wembley's pitch was invaded by thousands and the goalposts pulled down and broken in 1977; and unsuccessful attempts were then made to stop Scottish supporters obtaining tickets when the fixture was played south of the border. Northern Ireland's political problems fractured the 1981 tournament. In the end, England's games with Wales and Northern Ireland were not filling a quarter of Wembley.

Precious international dates, it was decided by England and Scotland, could be more profitably and usefully employed by fixtures with Continental opposition. The Welsh and Irish Associations protested bitterly that they faced financial ruin. But there was no going back and the Home International Championship passed uncomfortably into history. England continued to play Scotland and were joined by a foreign nation (first Brazil, then Colombia and Chile) in a three-cornered competition for a trophy named after Sir Stanley Rous; but this, too, had a limited future.

Little in football was now safe.

FA Cup

Year	Date	Winners	Runners-up		Venue	Attendance	Referee	Entries
1978	6 May	Ipswich Town	1	Arsenal	0	Wembley	100,000	DRG Nippard	469
1979	12 May	Arsenal	3	Manchester United	2	Wembley	100,000	R Challis	466
1980	10 May	West Ham United	1	Arsenal	0	Wembley	100,000	G Courtney	475
1981	9 May	Tottenham Hotspur	1	Manchester City	1*	Wembley	100,000	K Hackett	480
Replay	14 May	Tottenham Hotspur	3	Manchester City	2	Wembley	100,000	K Hackett	
1982	22 May	Tottenham Hotspur	1	Queen's Park Rangers	1*	Wembley	100,000	C White	486
Replay	27 May	Tottenham Hotspur	1	Queen's Park Rangers	0	Wembley	100,000	C White	
1983	21 May	Manchester United	2	Brighton and Hove Albion	2*	Wembley	100,000	AW Grey	479
Replay	26 May	Manchester United	4	Brighton and Hove Albion	0	Wembley	100,000	AW Grey	
1984	19 May	Everton	2	Watford	0	Wembley	100,000	J Hunting	487

①

②

③

① England's game against France in Bilbao on 16 June 1982 is only 27 seconds old ... and Bryan Robson of Manchester United scores the fastest goal in the history of World Cup finals. Jean Luc Ettori, the French goalkeeper, raises his hands desperately and Paul Mariner of Ipswich (11) and Jean Francois Larios (13) just watch. It was England's first game in the finals of a World Cup for 12 years. England 3, France 1.

② Trevor Brooking and Kevin Keegan wait for their first and only experience of World Cup final football – with 27 minutes remaining of England's game against Spain in Madrid, 5 July 1982. Brooking and Keegan had missed England's four earlier games because of injury, and they still were not perfectly

fit, but England manager Ron Greenwood sent them on as 'my two trumps'. Both went near to scoring but the game finished as a goalless draw. England were unbeaten – and out.

③ Kevin Keegan – described by Ron Greenwood as 'the most modern of modern footballers' and perhaps the first English player to turn his job into big business. One of the outstanding English players of the post-war period. Captain of England: 63 caps and 20 goals (1973–82). Played for Scunthorpe (1968–71), Liverpool (1971–77), SV Hamburg (1977–80), Southampton (1980–82) and Newcastle (1982–84). Honours: Liverpool – European Cup-winner 1977, UEFA Cup-winner 1973, 1976, League championships 1973, 1976, 1977, FA Cup-

winner 1974, FA Cup finalist 1977. With SV Hamburg – Bundesliga championship 1979, European Cup finalist 1980. Scored in his 500th and last League game to help Newcastle win promotion from Division Two in 1984. Football Writers' Association Footballer of the Year 1976, Professional Footballers' Association Player of the Year 1982, West Germany's Footballer of the Year 1978, European Footballer of the Year 1978 and 1979. Awarded OBE 1982. But, in a career full of honour and achievement, Keegan played only 27 minutes' football in the finals of a World Cup. He went on as a substitute in his last international, against Spain in Madrid in 1982.

BRITISH CHAMPIONSHIP
ENGLAND...................1
WOODCOCK
NORTHERN IRELAND...........0

①

① The British Home Championship: born 1884 ... died peacefully 1984. England face Northern Ireland for the last time in the oldest international tournament of all at Wembley, 4 April 1984. England won 1–0, but Northern Ireland took the title on goal difference. Of the 88 completed championships, England won 34 outright, Scotland 24, Wales seven and Northern Ireland three. The title was shared on 20 occasions.

② Headquarters: 16, Lancaster Gate, London W2 3LW. FA Christmas card, 1989.

③ Lilleshall Hall, Shropshire, a gift to British sport from South Africa. A public 'Tribute to Britain' fund swiftly raised more than a million pounds in South Africa after World War Two – an enormous sum of money then – which was presented to the Prime Minister to use 'for the good of Britain'. A committee under the Speaker of the House of Commons was appointed to spend the money and, among the schemes approved, was the setting up of a National Recreation Centre in the north of England. Nowhere suitable in the *real* north was found and Lilleshall was

bought. It was opened by HRH Princess Elizabeth on 8 June 1951. Lilleshall now houses the FA's GM Vauxhall National School, opened by HRH The Duke of Kent on 4 September 1984, and also the Rehabilitation and Sports Injury Centre (1986) and the Human Performance Department (1988).

②

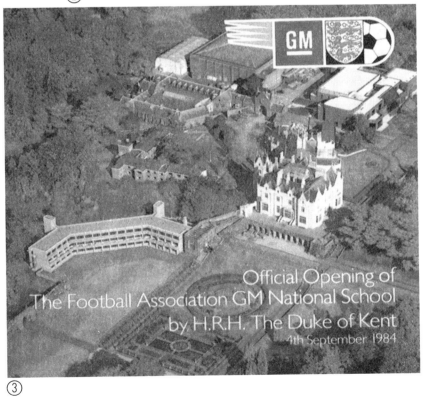

③

12

HEYSEL AND AFTER
1985–

The homespun game of football was now to know tragedy and sorrow beyond the alchemy of words. Cups and championships were still won and lost in the late 1980s; but these, above all, were the years of Heysel, Bradford and Hillsborough.

In all, 190 people died and more than 800 were injured in the three disasters. They emphasised beyond argument that in spite of all the lessons of the past, and all the enquiries, reports and commandments, there was still grave and inherent danger in the simple pleasure of watching a big football match.

Lord Justice Peter Taylor who, as a boy, had shared St James's Park with 50,000 others to cheer on Newcastle, conducted an exhaustive enquiry into the 1989 Hillsborough tragedy; and in his luminously honest report he listed old grounds, poor facilities, hooliganism, excessive drinking and poor leadership as the factors which marred football as a spectator sport.

'Amazingly, complacency was still to be found even after Hillsborough,' he observed. 'It was chilling to hear the same refrain from directors at several clubs I visited: "Hillsborough was horrible – but, of course, it couldn't happen here".'

'Couldn't it?' asked Taylor.

'I am satisfied from eye-witness accounts I have received that there have been many other occasions when overcrowding has led, at various grounds round the country, to a genuine apprehension of impending disaster through crushing, averted only by good fortune ... The lesson here is that Hillsborough should not be regarded as a freak occurrence, incapable of happening elsewhere. All those responsible for certifying, using and supervising sports grounds should take a hard look at their arrangements and keep on doing so. Complacency is the enemy of safety.'

Taylor's judgment was the ninth official report covering crowd safety and control at football matches, a line of well-intended strictures going all the way back to 1923 and the chaos at the first Cup final at Wembley. Yet, 13 different Prime Ministers later, television audiences of millions still witnessed horror inside football grounds. Taylor commented:

> There is no point in holding enquiries or publishing guidance unless the recommendations are followed diligently. That must be the first lesson. The years of patching up grounds, of having periodic disasters and narrowly avoiding others by muddling through on a wing and a prayer must be over. A totally new approach across the whole field of football requires higher standards both in bricks and mortar and human relationships.

The shameful calamities of Bradford, Heysel and Hillsborough touched the heart and conscience of the nation. Taylor touched its mind as well. His final report was a plan for radical modernisation of grounds and accommodation which signalled, among many other things, the beginning of the end for the old standing terraces and the coming of 'all-seater' stadiums. The report helped change attitudes as well, and emphasised the essential role of the Government and local authorities in redeveloping and re-arming the national game. Football was obliged to accept that it had no entitlement to survival and the Government began to recognise its ultimate responsibility for safety and control.

The catalyst was tragedy, however, and it would have been impossible to ignore the lessons of Bradford, Heysel and Hillsborough. But it is very doubtful if watching football will ever be free of all hazard. When a crowd, which is the equivalent in size to the entire population of a small town, gathers tightly around a couple of acres to watch a game that bares emotion and prejudice there will always be a random element of risk. The chances of trouble obviously increase when there is inefficiency and human error; and both were factors in the grotesque disasters of the 1980s.

Exactly 100 years after the birth of professionalism, 1985 was a year which showed the ugliest profile of English professional football to the world. The number of violent incidents mounted and, on 13 March, the modest home of Luton Town was the scene of a riot which beggared understanding. An army of Millwall fans invaded the pitch at Kenilworth Road during an FA Cup quarter-final and launched themselves into a battle with the police. Plastic seats were ripped out and used as missiles, skimmed lethally, and nearly 50 people, mostly policemen, were injured. Later, the Millwall fans rampaged through the town, damaging cars, homes and shops, and then wrecked their train on the way back to London.

Millwall were duly fined £7,500 and Luton were ordered to put up fences, which led to accusations that the FA was an ostrich with its head in the sand; and when, after an appeal, the sentences were quashed or scaled down Neil Macfarlane, the Minister for Sport, claimed that 'everybody concerned for the good name of football is astonished and dismayed'. But, as Ted Croker patiently pointed out, in an argument which did not arouse much sympathy, the FA could only find a club guilty of misconduct if it failed to take 'all reasonable precautions' – and Luton and Millwall had provided evidence to show they had done all they could.

The Luton riot did more than raise the hackles of a passing Minister of Sport. It engaged the direct gaze of Margaret Thatcher; and she recognised, perhaps for the first time since she became Prime Minister in 1979, that the national game had a problem which impinged on national life. On 1 April 1985, the senior aldermen of the FA and the League were summoned to 10 Downing Street where Croker, with a bold disregard for his own health, suggested to Mrs Thatcher that 'these people are society's problem and we don't want your hooligans at our sport'. Ministers and civil servants flinched – and Macfarlane, on his own admission, felt like diving for shelter under the table – but the Prime Minister's reply was placatory. 'Steady the Buffs,' she said.

Although some people might be inclined to dismiss it as 'merely a game', there are a number of reasons for believing that soccer is an economic and socio-cultural phenomenon of considerable importance. Laurence Kitchin captured some of this significance in 1966 when he described the game, not inaccurately, as the only 'global idiom' apart from science. The sociologists, Edgell and Jary, were elaborating on this basic idea when they postulated in 1975 that soccer is what they call an 'evolutionary universal', similar, they say, to science, industrialism, jazz and rhythm and blues in what they describe as its 'capacity to optimise biological gratifications and social ends'. That may be a bit of a jargonistic mouthful but the underlying idea appears to be basically sound. Arthur Hopcraft expressed it more circumspectly and more elegantly when he wrote that: 'What happens on the football field matters, not in the way that food matters but as poetry does to some people and alcohol does to others; it engages the personality.' ... In the context of a society that, for better or worse, has grown increasingly secular over the last 100 years or so, it has come to perform many of the functions that, in earlier times, were performed by church membership and church attendance.

Professor Eric Dunning speaking at a conference – 'Football into the 1990s' – at the University of Leicester, 1988. The conference was organised by the Sir Norman Chester Centre for Football Research (opened in 1987) and sponsored by the Football Trust.

The FA were given six weeks to produce a report on hooliganism, but only a fortnight later Mrs Thatcher told her Cabinet that football's authorities were not doing enough. While her understanding of the problems involved, and of the enormous investment in fences, segregation, closed circuit television and policing, appeared to be less than sure, her own involvement meant action. The idea of a national membership scheme for football, which would require every fan to produce an identity card before being allowed into a game, was mooted. A ban on the general sale of alcohol at grounds was also set in motion. It had been said that Britain's first woman premier had a Minister for Sport but no policy for sport; but now, it seemed, she could see a way forward for football. Nobody knew, of course, that Bradford and Heysel lay directly ahead. The woeful enormity of the two tragedies, which happened within 18 days of each other, was numbing.

Fifty-six people perished and more than 200 suffered burns, many of them serious, in the Bradford fire disaster at Valley Parade on 11 May 1985 – the last day of the League season and a day of celebration for the Yorkshire club. Bradford City had won the Third Division championship and a crowd of about 11,000, including civic dignitaries and even guests from twinned towns in Germany and Belgium, watched a parade and presentations before the start of the game against Lincoln City. Five minutes before half time a Mr Brownlie, sitting in Block G of the wooden main stand, felt heat on his right leg, rubbed it and said: 'Hell, it's warm down there.' Wisps of smoke rose from the floorboards and somebody poured a quarter of a cup of coffee through a crack. The police were called and the fire brigade were summoned, but the danger seemed small and people were reluctant to move.

The fire, said one witness, then spread faster than a man can run. Another said it was like a moving ball of fire. Yet another said the black smoke was like that caused by burning tyres. Hundreds of spectators jumped or clambered down onto the pitch. Others, including many elderly people, went to the rear. And the stand, which was 76 years old and had housed nearly 6,000,000 people in its time, was a raging inferno from end to end in less than five minutes.

Two days later, Mr Justice Oliver Popplewell was appointed to enquire into the disaster and his interim report was ready for Leon Brittan, the Home Secretary, by July. He noted that between 1977 and 1983, in the United Kingdom alone, there were 86 fires in grandstands. 'Safety levels must be improved quickly,' he warned. 'I am quite satisfied,' he reported on the Bradford tragedy, 'that the cause of the fire was the dropping of a lighted match, or a cigarette or tobacco on to debris beneath the floorboards.' Unburned rubbish found afterwards included a copy of the *Bradford Evening Telegraph and Argus* for Monday, 4 November 1968 and a wrapper for a packet of peanuts costing six old pennies.

Popplewell recalled that the Home Office published a guide to safety at football grounds in 1976. Known as 'The Green Guide', it recommended that all buildings should be inspected before and after every event; waste should be cleared as quickly as possible; every stand should have enough exits to permit orderly evacuation; the escape-time for a stand with a high fire-risk should be two-and-a-half minutes. Had the guide been complied with, the Bradford tragedy would not have occurred.

The long list of recommendations in Popplewell's interim and final reports called for more grounds to be designated under the Safety of Sports Grounds Act, the building of non-combustible stands, better evacuation procedures by police, tighter restrictions by the fire authorities, trained stewards and 'suitable and adequate' exits. He also championed a national membership scheme for fans. Some of his recommendations became law, some could not be enforced by legislation, but his broad message was always clear: the safety of the fans came before the interests of the clubs.

The Bradford fire, and all the sorrow and bitterness, recriminations and denials which followed it, made the routine business of League and Cup seem almost irrelevant. Everton, in fact, stylishly won the League championship for the first time in 15 years – the first stage of a tilt at a unique treble. Howard Kendall's team then won their first European trophy by outclassing Rapid Vienna 3–1 in the final of the Cup-Winners' Cup in Rotterdam; but they foundered in the FA Cup in which they were beaten by an extra-time goal by Manchester United's Norman Whiteside. Kevin Moran, one of United's central defenders, earned the unenviable distinction of being the first man to be sent off in an FA Cup final – and this was the 104th!

Some 20,000 fans had followed Everton to Rotterdam, and their behaviour was not much short of impeccable. A fortnight later – on 29 May 1985 – nearly as many headed for Brussels. This was the red half of Merseyside, bent on watching Liverpool face Juventus of Turin in the final of the European Cup. Confidence was high: Liverpool, the holders, were aiming for their fifth victory in the Champions' Cup and English clubs had won it seven times in the previous eight years. The advance word was that Liverpool's fans would cause little trouble. Their record in Europe over 22 years was good.

The headlines next morning, however, were not about a game of football. 'Bloodbath – Soccer hits the ultimate depths', said the *Daily Mail*. 'Brussels counts soccer riot dead', declared the *Guardian*. 'The Final Shame', added the *Daily Mirror*. 'The game has gone', concluded *The Times* in a leader article. Pages were devoted to description, pictures, analysis and comment. The civilised world, in any case, had witnessed much of the disaster on their television screens. Thirty-nine people were killed, most of them Italian, and more than 400 were injured in a riot shortly before the game was due to begin in the Heysel Stadium in a northern suburb of Brussels.

The build-up to the calamity began early in the day: there was heavy drinking, theft, damage and dislocation of traffic by about 2,000 British supporters in the centre of the city. Tickets were on sale before the match, and many fans found their way into the stadium without paying. The plans for segregation were useless. Alcohol was on sale outside the ground and the searching of fans by police was so superficial that sticks, iron bars, bottles and stones were taken inside. Missiles were soon thrown at the police and fencing in the old stadium was shaken and broken. Fans, mainly Juventus supporters to begin with, charged forward and retreated. The trading of insults increased and English fans fired rockets and flares towards the Italians. Then, at around 7·15pm on that pleasant evening in Brussels, Liverpool fans made the first of three concerted charges. It was repulsed, and so was the second. But the third saw Juventus supporters turn and run for safety. There was no way out. An old wall collapsed under the pressure, and fans tumbled and trampled over each other in the panic and crush. Bodies lay unattended as police, hitting out with truncheons, attempted to clear the area – and were met by hooligans with sticks and iron bars. 'It was like a war . . . no, worse than a war because there was no reason for it,' said one Liverpool father, who watched it all from a few yards away. 'It was terrible and disgusting.' And it was watched by television viewers in 80 countries.

The match was still played, an hour and a half late, because UEFA dared not risk turning nearly 60,000 fans, many of them drunk, out into the streets. This would undoubtedly have led to more trouble and, once news of the deaths had spread, violent reprisal. Morally the game should have been cancelled . . . responsibly, it had to go ahead. It was a macabre event.

The Belgian government and Belgian FA, local authorities, UEFA, the police, profiteers and the National Front were all blamed. Drunkenness, poor segregation, the method of selling tickets, inadequate searches, weak walls and barriers and lack of co-operation and communication were isolated as contributory reasons. Enquiries proliferated, and inquests and litigation were to carry on for years. A Belgian parliamentary commission made it clear, however, that 'it was the British supporters who mounted the disastrous charge . . . they bear the main responsibility for the terrible events that followed and this must remain the case whatever blame might be attributed to others for having aggravated the matter'. Mr Justice Popplewell also embraced the Heysel disaster in his final report: 'I cannot too strongly or too frequently emphasise that if hooligans did not behave like hooligans at football matches there would be no risk of such death or injury.'

Bert Millichip and Ted Croker were high over the Atlantic during the hours of madness at the Heysel. They were on their way, via Miami, to join England's players, who were in Mexico City for matches against Italy of all countries, Mexico and West Germany as part of their preparation for the 1986 World Cup finals – with their qualification already looking a good bet. Millichip and Croker were sitting happily in the transit lounge in Miami when they received a call from BBC Radio's sportsroom in London asking for their comments on the disaster in Brussels. They immediately agreed to catch the morning plane back to London. A British Embassy message confirmed the wisdom of their decision: the Prime Minister wanted to see them immediately.

Millichip and Croker did the round trip from London to Mexico and back again in 36 hours; and, by the time they landed, they had decided, provisionally, to withdraw England's clubs from European competition for the following season. Arthur McMullen, the vice-chairman of the FA, agreed. Jack Dunnett, the president of the Football League, disagreed: 'Why pre-judge? Why over-react?' he asked. But further telephone calls gave Millichip and Croker the mandate they needed. They knew that UEFA would impose a ban in any case and soon learned that Mrs Thatcher, after a two-hour meeting with her ministers, had made it clear she expected the FA to withdraw.

Mrs Thatcher punched her full and formidable weight when she met football's leaders again at Downing Street two days after the disaster. She gave the impression that she believed it would be no great loss to mankind if the professional game was stopped altogether. Millichip and Croker emphasised that Government money was needed to make grounds safe and urged, as the Chester Report had done 17 years before, that a football levy board, similar to the one in racing, should be set up. Mrs Thatcher curtly cited the 'enormous' transfer fees being paid for players and quoted the £800,000 Everton paid Leicester for Gary Lineker. Football, she stressed, must put its own house in order.

The FA announced formally that Everton (League champions), Manchester United (FA Cup-winners) and Liverpool, Norwich, Southampton and Tottenham (who had all qualified for the UEFA Cup) would not be entered for European competition the following season. On 2 June 1985 UEFA banned all English clubs indefinitely; and, 18 days later, they declared that even when the other clubs were re-admitted Liverpool's ban would run for another three years – three years in which they qualified! Juventus were ordered to play their next two European games behind closed gates and Belgium was banned from staging the final of the European Cup and European Cup-Winners' Cup for ten years. FIFA weighed in by imposing a worldwide ban on English clubs, but later allowed friendly games.

Four of the clubs banned from Europe – Everton, Manchester United,

Norwich and Southampton – attempted to get a High Court injunction against the Football Association which, if successful, would have obliged the FA to enter them for European competition the following season. The move was ill-advised and out of step with general opinion; and the FA's action was confirmed as 'justified'. The Government followed up quickly by promising tougher measures on alcohol, crowd limits, security and the powers of the police. Mrs Thatcher, in a letter to the FA and League, made it very clear that she expected them to produce – 'urgently' – a membership card scheme.

English football had reached the lowest point in its history. It had introduced the game to the rest of the world; but now, a century and more on, its own clubs were forbidden to travel the world. All the game's problems had come to a head: hooliganism, safety, finance, television, internecine struggles for power and attendances which, in the League in the season after Heysel, dropped despairingly to under 17,000,000. The professional game had become a political issue, moreover, and there were well-founded fears that it would not survive in its old and loved form. The remaining years of the decade were going to test its spirit and fibre, its structure and viability, its leaders and players, its hold on its public and its place in society.

Neil Macfarlane was replaced by the affable Richard Tracey, who was succeeded by Colin Moynihan as the Minister for Sport – or, more precisely, as the Parliamentary Under-Secretary of State with responsibility for sport at the Department of the Environment. A national membership scheme, they dutifully insisted on Mrs Thatcher's behalf, was the main plank of reform. The police did not agree, nor did several working parties, nor did the FA or the League who, in an early memorandum asked for by the Prime Minister, described the idea as 'entirely valueless'. 'Is it worth the trouble involved', the memorandum continued, 'in issuing nearly 6,000,000 cards and putting the details on a computer (bearing in mind that merely to go to one game per season requires a card) to combat the violence of no more than 10,000 spectators a season out of 22,000,000 spectators?'

Arguments against the plan did not change over the next three or four years. Adapting grounds and setting up and maintaining the technology would be an awesome task; and so would the processing of millions of applications and cards, together with replacing those which were lost, stolen or unreadable. The distribution and updating of the membership list would need a big and well-trained staff. Delay at the turnstiles would cause frustration and trouble. Safety would be further threatened, the casual supporter would be driven away and the cost would be crippling. There was no guarantee that this sledgehammer of a scheme would crack its nut. Would the hooligan allow himself to be defeated by a computer?

Voluntary individual schemes, with privileges and reserved areas for members and families, the FA and League agreed, could be a way of forestalling heavy legislation; and some clubs moved successfully in this direction. Luton Town went the whole way. They made their move against hooliganism and solved the problem of segregation posed by a small and limited ground by introducing a 100 percent membership plan and a ban on away supporters. Their decision neatly split opinion and cost them their place in the League Cup (then sponsored by the retail division of the Littlewoods Pools company), because the rules required visiting clubs to have a quarter of all available tickets. The threat of a national membership scheme hung over the game for nearly five years, and there was going to be another major disaster and another Government enquiry before it was removed.

① Off the map. UEFA Congress in West Germany, 1988 – and the British Isles are omitted from UEFA's insignia as president Jacques Georges of France addresses delegates. 'An error,' said UEFA – and no reflection on the ban on English clubs from European competition.

② Commercial co-operation.

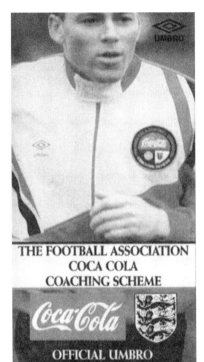

①

②

③

① Kevin Moran of Manchester United becomes the first player to be sent off in an FA Cup final – and United's meeting with Everton at Wembley in 1985 was the 104th final. Referee Peter Willis, from Meadowfield, County Durham, points to the dressing room and Moran is restrained by fellow Republic of Ireland international Frank Stapleton. The final was 82 minutes old when Moran, a central defender, was dismissed for a 'professional' foul; but United, with ten men, won the Cup with an extra-time goal by Norman Whiteside.

② Dave Beasant of Wimbledon becomes the first goalkeeper to save a penalty in an FA Cup final at Wembley, 14 May 1988. John Aldridge of Liverpool strikes and directs the ball firmly but Beasant, 6 feet 4 inches tall, brilliantly turns it past his left post. Liverpool were 4–1 on favourites and victory would have given them the League and Cup 'double' for the second time in three seasons; but Wimbledon, a non-League club only 11 years before, won the Cup for the first time with a headed goal by Lawrie Sanchez nine minutes before half time. Beasant, Wimbledon's captain, also became the first goalkeeper to lead a side up Wembley's steps to lift the FA Cup.

③ The climax of the most exciting semi-final day in the history of the FA Cup, Palm Sunday, 8 April 1990, when 13 goals were scored in the two matches. Crystal Palace reached Wembley for the first time by beating Liverpool 4–3 (after losing 9–0 and 2–0 to the Anfield club in the League) at Villa Park; and then Manchester United and Oldham Athletic of the Second Division drew 3–3 at Maine Road, Manchester. Both matches went to extra time. The picture shows Alan Pardew celebrating his winning goal for Palace in the 109th minute. Manchester United beat Oldham 2–1 in their replay at Maine Road, again after extra time, and won the Cup for the seventh time by overcoming Palace in a final which went to two matches (3–3, 1–0).

①

②

① Seconds remain of the last League match of season 1988/9 – and Michael Thomas of Arsenal scores the goal which wins the championship at Anfield. Steve Nicol (centre) and Ray Houghton (obscured) lunge and Bruce Grobbelaar (left) dives but Thomas's goal gave Arsenal the 2–0 victory they needed in the most dramatic climax of all to a League season. Liverpool would have been champions had they avoided defeat by two goals and Anfield fans were already saluting their team when Thomas struck. The two teams finished level on points and goal difference – but Arsenal scored more goals. It was Arsenal's first championship for 18 years and in 1991 they won the title again under the strong and intelligent stewardship of George Graham. This, too, was a remarkable triumph: Arsenal had two points deducted by the FA in mid-season for their part in a brawl during a game against Manchester United. Arsenal's success was achieved, moreover, with the help of eight players who were graduates of the club's youth scheme.

② Football discipline. Lou Macari runs the media gauntlet outside FA headquarters at Lancaster Gate, 12 February 1990. Macari, once a forward of skill and verve with Manchester United and Scotland, was fined £1,000 and censured for his part, as manager, in the Swindon 'betting' affair in 1988. Swindon won promotion to Division One, via the play-offs, in 1990 – but were relegated to Division Three by the Football League and then, on appeal, reinstated in Division Two by the FA. The FA Disciplinary Committee is usually busy. In season 1990/1 60 commissions dealt with 250 cases ranging from field offences to financial irregularities. The FA itself handles cases involving players from the Football League and the other senior leagues in football's 'pyramid'.

The 1980s saw football and television lock antlers and come near to destroying the Football League. In the beginning, there was only BBC TV's 'Match of the Day' (first broadcast on 22 August 1964) which showed the highlights of two or three games on Saturday nights and was ritual viewing for nearly a quarter of the population. Then Independent Television wrestled BBC's Saturday hold from them in 1978 and the two alternated coverage between Saturday nights and Sunday afternoons. BBC and ITV stuck solidly together in negotiation, and football, faced by a cartel, bargained without much success. Regular live television began in 1983, the year in which Canon, the giant Japanese camera and computer firm, became the first sponsors of the Football League. Football needed sponsors; and sponsors demanded exposure on television.

The League was still convinced it was not getting the proper rate for its product, however, and the major clubs were unhappiest of all – especially Liverpool, Everton, Manchester United, Arsenal and Tottenham who became known as the 'Big Five'. They wanted more power and more of the money they earned: they were fed up, they said, with the tail wagging the dog. They threatened to break away and form a 'Super League', together with a few other hand-picked clubs, and their resolution hardened after the Heysel disaster. There was no prospect of European football, gates were falling, sponsors were worrying and, with negotiations with the BBC and ITV breaking down completely for the first time, there was no football on television during the first half of season 1985/6. Television, to make matters worse, did not seem to worry. 'Football has too high an opinion of itself,' said a BBC executive.

The day of a self-perpetuating 'Super League', with selection of members based on wealth, facilities, tradition, size of crowds and appeal to television, seemed imminent. It looked as if the oldest football league in the world was going to lose its head. The 'Big Five' spoke about 'sensible restructuring' and the 'long-term good of the game'; but the rest of the League knew it was money and power they would have to concede if the split was to be avoided.

The Football Association was not directly involved, but any league – super or headless – would have been subject to its authority; and that authority, in the event of a split, would probably have been strengthened. Ted Croker, speaking personally, said he did not think it possible any longer for the League to support 92 clubs with full-time players. The FA secretary was immediately identified in the press as a possible chief executive of the Super League.

There was strong opposition in the Second Division, from the media generally and, importantly, from Gordon Taylor, the secretary of the Professional Footballers' Association, who said he did not believe 'the leading players in the game would sell their less well-paid colleagues down the river'. Taylor, an intelligent, articulate man of good conscience with a muscular sense of tradition, knew his members. They made it clear at their annual meeting in 1985 that they were not in favour of a Super League and that they would strike if the livelihoods of any PFA members were threatened. Taylor's role continued to be a central one. His cool common sense saw him succeed as umpire and mediator, and even as a go-between, in the heat of all the argument. His strength, above all, was that he put the good of the game as a whole before everything. It was a battle between paymasters but, ironically, here was a union man acting as peacemaker.

It became apparent that some chairmen now had reservations about torpedo-ing the Football League just a couple of years before its 100th birthday. Revolution-ary talk is one thing, revolution itself quite another. A short-term agreement saw football return to the nation's screens in December 1985 and, in that same month, with Taylor again present, representatives of all four divisions of the League met at a hotel near Heathrow airport and worked out a package deal. It was to be amended and condemned, refined and challenged, and booted lustily towards touch in the next few months; but, broadly, it was accepted by the clubs at an extraordinary meeting on 28 April 1986. The First Division was richer and more powerful, with weightier votes and a bigger share of income, which meant the 'super' teams had got their way in the end. Play-offs were introduced, which helped compensate clubs in the lower divisions, and there was automatic promotion and relegation between the club at the bottom of the Fourth Division and the winners of the G M Vauxhall Conference, which became the League's 'fifth' division.

There was a lull in the hostilities, but then satellite television came over the brow of the hill – and firing resumed. British Satellite Broadcasting (BSB) needed some major acts for its coming battle with Sky channel and, early in 1988, it made an exclusive offer for League football, which started at £5,500,000 and was eventually doubled. ITV decided it could not lose such an important battle against new rivals and secretly offered over £1,000,000 each to the 'Big Five' and more than £2,000,000 for another five clubs to make up an 'ITV Superleague'. Aston Villa, Newcastle, Nottingham Forest, Sheffield Wednesday and West Ham – a tidy re-gional spread – completed the 'Big Ten'.

So, almost at a stroke, the League was divided, if not yet conquered. Self-interest ruled. Philip Carter of Everton, the president of the League, and David Dein of Arsenal did not alert their fellow members of the League management com-mittee to ITV's overtures – and this while the official deal with BSB was moving towards agreement. The League's unity was threatened again, the spectre of a breakaway rose once more and the old BBC-ITV cartel was at an end. Football, which television decided was surplus to requirements in 1985, was suddenly an irresistible commodity.

News of the ITV offer leaked out, and a marriage between BBC and BSB was hastily arranged, still solidly supported by the rest of the League. The 'Big Ten' decided they were going to accept the ITV deal whatever the cost. Injunctions were taken out, media criticism hit higher notes and compromises were floated, with Gordon Taylor, at the urgent request of the League Management Committee, driving from Lancashire to Plymouth to help their deliberations. Taylor also spoke to the 'Big Ten' and Carter insisted it was not their intention to desert the League.

When ITV increased their offer to £11,000,000 a season in a deal to include the whole of the League, there was now a slow change of minds among the rest of the First Division clubs. What had they to sell to BBC/BSB without the 'Big Ten'? How would sponsors regard a League shorn of its best clubs? The ITV package was accepted – by which time the BBC/BSB partnership had begun separate negotiations with the Football Association for the FA Cup and international matches. It was to be worth £30,000,000 over five years and, as value for money, many considered it a more attractive deal. Carter and Dein were removed from the Management Committee for their 'double' role in television's battle for football; but it was now clear that this was only part of a bigger war. British television was entering a new and infinitely more competitive era.

Football's market-place was changing, and so were attitudes, and this was reflected by the FA's willingness in November 1987 to consider sponsorship of the FA Cup, the oldest, most venerated and best-loved asset in its weighty portfolio. The news aroused furiously emotive comment. 'Is nothing sacred?' was the general theme and, indeed, Ted Croker in his autobiography, *The First Voice You Will Hear is . . .* (published earlier in 1987), sided firmly with the traditionalists. 'Some of the magic would disappear,' he wrote. 'The Cup sells itself. FA policy is against the whole concept. I cannot see that changing.'

An offer by way of an agent from Elders, the Australian brewing company, prompted second thoughts. They wanted to use the Cup to promote their Foster's lager and they were prepared to pay £20,000,000 over five years. There were immediate reservations about linking the Cup with alcohol but, given the pressing need for funds at all levels of the game, there was broad approval for the offer at Lancaster Gate. Later, as the arguments raged, some councillors changed their minds. Elders wanted the FA Cup to become the Foster's Cup and, before this became a major hitch, as it undoubtedly would have done, the deal foundered at the negotiating table. The Australian stock market took a nasty fall and the Elders' offer suddenly became £10,500,000 over four years. It was not enough. Another brewer offered £18,500,000 over five years. This, too, was rejected. The FA wanted

£27,500,000 over five years. Croker announced the FA had 'insufficient common ground' with the would-be sponsors.

In step with the changing times, and in pursuit of efficiency, the FA invested £65,000 in an examination of the Association by a London firm of management consultants – 'with particular consideration to the top structure of the Association, including salaried staff, and its various relationships with Council'. It took the Knightsbridge specialists most of 1987 to prepare their report – entitled 'The Football Association – organising for the future' – and it recommended sweeping changes. It suggested the FA secretary be replaced by a chief executive or general manager with more responsibility and power, who would take his place on a Board of Management on which the League president would also sit. The Council was said to be 'out of touch with what is essentially a young person's game . . . and too large and unwieldy to operate effectively'. It recommended that members should be under 62 when elected and should retire when 72. It also criticised the absence of 'soundly formulated budgets and plans'.

The report surfaced at a Council meeting at Plymouth on 9 July 1988 and was given a lengthy hearing; but the weight of opinion was against it while conceding that several recommendations were worthy of 'further consideration'. The report was too radical. It wanted too much. By then, in fact, the FA had already acquired its next chief executive. Ted Croker was to retire early in 1989 after nearly 16 roller-coaster years as secretary, during which the FA's turnover increased by nearly 500 percent and the number of clubs affiliated to the FA rose from 37,000 to 42,000. Among those interviewed as possible successors to Croker were three senior members of the FA staff – Charles Hughes, Glen Kirton and Adrian Titcombe – but the eventual choice was a surprise even in the game's best-informed circles.

Graham Kelly, the secretary of the Football League, it was announced on 7 June 1988, would be moving to Lancaster Gate as chief executive and secretary – a bridge never crossed before. Kelly and Croker had worked together for ten years, mostly harmoniously, on all the game's major issues, although the priorities of their employers were not always in step. Kelly also had a good knowledge of accountancy and company law and, like Croker, he was well versed in the ways and smallprint of UEFA.

Kelly, a large and museful Lancastrian with a perceptive eye for detail and a wry sense of humour, a negotiator rather than a fire-eater, became the youngest secretary of the League at the age of 33 and was 42 when he moved to the FA. He worked for a bank before joining the League and then learned the business of football administration under the street-wise tutelage of Alan Hardaker. Kelly was recommended to the FA by Philip Carter, when the Everton chairman was president of the League, and his interview at Lancaster Gate was considered excellent. His appointment, in the face of stiff opposition, was not cut and dried but he was chosen by a clear majority. Kelly settled himself into Croker's chair in the FA secretary's second-floor office in February 1989. That chair would soon be one of the hottest in the country.

Football's backcloth in the late 1980s was a tapestry of tragedy, divisive struggles for power, endless crises, wearisome acrimony and erosive criticism. Yet, remarkably, the game itself continued to attract and surprise; and, after inevitable antipathy in the season following the Bradford and Heysel disasters, gates began to increase again. They were still rising as football moved into the 1990s.

There were reservations about the quality of English football. It was said to be short of adventure and fantasy, too fast and too defensive, a victim of frightened managers and poor coaches, a product wrapped in dull orthodoxy and soaked in sweat. It was ever thus, of course. Herbert Chapman asked 'Where is the skill? Where are the personalities?' in the early 1930s. 'There is a terrible dearth of players,' observed Raich Carter in 1950. 'Too much coaching, too little character,' reproved Billy Walker, the manager of Nottingham Forest, at the start of the 1960s. 'Football has become too grim . . . a smiling player is a rare player,' said Sir Matt Busby of the mid-1970s.

One team above all, though, found a way through the critical crossfire of the 1980s. Liverpool were still the standard-bearers and the standard-setters. Joe Fagan, another Anfield insider and a likeable professional of the old school, had succeeded Bob Paisley as manager in 1983 and then stepped aside after the Heysel disaster for Kenny Dalglish who became player-manager. Dalglish had been a Liverpool player for eight years, a forward of arresting brilliance who would soon win his 100th cap for Scotland, a man of character and reserve, and his elevation to manager simply emphasised the confidence of the club in their staff and system. Nothing deflected their pursuit of success. In Fagan's first season as manager Liverpool won the European Cup, the League championship (for the third season running, equalling the record of Huddersfield and Arsenal) and the League Cup (for the fourth year running) – the only time an English club has won three major trophies in one season. And in Dalglish's first season as Liverpool's player-manager, 1985/6, they completed the League and FA Cup 'double', the fifth club to manage it in all, the third of the 20th century. Liverpool, however, were more than just winners. They had that elusive but unmistakable thing known as 'style'. Discipline, fitness and pride were important; but so were self-expression and simple harmony. Their team was a perfect frame for the best talent in the land. Liverpool's hand was completed by good husbandry and by their supporters' booming passion for the game. A lesser club might have been destroyed by the tragedies Liverpool endured in the late 1980s.

It was also a period notable for success stories of a kind normally found on fiction shelves. Coventry City won the first major trophy in their 104-year history by beating Tottenham in the 1987 FA Cup final with the help of an own goal in extra time by Gary Mabbutt. It was Tottenham's eighth final – and the first they had lost. Twelve months later Wimbledon also won the Cup for the first time and their tale was even more remarkable.

Wimbledon, hidden away in London's southern outback, had climbed from non-League football to the First Division in only nine seasons (1977–86), and then finished sixth in their first season in the top form. Their route to the 1988 final was a modest one but their opponents at Wembley were Liverpool – of all teams – and the soothsayers gave Wimbledon considerably less than no chance. Liverpool had just won the League title for the 17th time and were the hottest favourites since the war. Wimbledon's fans were outnumbered by about four to one and their combative playing methods, a Battle of Britain style based on aerial forays and dauntless pursuit, had few admirers outside the family circle. The plot proved a simple one, though. Lawrie Sanchez scored for Wimbledon in the first half; and Dave Beasant, their 6 feet 4-inch goalkeeper, saved a penalty by John Aldridge in the second half, the first penalty ever missed in a Wembley FA Cup final. 'Game, set and match' called the *Sunday Express* headline next morning.

In the weeks of heart-searching which followed the Heysel disaster, there were whispered suggestions that England's national team, as well as her clubs, should be banned from travelling. Withdrawal from the World Cup and European Championship was considered at Lancaster Gate, but there was a strong feeling that this would be harmful over-reaction. The record of England's fans abroad was undeniably poor, but there had only been one sanction, after the riot in Turin during the 1980 European finals. England also faced a run of home games. The theory that England's hooligans would switch their 'allegiance' from club to country would not be tested for almost a year.

England, barring nasty mishap, had already qualified for the 1986 World Cup finals by the dark day of the Brussels calamity. They had beaten Finland 5–0 at Wembley, scored eight in Turkey, overcome Northern Ireland with a goal by Mark Hateley in Belfast (the morning-after consensus was 'lucky England . . . plucky Ireland', but this was a key victory), drawn 0–0 with a talented but desperate Rumania in Bucharest and then drawn again, 1–1, with a surprisingly resilient Finland in Helsinki. Eight points were in the bank after five games, with Wembley dates against Rumania, Turkey and Northern Ireland to come.

England's summer tour to Mexico City in 1985 was heavily significant: their opponents were Italy, the world champions, Mexico themselves and the redoubtable might of West Germany. But to begin with, on their first full day there, Bobby Robson and his players settled down to watch the European Cup final in the Heysel. The hotel's big television screen stayed blank for more than an hour and the England squad talked and fidgeted until, at last, a picture was shown of Liverpool and Juventus about to kick-off. Reports of trouble began to reach them, but much was regarded as exaggeration. Then, by way of news flashes and telephone calls, the full horror of the day unfolded.

The mood was one of outrage and bewilderment as the attention of the international media focussed on the Camino Real Hotel. There was an immediate feeling that the tour could not possibly continue but, after quiet discussion and then consultation with Italian officials, it was decided the game between England and Italy in the Azteca Stadium five days later – on 6 June 1985 – should go ahead. The Italians agreed that cancellation of the game would only widen the breach between the two countries. The match, if played, would be a gesture of sympathy and understanding. Both parties attended a memorial service.

Bert Millichip and Ted Croker returned to Mexico City after meeting Mrs Thatcher, and the FA chairman made it clear in the dressing room before the game with Italy that he expected nothing less than perfect behaviour. Any player who was out of line would be sent home on the next plane, no excuses, no exceptions. The teams walked out onto the pitch in near silence, with English and Italian players alternating, and then stood shoulder-to-shoulder in tribute. No England side before or since has played under such duress or in a match of such sensitivity. In that team, moreover, were three players who were earning their living in Italy, Ray Wilkins and Mark Hateley (both AC Milan) and Trevor Francis (Sampdoria). Italy won 2–1 with the help of a late and very debatable penalty; but, much more importantly, England's behaviour was impeccable. They then lost 1–0 to Mexico and, with Kerry Dixon of Chelsea scoring twice, beat West Germany 3–0.

②

① The *Liverpool Sunday Echo* on the morning after the Hillsborough tragedy. A leader article inside had this to say: 'This is a time when all of us must join together to share our neighbours' grief. Later there will be a time for anger that such a tragedy could be allowed to happen … in the meantime what can anyone do on this bleak April morning other than offer our help, our prayers, and our profound sympathy to the families and friends of those who died in the horror that yesterday was Hillsborough.'

② The *Sunday Times* view (28 January 1990) of Lord Justice Taylor's rejection of a compulsory national membership scheme for football supporters. Margaret Thatcher and Sports Minister Colin Moynihan head for the dressing room. All the recommendations of Taylor's report on the 1989 Hillsborough tragedy were accepted by the Government.

①

②

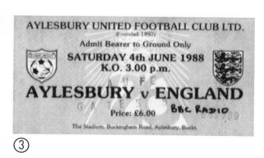

③

AYLESBURY UNITED FOOTBALL CLUB LTD.
(Founded 1897)

Admit Bearer to Ground Only

SATURDAY 4th JUNE 1988
K.O. 3.00 p.m.

AYLESBURY v ENGLAND

Price: £6.00

The Stadium, Buckingham Road, Aylesbury, Bucks.

① Gary Lineker completes his hat trick against Poland in the heat of Monterrey in the 1986 World Cup finals. His six goals in Mexico gave England dignity and a place in the quarter-finals after a dreadful start – and set him apart as the tournament's leading scorer. Lineker did not get the match-ball to mark his hat trick against Poland: it was snaffled by referee Andre Daina.

② Bryan Robson equalises for England against Holland in Dusseldorf in the European Championship finals, 15 June 1988. But Marco Van Basten completed the first hat trick against England for 29 years to give Holland victory by 3–1 – and for the first time England lost all their matches in the finals of a major competition.

③ New fixture. England flexed their muscles before the 1988 European Championship finals in West Germany by playing Aylesbury, the champions of the Beazer Homes League (Southern League). A record crowd of 6,031 and the nation's media watched England win 7–0.

England rounded off their qualification for the World Cup finals in the summer of 1985 without much difficulty, but also without much conviction. Their Wembley games with Rumania (1–1), Turkey (5–0) and Northern Ireland (0–0) gave them, finally, top place in their group with 12 points from eight games. Matches in Egypt and Israel (both new opponents at full international level) and against the Soviet Union in Tbilisi, down in the deep south of Georgia, were all won – trips early in 1986 which promised reasonable weather and were beyond the purse of most supporters. Scotland were also beaten, 2–1 at Wembley, and, by the time England left for acclimatisation in the Rocky Mountain heights of Colorado Springs, nearly a month before the start of the World Cup, Bobby Robson was convinced his party was 'the best prepared ever'.

There would be criticism that England's preparation was too long. Ted Croker believed it should have been a fortnight shorter, particularly as England's base for their three first-round matches, against Portugal, Morocco and Poland, was to be in Monterrey in the north of Mexico, which was little more than a thousand feet above sea level. But Robson and Vernon Edwards of Watford, who had been England's doctor for nine years, were adamant that their schedule was the correct one. If and when England reached the second round, the pair argued, they could suddenly find themselves playing at high altitude. 'It's better to have training at height in the bank,' they said. Expense was not at the root of the argument – the FA paid for the players' wives and girlfriends to join them for a week in Colorado.

But diligence is not always the mother of good fortune. Bryan Robson, England's captain and a central and talismanic figure in all Bobby Robson's calculations, dislocated his right shoulder in a warm-up game against Mexico (won 3–0) in Los Angeles; and later, in practice, he aggravated an old hamstring injury. Gary Lineker of Everton, the Footballer of the Year, the League's leading scorer and the sharpest weapon in England's attack, badly sprained his left wrist in another friendly international against Canada (won 1–0) in Vancouver. And, soon after the party had moved to Monterrey ten days before their first World Cup game, Vernon Edwards suffered a serious heart attack.

Dr Edwards had prepared and worked – perhaps overworked – for the finals for nearly two years, but he was more than the team's physician. He was a father-figure, a large and amiable man who was always ready to advise or listen – 'losing him', Bobby Robson said, 'is like losing one of my best players.' Edwards spent a week or so in hospital in Monterrey and, all too obviously, it was the end of his World Cup involvement. 'Sorry to let you all down but if you want to do anything for me go out and win the Cup,' he said. John Crane, the Arsenal doctor, flew out to take his place.

Lineker had a light cast put on his injured wrist: ahead of him was an outstanding World Cup. Bryan Robson simply hoped for the best about his shoulder, his hamstring and everything else about a body which had let him down too often to be trusted: for him it was to be a World Cup of mounting frustration. His shoulder dislocation in Los Angeles was his third, and his inclusion in the England squad was an obvious gamble. Bobby Robson considered it was worth taking, however, although he conceded that his captain's all-action, all-purpose style meant he had to be 100 percent fit to be properly effective. But he refused to admit the extent of Bryan Robson's injuries, or even admit his own grave doubts, and he was bitingly rebuked by the media. The shoulder should have been operated on months before, but that thought was of no help in Mexico.

England's base was just outside the quiet university town of Saltillo, an hour's snaking drive from Monterrey. The hotel was the smaller sister of the Camino Real in Mexico City and was perched beside the road to the American border and in the shadow of the grey Sierra Madre mountains. The temperature in Monterrey often approached 100 degrees Fahrenheit and, worse, the humidity was cloyingly high. But England's meticulous preparation and their long period of acclimatisation gave them a firm foundation. Confidence, justifiably, was high. They had not been beaten for a year and Robson had a settled squad in which he had faith. 'Alf Ramsey became a "Sir" when he won the World Cup ... will you become a "Sir" if you win this one?' Robson was asked by a Mexican reporter.

Robson picked the side he said he had 'always wanted to play' for England's game against Portugal in the Tecnologico Stadium in Monterrey on 3 June 1986. Peter Shilton, age irrelevant, was an automatic choice in goal. Gary Stevens of Everton, a natural athlete and a formidable tackler, and Kenny Sansom, who still had no rival, were the full backs. Terry Fenwick of Queen's Park Rangers, a pocket battleship, was Terry Butcher's partner in central defence. Glenn Hoddle, Ray Wilkins and Bryan Robson (with a shoulder harness) promised to fill the midfield with skill, order and drive. And in attack there was the stiletto threat of Gary Lineker (now with a strap around his wrist), the stately height of Mark Hateley and the artful dodging of Chris Waddle of Tottenham. It was an adventurous format in the context of a tournament which, in its early stages, was ruled by caution.

England's confidence was given an unexpected lift, moreover, by news which filtered across from Portugal's hotel on the other side of the road in Saltillo. The Portuguese players were threatening to strike over the size of their bonuses and expenses, and they protested by wearing their shirts inside out during training. It seemed to be the action of players without hope: the promise of jam later in the tournament did not appeal to them. Presidential words from home about the 'national prestige of Portugal' persuaded them to be there for the kick-off, however, and their game-plan was simply one of containment and hope. It worked, too. The ball belonged largely to England, but chances were missed, principally by Lineker, Hateley and Robson, until Portugal at last got an attack going with only 15 minutes left. The previously anonymous Diamantino levered the ball over from the right and Carlos Manuel, happily unfettered, scored from close range. The English defence, to a man, was absent without leave. England 0, Portugal 1.

Sleep at Saltillo was disturbed by the sound of the critics cocking their pistols and sharpening their knives. Bobby Robson put on his bravest face and Don Howe, his coach and confidant, said: 'Portugal won't win the World Cup like that but we can with our way.' But England had to profit from their second game, against Morocco, who had held Poland to a goalless draw without difficulty. Bobby Robson decided against change: one poor performance did not mean he had a poor side. Yet England's hopes, the product of two years' work and planning, seemed to disappear in five minutes late in the first half of their first-ever meeting with Morocco. First Bryan Robson fell awkwardly and dislocated his shoulder for a fourth time. Steve Hodge took his place. Then, as the side adjusted in a pitch temperature of more than 100 degrees Fahrenheit, Ray Wilkins reacted to a decision against him by throwing the ball in the direction of the referee who was a Paraguayan called Gonzalez. The ball hit the referee and Wilkins, who had already been cautioned, was sent off. But even though they faced only ten men, Morocco set their sights on nothing more than a draw. England 0, Morocco 0. Ray Wilkins – 'I feel a fool' – was suspended for two games.

Gloom hovered like a dark cloud over the chalets and lawns of England's hotel. Bobby Robson was pictured as a man in despair, photographed listening to his radio, head down, hand over ears. England, it was whispered, were training too hard: they were leaving their zip on the practice field. And, in a long and honest discussion up in the mountains, beside a monastery at Los Pinos, some of the senior players made it clear that they wanted a different, more flexible shape to the side – with four men in midfield. Bryan Robson, in a television interview, hinted at the general feeling by saying: 'We need a more careful style . . . to get people back behind the ball, defend in numbers and attack on the break.' There were stories of rebellion and a split in the England dressing room but Bobby Robson, after watching the interview again, decided immediately there was nothing wrong with it. 'If you're going to write stuff like that, that's scandalous. Just don't come near me,' he told reporters.

Bryan Robson wanted to play against Poland, but England's manager felt this was a gamble he was not entitled to take for a game being described as their most important for four years. So, with Wilkins suspended, Bobby Robson's hand was radically changed. He dropped Mark Hateley and Chris Waddle; brought in Peter Beardsley, a mobile little phantom, to partner Gary Lineker; and lined up Trevor Steven, Glenn Hoddle, Peter Reid and Steve Hodge in midfield. Reid was wise and tenacious, a canny prober of weaknesses, while Steven on the right and Hodge on the left provided pace and flexibility. Lineker, Reid, Steven and Stevens were all Everton players, a backbone of understanding.

So, once again, Poland stood four-square in England's path, and memories were rekindled of Tomaszewski's famous game in 1973 when Alf Ramsey's side was edged out of the World Cup. This time it was different. Ways were found around the flanks of the Polish defence; passes were played into Beardsley who drifted and manoeuvred and took opponents with him; Mlynarczyk, in the Polish goal, was no Tomaszewski; and this time, too, Lineker was sweetly on song. He became the first England player since Geoff Hurst in 1966 to score a hat trick in the finals of a World Cup. His three goals all came in the first half and all were the product of late, quick movement, perfect timing and finely engineered contact. England were out of jug. Champagne and a mariachi band were waiting for them back at Saltillo. 'When I woke up,' said Lineker next morning, 'I thought I'd been dreaming.'

Morocco topped the group, more evidence of the rising quality of African football, but this meant they stayed in Monterrey to face West Germany in what was now the sudden-death stage of the tournament. England were happier with their reward for finishing second: a date with Paraguay in the Azteca Stadium in Mexico City.

The Mexican capital was snarled by traffic jams, cuddled by fumes and still coming to terms, mournfully, with the disastrous earthquake which hit the city in September 1985. The hotel England moved into, a big commercial box beside a dual carriageway, was no home from home either. One player described it as 'a combination of Fawlty Towers and Brands Hatch'. Three days later, England moved to another hotel, so near to the airport that it sometimes sounded as if a plane was taking a short cut through the dining room, but it was private, pleasant and, as another player put it, 'a bit of heaven compared to that other place'.

There were no complaints, either, about England's training camp, the Reforma Club, which had been built by the English 100 years before, a slice of Old Blighty sited and designed for peace and deliverance. It was heaven on a hillside, a bolt-hole away from the sludge-like air of the city, a place with tennis courts, a cricket pitch, a mighty swimming pool and a fortress-sized club house with pictures of the Royals on the walls. It was here that travelling Victorians first introduced the game of football to Mexico.

One change was necessary for the game with Paraguay, Alvin Martin of West

Ham replacing Fenwick who was suspended, and against a team of engaging ability but erratic temperament, England again looked very good. Shilton made two masterly saves early on but, once he had established he was not going to be beaten, Lineker, Beardsley and Lineker again scored with impudent efficiency. Lineker received some cruel treatment, but his temperament, like his eye for a chance, was admirable.

England had reached the quarter-finals of a World Cup for the first time since Alf Ramsey's ill-fated visit to Mexico in 1970. Their opponents were Argentina and nobody suggested this was just an ordinary game of football. The Falklands and 1966 surfaced almost hourly in the three clear days before the game. There was no avoiding the fact that the two countries had been at war only four years before; and the memory of their quarter-final meeting during the World Cup in England, when Rattin was sent off and Ramsey described the Argentines as 'animals', was sharply invoked.

Politics and sport fused: every interview and news conference was an exercise in official diplomacy. Argentine politicians called for a minute's silence before the game as a mark of respect to those who had fallen in the Falklands. John Morgan, the British ambassador in Mexico City, suggested a message urging moderation be read to the supporters of the two nations before the game. Ted Croker immediately made the point that neither set of fans had caused any trouble during the tournament. 'Why risk provoking it?' he asked. 'High Noon' shouted the *Daily Mirror's* headline; but Croker was right. The only incidents on the terraces were minor.

The footballers of England and Argentina then gave the history of the World Cup one of its great controversies. England made only one change, Fenwick for Martin, and the first half was largely an exercise in containment. Then, in five minutes soon after the interval, a little pillar-box on legs called Diego Maradona changed everything. Maradona was Argentina's captain, a square figure with muscles, it seemed, on his eyebrows and kneecaps, a dandy with an ear-ring and coiffured bonnet of black hair. But he could play football, beautifully, and words like colossal (even at 5 feet 6 inches) and sensational followed him through his career.

Genius does what it must, and Maradona proceeded to win the game with sleight of hand and foot. First Hodge looped the ball back to Shilton, a dangerous move which invited a challenge from Maradona. He rose with Shilton and two hands went up. Shilton's clenched fist was just short, but Maradona's left wrist made contact and the ball spun into the net. Some recognised a handball immediately: television later confirmed it for everybody. The Tunisian referee, Ali ben Naceur, saw only a goal. 'A little bit of the hand of God . . . a little of the head of Maradona,' Argentina's captain was to say later; but that was after he had scored a second goal of coruscating brilliance. He just ran through the English defence, with swaying hips and subtle changes of gear, before slipping the ball past Shilton who had been wrong-footed on to his backside.

England's World Cup was not over yet, however. Barnes and Waddle replaced Steven and the injured Reid and, with ten minutes left, Barnes moved sinuously past two Argentine defenders before providing Lineker with his sixth goal of the tournament. The ploy seemed a good one and so, with three minutes left, Barnes tried again, cutting his centre to the far post. Lineker was there, right on cue, and for a split moment the crowd thought he had scored. But, as Lineker said afterwards: 'The goal was there, the ball was there and I was there . . . and the next thing I was seeing stars in the back of the net.' The ball was out, though, and so were England.

'The hand of God' goal was an authentic sensation, a rival in its way to Hurst's 'ball on the line' goal in the 1966 final. Maradona and Argentina went on to beat West Germany 3–2 in a splendid final, the last act of a tournament which began dourly, but was well served later by France, Denmark, the Soviet Union, Belgium, Spain and, yes, England. Again, too, an England player left a singular mark on the event. In 1982 Bryan Robson's goal in 27 seconds against France was the fastest in the history of World Cup finals. In 1986 Gary Lineker was the leading scorer with six goals – and, mightily impressed, Barcelona bought him soon afterwards for £2,750,000.

The Mexican experience convinced Bobby Robson that he had the players to make a positive bid for the 1988 European Championship. His opinion seemed confirmed by England's record over the next two years during which there were only two defeats, both in friendlies, in 17 games. Yugoslavia, Northern Ireland and Turkey were in England's qualifying group and their record was the best in the tournament: they scored 19 goals in six games and dropped only one point. Their right to be in West Germany in June 1988 was finally confirmed by a 4–1 victory over Yugoslavia in Belgrade, all four goals coming in a devastating first 25 minutes, which Bobby Robson was to describe as 'one of the best displays and results' in his whole time as England manager. Better even than England's 4–2 victory in Madrid on 18 February 1987, Spain's first home defeat in three years. Lineker of Barcelona scored all four – and that, for Madrid, was the last and most painful twist of the knife.

So England turned to the finals – a compact 15-day rodeo involving seven group-winners and the hosts – with a squad that was confident and battle-hardened. They discovered for themselves, however, that it is often better to travel hopefully than to arrive. For the first time in their history, England lost all their games in the finals of a major tournament.

On the morning of their first match, against the Republic of Ireland, several papers tipped England to win the tournament. On the morning after their third and last match against the Soviet Union, just seven days later, the papers wanted Bobby Robson's head on a platter. England lost 1–0 to a combative Republic of Ireland, managed by that most Irish of Englishmen, Jack Charlton, one of the class of '66, in Stuttgart; lost 3–1 to Holland, sunk by a hat trick by Marco Van Basten of AC Milan, in Dusseldorf; and then they keeled over against the Soviet Union, again losing 3–1, in Frankfurt.

Reasons and excuses merged . . . the missed chances against the Irish, the two shots which hit wood against the Dutch, the unforced errors against the USSR, the tiring effects of a long domestic season, the absence through injury of Terry Butcher and the lack of edge in Gary Lineker's game which was to be explained, quite legitimately, by a diagnosis that he was suffering from hepatitis. All this, moreover, in a week in which England's supporters again caused highly publicised trouble. It was no consolation that Holland and the Soviet Union, two of the sides which beat England, contested the final – with the Dutch winning their first major honour by 2–0.

Bobby Robson was left to endure what he described as 'the worst summer of his life'. He became convinced that some papers wanted England to fail, just to give credence to their campaign to have him sacked. That campaign, ironically, merely strengthened the resolve of Bert Millichip and his senior FA colleagues to stand by their manager. 'We can absorb the pressure. Can you?' said Millichip to Robson. 'Yes,' replied Robson. 'Then get on with the job, Bobby, get us to the World Cup finals again,' said the FA chairman.

Robson duly obliged; but his journey to Italy had only just begun when the Hillsborough tragedy tore at the heart of the city of Liverpool and at the conscience of the nation. The date was Saturday, 15 April 1989 – FA Cup semi-final day – and it was the worst disaster in the history of British sport. Ninety-five Liverpool supporters died and nearly 200 were injured.

Spring sunshine warmed the way of 53,000 Liverpool and Nottingham Forest fans as they eased towards Hillsborough, two-and-a-half miles to the north of Sheffield's city centre. The mood was relaxed and the route familiar: the two clubs had met at the same stage of the tournament on the same ground a year before. Sheffield Wednesday had spent £1,500,000 on improving their home in the previous four years. More than 1,100 policemen waited confidently.

By 2·30, however, half an hour before kick-off, there were signs of trouble at the Leppings Lane end of the ground. The crowd built up, impatiently pressed from the back and confined between a wall and too few turnstiles. Help was summoned, but the pressure became so severe that a police horse was lifted bodily from the ground. At 2·52, a gate into the ground was opened to relieve the crush. Two thousand fans surged down a sloping tunnel and into pens already full. Supporters at the front shouted and pleaded for help as they were squashed against the perimeter fence. The semi-final started and there was more pressure from the back; and, as the rest of Hillsborough enjoyed the game, unaware of anything wrong, the tragedy took place. Lord Justice Taylor in his report described how 'the dead, the dying and the desperate became interwoven'.

The game was abandoned after six minutes, but by then the scene was one of numbing horror. Fans watched relatives and friends die. A powerful barrier was broken and twisted, steel bent like a pipe-cleaner. Fans clambered over bodies to escape. Advertisement hoardings were torn down and used as stretchers. Ambulance men and women cried as they did their best. There were appeals for doctors. Despair turned to anger and screamed recrimination. The gymnasium became a mortuary.

And Liverpool wept, a great city united in its sorrow. 'The tragedy has brought us to our knees, not in defeat but in prayer,' said the Roman Catholic Archbishop of Liverpool, the Most Reverend Derek Worlock. Anfield itself became a place of mourning, a shrine, the pitch in front of the Kop covered in red, white and blue flowers as an endless queue of people from all over the country moved silently around its edge. The only sound was that of the wind tugging at the cellophane wrapping on the wreaths: it sounded, eerily, like distant applause. Seven days after the disaster, at six minutes past three, the city came to a halt. Traffic stopped and shoppers bowed their heads as Merseyside observed a minute's silence. Church bells tolled in Nottingham and Sheffield as well as Liverpool; and a chain of football scarves, a mile long, linked Anfield and Goodison Park.

> It's all changed now, which is why it mattered to those young men from Liverpool that they should be there to support their team. What other group is going to troop the colours for them, present them with scarves and emblems? To what other section of society should they owe allegiance? Not to country; we're going into Europe. Not to community; we're all isolated, shut in little boxes, high-rise or low, watching another box. Not to God; science has got rid of him. Not to guilt; Freud shoved that out of the window.
>
> *Beryl Bainbridge, author and journalist, after the Hillsborough disaster, 1989.*

Lord Justice Taylor was appointed to enquire into the tragedy: he spoke to 179 witnesses in 32 days. But first the Football Association pledged £250,000 to the disaster fund and faced the sensitive question of whether the FA Cup that season should be allowed to continue. It decided, according to its minutes, 'to give a clear indication of its position at the earliest opportunity'. The staff at Lancaster Gate were sounded: only one of more than 50 said the Cup should be stopped. Newspaper polls suggested the big majority of people believed the tournament should run its course. Dozens of telephone callers agreed. Graham Kelly, coping honestly and sympathetically with dozens of television, radio and newspaper interviews, said he thought it would be a fitting memorial to carry on.

Forty-eight hours after the disaster the FA decided the Cup should continue. The date for the semi-final between Liverpool and Nottingham Forest would be Sunday, 7 May 1989 and it would be played at Old Trafford. They were accused of 'inhumanity' by several papers and Peter Robinson, Liverpool's chief executive, described the decision as 'insensitive'. Kelly said he understood the criticism, but the FA felt it was imperative to make decisions so that everyone could make plans in the light of them. But there was shared condemnation of a crass comment by Jacques Georges, the president of UEFA, that the Hillsborough tragedy again showed English supporters to be 'beasts'. Glen Kirton, the FA's head of external affairs, went to see him to ensure that the rift with the European authority was not widened. Even then Georges refused to apologise.

Liverpool, understandably, wanted to get things absolutely right. They shared the pain and anger of their city and Kenny Dalglish said simply: 'Football is irrelevant.' There were suggestions that the Cup final should be played at the start of the following season and that the trophy itself should be given to Merseyside. A fortnight of anguish after the tragedy, however, Liverpool agreed to play. The shadow of Hillsborough reached all the way to Old Trafford and a subdued Nottingham Forest seemed party to a feeling that a place in the final was Liverpool's right. John Aldridge scored twice in the champions' 3–1 victory and so a final born of tragedy belonged to Merseyside. Some 37,000 tickets went to both Liverpool and Everton, who had been waiting joylessly since their victory over Norwich in the other semi-final at Villa Park.

It was referred to as the 'Requiem Cup Final' and was, perhaps, the most private of all Wembley's big occasions. The crowd sang 'You'll Never Walk Alone' as they had never sung it before, and the players produced a stylish and dramatic final which Liverpool won 3–2, with Ian Rush of Wales, who had come on as a substitute, scoring twice in extra time. But even such a day as this was flawed. The fences at Wembley, a symbol of the disaster at Hillsborough, were taken down for the game and hundreds of fans abused their freedom by persistently invading the pitch. The terraces shouted 'Off . . . off . . . off', but here was a depressing reminder of the reality of the times. The fences went up again.

Liverpool then turned their attention to the League; and a season shared by torment and triumph produced one more piece of towering drama. Liverpool faced Arsenal, champions against challengers, at Anfield in the last match of the season, needing only to avoid defeat by two goals to win the championship – and to become the first club to complete the League and Cup 'double' twice. Anfield swelled with noise and expectation, but George Graham's Arsenal took the lead seven minutes after half time, a controversial goal by Alan Smith, and then, with only seconds of the game and season left, Michael Thomas pushed forward quickly between closing defenders to score from ten yards. Arsenal were champions for the first time in 18 years after, arguably, the most exciting finish in the history of the League.

In 1989, the Government unwrapped its Football Spectators Bill, which provided the framework for a compulsory national membership scheme with a membership authority to plan and run it and a licensing authority to inspect, license and monitor grounds. It also contained measures for preventing convicted hooligans from travelling to key matches abroad – a change of direction by a Government which had always insisted this was against civil rights. The target date for introduction was spring 1990 and football, it was made clear, would be footing the bill.

Football's opposition to the bill was so implacable that the FA and the League considered stating their case in a £60,000 advertisement in a national newspaper. The Government's hand was strengthened, however, when UEFA at last made the decision to re-admit English clubs into Europe from season 1990/1. English football had waited for the call for four years and UEFA noted 'the enormous efforts made by the English football authorities'; but UEFA also insisted that re-admission was subject to Government support. Colin Moynihan, the Minister for Sport, said immediately that this support would only be given when the Football Spectators Bill became law.

Then came Hillsborough, and the Government halted the bill's progress until the publication of Lord Justice Taylor's interim conclusions. His 71-page report left few unscathed. The failure of police control, he made it clear, had been the main reason for the disaster. He also criticised Sheffield Wednesday and Sheffield City Council and added that 'a drunken minority of fans' had aggravated the problems which led to the tragedy. The FA's choice of ground was 'not causative of this disaster'. The report urged that the capacity of terraces of grounds should be cut by 15 percent.

Lord Justice Taylor's final report, the result of 'wider and deeper' investigation, pointed English football towards a new future – and his main recommendation was the beginning of the end for the culture of the terraces. He recommended that First and Second Division grounds should be 'all-seaters' by 1994 and the rest of the League by 1999. He also, after detailed analysis, rejected the Government's national membership scheme on the grounds of effectiveness and safety.

The Government bowed. David Waddington, the Home Secretary, told the House of Commons that all the recommendations of the Taylor Report would be accepted, and that it had been decided not to proceed with the national membership scheme. John Major, the Chancellor of the Exchequer and soon to be Prime Minister, announced in his Budget on 20 March 1990 that the tax on football Pools betting would be cut by 2·5 percent and that £100,000,000 would be available over five years to help clubs turn their grounds into all-seaters. The highly respected Football Trust, created in 1979 to help football at all levels and a body experienced in supporting and funding clubs, was given the responsibility of allocating the money. The clubs were surprised and grateful for the Government's munificence; but, as they turned towards what Bert Millichip called 'a new era', they estimated that the bill for providing seats for all would be more than £300,000,000. It was going to be a hard road.

①

②

③

④

① Battle order. England's dressing room in Turin before their semi-final with West Germany in the 1990 World Cup finals – one of the tournament's outstanding games.

② Chris Waddle curves the ball high and wide – and England's dream of winning the 1990 World Cup is over. Waddle's kick was England's fifth and last in the penalty shoot-out against West Germany in their semi-final in Turin; and, as Stuart Pearce's attempt had already been saved by Bodo Illgner, West Germany won by four penalties to three.

③ Paul Gascoigne after England's defeat by West Germany in the semi-finals of the 1990 World Cup finals – the game which made him a household name and arguably, for a while, the most famous man in Britain. He shed a tear after receiving his second caution of the tournament during the semi-final – a booking which meant that, if England won, he would not be able to play in the final. His tears endeared him to a million mums. 'Gazza' was born. The 23-year-old cherub from Gateshead, who moved from Newcastle United to Tottenham for £2,000,000 in 1988, was still a brilliant and audacious player; but now, too, he was a commercial goldmine, a darling of the tabloids, a lad about town, BBC TV's Sports Personality of the Year and a fitting subject for both heavy analysis and Madame Tussauds. He moved to Lazio (Rome) for £5.5 million in 1992.

④ Bobby Robson with the Fair Play trophy which was presented after the 1990 World Cup final in the Olympic Stadium in Rome – 'a magnificent achievement,' said Robson, 'when you consider the intensity of England's seven games and the fact that we played three periods of extra time and still finished with fewer cautions and fouls than any other country.' Robson became PSV Eindhoven's manager a few days after the final – and guided them to the Dutch championship in his first season.

①

(1) Steve Bull of Wolverhampton Wanderers – the fifth Third Division player to win a full international cap for England since World War Two. He made his debut as a substitute against Scotland at Hampden, 27 May 1989, Scotland 0, England 2 – and marked the occasion with a goal. Bull, well named, a striker of intimidating strength and courage, scored 37 League goals and led Wolves to the Third Division championship that same season.

(2) Jack Charlton, one of England's heroes in 1966 and the man who led the Republic of Ireland to their first World Cup finals in 1990. The Republic drew 1–1 with England in their first match in Cagliari – and went on to reach the quarter-finals. Charlton is pictured at the moment of defeat by Italy in Rome.

(3) Marked man. Gary Lineker of Tottenham Hotspur is accorded due respect by Hungary at Wembley, 12 September 1990. Lineker, captaining England for the first time, scored the only goal of the game.

(2)

(3)

England had to skirt a rock or two on the way to Italy, although they were undefeated and did not concede a goal (a record equalled only by South Korea among all the nations with their sights on the finals) in their qualifying matches against Sweden, Poland and Albania. England and Sweden locked themselves up in two goalless draws and both beat Albania – the 50th country England had met at full international level. Both, too, beat an unimpressive Poland at home; but, while Sweden won in industrial Chorzow, the best England could manage there was yet another scoreless draw, with Shilton again in undeniable form. Sweden and England qualified.

Bobby Robson, keen to test the fibre and sinew of his players, asked the FA to provide 'the best opposition available' for England's warm-up matches. They came up with Italy, Yugoslavia, Brazil, Czechoslovakia, Denmark and Uruguay – a list which included five other 1990 finalists, with Italy, Brazil and Uruguay having won, between them, eight of the previous 13 World Cups. All were at Wembley, which meant there was no risk of crowd trouble abroad; but there was a risk, of course, of some embarrassing results. England's manager believed, however, that his players should be able to cope with the best in the world at Wembley if they were going to make any headway in Italy. He was prepared for a defeat or two in the interests of further education.

Four of the games were won, one drawn and one lost. The first against Italy was goalless and the last against Uruguay was lost 2–1 which was England's first defeat in 18 games since the 1988 European finals. But Yugoslavia (2–1), Brazil (1–0), Czechoslovakia (4–2) and Denmark (1–0) were all beaten. David Platt of Aston Villa won his first cap against Italy. A goal by Bryan Robson after 38 seconds against Yugoslavia was the fastest England had ever scored at Wembley and paved the way for their 100th win in the stadium. A capacity crowd of 80,000, all seated for the first time, saw a goal by Gary Lineker defeat the Brazilians. Steve Bull of Wolves scored two of the four goals against Czechoslovakia; but the talk was of 22-year-old Paul Gascoigne of Tottenham, who had a decisive foot in the first three goals and then scored in the last minute. Lineker, always Lineker, scored another of his winners against Denmark. And then Uruguay spoiled things, England's first defeat at Wembley for six years, but it was a game full of bright and well interpreted ideas and, in Bobby Robson's opinion, 'great education and no disgrace'.

Bobby Robson had by then named his squad. Shilton, permanent as a church column, Bryan Robson and Terry Butcher were there from the 1982 World Cup; so were Gary Lineker, who was now with Tottenham, Peter Beardsley, John Barnes, Chris Waddle, Trevor Steven, Steve Hodge, Gary Stevens and Chris Woods from the 1986 World Cup; and so were Mark Wright, Stuart Pearce, Steve McMahon and Neil Webb from the 1988 European finals. And, facing their first major tournament, were Des Walker of Nottingham Forest, Paul Parker of Queen's Park Rangers and Tony Dorigo of Chelsea, injecting new pace into the defence, Paul Gascoigne and David Platt, bridging the divide between midfield and attack, and the predatory Steve Bull.

It was a familiar and seasoned band with only two gambles, Bull and Wright. Bull was a Second Division player but, uniquely, he had scored 50 goals in two successive seasons for the rising Wolves and he had all the mandatory qualities of 'a typical English centre forward'; and Bobby Robson decided a battering ram might be handy. Wright was a fitness risk. The Derby centre half, long in leg and ability, had a thigh injury and, later, a ricked neck which required a soft collar; but England's manager believed Wright's control and distribution could be key factors.

Sardinia, a long fist of an island which even friendly guide books find it difficult to gush about, was England's first base; and their month's confinement in this western outpost of Italia '90 was partly the work of Sophia Loren, film star, international ornament and official 'godmother' of the World Cup, who had taken a starring role in the Roman draw six months before. The draw, part circus, part chaos, was choreographed for television and – by way of glass bowls, plastic balls and little slips of paper – it despatched England, the Republic of Ireland, Holland and Egypt to the 'Island' group of Sicily and Sardinia. The media estimated that 50,000 English, Irish and Dutch fans would be heading that way, and classified the islands as potential war zones.

Then, sensationally, just 24 hours before England's departure, the *Today* newspaper declared that Bobby Robson had resigned because an old chapter in his private life was to be dressed up in another tabloid paper. Robson, claimed *Today*, had given hand-written letters of resignation to every member of the International Committee at the annual meeting of the FA the day before. The FA hastily summoned a news conference at Lancaster Gate which began – and nearly ended – with a thunderous volley of snapping cameras. Speech was almost impossible and Robson and Kelly threatened to walk out unless the photographers left.

'The story,' fumed Robson, 'is garbage. Appalling. If anyone can show me one of those letters I'm supposed to have written I'll hand over a million pounds. I have not resigned, everyone's morale is high and I am going to attempt to win the World Cup with a decent bunch of players. Do you honestly think I'd throw away all we've been working for because of a situation 13 years ago?' But Robson did confirm that he would be leaving the FA after the World Cup. 'I'm going because I didn't think there was a job here,' he said. Robson explained that Bert Millichip had not been able to give him any guarantees about his position, and this had coincided with an offer from PSV Eindhoven of Holland, one of the most ambitious clubs in Europe, which offered security and a new challenge. He had two more cordial meetings with Millichip, but nothing changed. The International Committee had decided it must keep its options open. Robson decided to take the PSV job and to tell England's players three days after their arrival in Sardinia; but there are few secrets in football.

Robson was not the first international manager, and would not be the last, to change direction after a World Cup. He was sure the news would not undermine the players' determination in Italy, and his instinct was right. Players are used to change, to new managers, new clubs and new team-mates, and, in any case, this was one of the biggest shows on earth. Twenty-four nations would be involved in 52 games with a television and radio audience so vast that its size could only be guessed at, and with enough newspaper hype to girdle the globe.

Wives and girlfriends joined the England squad for a week at the Is Morus Hotel, about 30 miles from the capital and port of Cagliari, a small, cosy place with white walls and white furniture which only just belonged to the 20th century. There was no traffic, no television or radio in the rooms, no shops and – without official say-so – no visitors. There was a grand piano in the lounge bar, cricket on the beach and a 23rd birthday cake for Paul Gascoigne; and he finished his speech by saying 'and here I am . . . a legend'. Then the girls went home and the real business began.

England crossed the Mediterranean for a first international with Tunisia in blinding light and on a bumpy pitch, and were a goal down with only 90 seconds left when Bull, a late substitute, a one-man cavalry charge, headed an equaliser. There was suddenly an inner lining of doubt, and Terry Butcher did not temper the criticism by throwing down his shirt after being booked and substituted. England returned to new headquarters in Sardinia – the Is Molus – a mile or two inland from the Is Morus, a golf hotel with a championship course and a view over lawns, flower beds and a pool to a distant Phoenician fishing village.

It was a delightful hermitage which seemed to divorce them from the rest of the World Cup on the mainland – but it was also the first base of a climb which was to take them all the way to the semi-finals. In six matches they lifted the spirit of English football in a way that had not been matched since the triumph of Alf Ramsey's team in 1966. 'Bring Them Home!' demanded the *Sun* newspaper after England's first game against the Republic of Ireland proved to be a dreadful dogfight. When they did return home, four weeks later, it was to an ecstatic reception by more than 100,000 people who found their way to Luton from all over the country.

It was, on nearly all counts, a remarkable achievement. No other England squad, for example, had been so slated or lampooned by its popular press. There were even attempts to introduce scandal into the scenario. One story claimed that a liaison girl at England's hotel had been 'liaising' too closely with several of the players. 'Sheer rubbish, utter fabrication, I'm mad, furious,' declared Bobby Robson. 'Seething . . . what are they trying to do . . . that's it,' said the players. There was talk of lawyers and the Press Council. Heavy frost developed into a big freeze: communication between the players and the press broke down. The rift itself became a story. David Bloomfield, the FA's press officer, found himself with a job that was on the sunless side of impossible. But Bobby Robson kept on talking and the thaw began when success became the best story of all.

England's first step, however, was painful. Bobby Robson sent out his most ambitious team for the opening game against the Republic of Ireland in the Sant' Elia stadium on the waterfront of Cagliari. Lineker and Beardsley had Waddle and Barnes outside them and Bryan Robson and Gascoigne behind them, with Stevens, Walker, Butcher and Pearce protecting Shilton. But the Republic's side, too, was 'Made in Britain', and, on a night of lightning, thunder, wind, rain, clacking helicopters and suffocating security, the game presented British football at its lumpish worst, a game of sweat, hassle, clout and counter-clout. Lineker scored after eight minutes and Kevin Sheedy of Everton equalised for the Republic a quarter of an hour from the end.

Next day, well aware that he and his players were being described in the morning prints as bunglers and simpletons, and most things in between, Bobby Robson was cordially invited to discuss the health and future of English football. Was he worried? How was he going to change it? Could he change it? 'I've answered 2,000 questions in the past two weeks, but I didn't come here for this,' said England's manager. 'Watch us play Holland and then ask me.'

What Robson did was play a sweeper, a third central defender, with a brief to provide not only extra depth and cover but also a first point of attack. It was a standard position in mainland Europe, but Peter Shilton, who would be making international history in the game by winning his 120th cap, confirmed it would be the first time in 20 years he had played behind 'a proper sweeper' for England. It was a brave move by Robson. He was trying something new against a Dutch side which had beaten England 3–1 on the way to winning the European Championship two years before; a side with two of the game's grandees, the dreadlocked Ruud Gullit and the lethal Marco Van Basten; and a side with several players from the PSV club he was soon to manage. And, with Holland having drawn 1–1 with Egypt in their first game, the World Cup future of both countries was on the line. It worked beautifully. The result was a goalless draw, but England's new base gave them a shape and confidence which showed in their use of the ball on the ground and the design of their movements. Wright slotted comfortably into his new international role and

England had the better chances in a game of wit and quality. There was, though, one sad and familiar sight. Bryan Robson limped out of the game midway through the second half with Achilles' tendon trouble, and David Platt entered the finals for the first time.

Next day the Republic of Ireland and Egypt also failed to score in Palermo which meant the first four games in the 'Island' group had been drawn and all four sides had an identical record. Qualification by drawing lots was a possibility. England, in short, needed to win their last game against Egypt, and Bobby Robson decided not to play a sweeper because their opponents were unlikely to use more than one forward player. He dropped Butcher for the first time in their long partnership together, brought in the tenacious McMahon for Bryan Robson and decided that Bull would lead from the start – which again meant no place for Beardsley. In the event, Bull was ineffectual, the game was graceless and England won with Mark Wright's first international goal, scored with a marvellously athletic header 13 minutes into the second half from a measured free kick by Gascoigne. The Republic of Ireland and Holland drew 1–1 in Palermo and, in the draw to decide second place, the combined luck of the Irish and Jack Charlton did not let them down.

England, however, were top of the group after a month in a Lotus land of solitude, high security, growing, if unadmitted, boredom and a sullen, sometimes even venomous, relationship with the press. Ahead of them was the real World Cup, sudden death, the agony of penalty shoot-outs and the survival of the fittest – or the toughest or the meanest or the luckiest.

Bryan Robson would not be part of it. For the second World Cup running, injury prevented England's captain from making the impact his quality and character deserved. But, before he accepted the inevitable, he made one last and unorthodox effort to get himself fit. He enlisted the services of Olga Stringfellow, a faith healer from Hartley Wintney in Hampshire, a small, slight lady in black, who had helped him before. The FA medical team was uncomfortable about it – and the foreign press was amazed – but Bobby Robson argued that it was probably his captain's last hope of playing in his last World Cup and 'if it doesn't work, well, we can't be accused of not trying'. Olga did her best, but Bryan Robson's Achilles' tendon did not improve – and early on the day that England moved to the mainland, the player Bobby Robson called his 'Captain Marvel' returned home for specialist treatment. As he left the Is Molus Hotel, Bobby Robson took a kick at an autographed ball he was carrying in a string bag. 'That's how mad I feel,' he said.

England's opponents in the second round, the knockout stage, were Belgium in the old Renato Dall'Ara Stadium in Bologna. Belgium had finished second in their group behind Spain, but it was an interesting piece of match-making. If the old pile of dust known as history was worth anything, England were already through to the quarter-finals: they had played Belgium 17 times in the past and lost only once. Belgium, though, had developed into formidable competitors during the previous decade (European finalists in 1980, World Cup semi-finalists in 1986), and they were a side whose method was based on defence and patience and an ability to punish opponents' mistakes. Robson was in two minds about playing a sweeper, but the players, in their bright, modern hotel 20 minutes from the city centre, made it clear that they were more comfortable with three central defenders – and Robson decided their opinion was important. Back came Butcher as captain, McMahon's stern qualities were again employed in midfield in place of Bryan Robson, and Waddle and Barnes were invoked to do justice to their talent in forward areas.

It proved to be a superb game. Belgium started brightly, with the stylish and inventive Scifo prominent, and the evergreen Ceulemans hitting a post; but Shilton made two critical saves and, after half an hour, it was England, their shape strong, their confidence growing, who had the edge. Barnes, emphatically, and Lineker, in the blink of an eye, both found the net, but both were ruled offside. Waddle, with his sways and shuffles, promised to be a match-winner. Gascoigne's ability influenced and adorned the game. Parker's purpose emphasised why he had been Robson's choice at right back from the Holland game onwards. Robson sent on Platt for McMahon, a positive move, but then had to replace Barnes with Bull. Barnes had groin trouble, and, with Walker carrying a leg injury and Lineker feeling an injured toe which had needed a painkilling injection, England were on dangerous ground as the resilient Belgians carried the game into extra time. A penalty shoot-out looked inevitable but, with less than a minute left, Gascoigne found the will to make one more challenging run. He was fouled, a free kick was given and Gascoigne himself, after a moment's hesitation, looped it towards the right post. Platt was there: his angle was awkward and the height of the ball difficult, but his timing was sweet, his contact precise and his volley on the turn swept the ball into the net and England into the quarter-finals.

It was the last game of the second round and now, at last, the World Cup had taken shape. Brazil were out, as were Holland, but West Germany, Argentina and Italy themselves were all through; and so, doughtily, were the Republic of Ireland who overcame Rumania by way of the tournament's first penalty shoot-out. Cameroon were also there, the new standard-bearers for Africa. They were the 'characters' of the finals, vibrant and skilful, but also hard and not overburdened by conscience. Their star was in keeping with their image, Albert Roger Milla, aged 38, who had been summoned from the Indian Ocean island of Reunion, where he was playing amateur football. Cameroon did not ask him to play full games. They just sent him on as a substitute to score crucial goals – which he did and then celebrated by wiggling his hips in front of a corner flag as if inviting it to dance. And Cameroon were England's opponents in Naples in the quarter-finals.

England moved to a hotel in Amalfi, a favoured place for wedding receptions which looked like a wedding cake itself – white, tiered and perched on a cliffside. The bay below was so blue that sea and sky seemed part of each other. England were now third favourites, behind Italy and West Germany, but it was not until Robson telephoned Robson that England's manager had a first real inkling of the World Cup fervour at home. Bryan Robson, whose tendon had already been operated on, said 'the whole country was singing'.

The Republic of Ireland ran out of road at last, beaten in Rome by the host country and a goal from 'Toto' Schillaci of Juventus, a little Sicilian with wild eyes and an india-rubber face, who was as central to Italy's hopes as Paolo Rossi was in 1982. Jack Charlton had taken his players to the last eight of their first World Cup finals by way of three draws and a penalty shoot-out; but it was honest reward for the best and happiest army of supporters in Italy. Argentina overcame Yugoslavia in another penalty shoot-out, and England discovered who their semi-final opponents would be if they got past Cameroon, when West Germany beat Czechoslovakia with an orthodox penalty. The World Cup was being won from the penalty spot; and there were more to come.

Bobby Robson made only one change from the side which beat Belgium. Platt, the hero, took the place of McMahon, and the Aston Villa player found himself at the heart of a game which filled the San Paolo Stadium with raw drama and nail-ruining excitement. Naples, with all its beauty and ugliness, was a perfect setting. Platt put England ahead in the 25th minute, a lovely header from a centre by Pearce, but Cameroon, skilfully, brawnily and with the crowd thunderously behind them, began to look the better side. England were prone to error, they lacked harmony, and Robson told them at half time: 'Carry on like this and we're out.' He sent on Beardsley for a struggling Barnes; and Cameroon introduced Milla the sorcerer. In the space of four minutes midway through the second half, Milla and Cameroon pointed England firmly in the direction of home. Milla was tumbled by Gascoigne and Kunde scored from the penalty spot. Then Milla again: he conjured a pass which sent in Ekeke, a new substitute, for a second Cameroon goal. Cameroon 2, England 1 and, although Bobby Robson sent on Trevor Steven for Butcher, a last gamble, he was to admit later he thought it was all over.

England needed a break and, with eight minutes left, they got one – their first penalty for four years. Lineker was fouled by Kunde and it was Lineker who scored

HEYSEL AND AFTER 1985–

from the spot. What was he thinking about as he prepared to take the kick? 'Actually, my brother in Tenerife,' he revealed, 'and what he would say if I missed.' Extra time was almost there, but not quite. Mark Wright sustained an ugly three-inch wound over an eye, went off and – part folly, part heroism – returned to do what he could.

Now it was extra time. 'Do you want to win?' demanded Robson before the restart. 'Do you want a place in the semi-final?' They did. Cameroon still used their clever angles and still pushed forward, but there was more to the game now than art and science. It was a battle in which heart and muscle also mattered – and in the 105th minute it was English heart and Cameroon muscle which decided everything. Gascoigne, tiring but stubbornly competitive, found Lineker who was quickly and mercilessly floored. It was a penalty, undoubtedly, and Lineker again prepared to take it; and this one, even more than the first, showed the mettle of the man. He had taken a painful tumble and now, seconds later, England were depending on his nerve and his eye. Thomas Nkono, Cameroon's goalkeeper, dived for the corner Lineker had chosen for his first penalty. This time, though, Lineker hit it hard and straight. It was enough. Cameroon 2, England 3. Cameroon did a lap of honour, and no-one begrudged them that. On the night, perhaps, they had been the better team. For three weeks, certainly, they had given the tournament colour and a touch of fantasy. They were heroes of a continent as well as their country: the first African nation to reach the quarter-finals. But England, for the first time, were in the semi-finals of an overseas World Cup.

> If we had beaten England and reached the semi-finals, Africa would have exploded. There could even have been deaths. The good Lord knows what He did and I thank Him for stopping us in the quarters. That allowed some calmness.
>
> *Roger Milla of Cameroon after their 3–2 defeat by England in the quarter-finals of the 1990 World Cup in Italy.*

Now it was Turin; and a date with West Germany just three days later. England moved to the Hasta Hotel, a secluded place on a hillside at Asti about 20 miles from the city where Ron Greenwood's squad had stayed during the European finals in 1980. Robson's first press conference there was a measure in itself of England's success. It was an international occasion attended by 300 reporters, with representatives from Brazil, Israel, Australia, Ecuador, Thailand and another dozen nations. The Italian reporters could see only one final: Italy against West Germany.

'What do you think of that?' asked one. 'Not much,' said Robson. 'Do you feel like David waiting to meet Goliath?' asked another. 'I'd like to answer that,' replied Robson, 'but it would make headlines all over the world.'

England's supporters were now converging on Turin. There were beleaguered but wearily determined survivors from Sardinia, Bologna and Naples and also new arrivals from home bent on sharing a rare occasion. They numbered altogether nearly 5,000 and, after the FA had tracked down and explored every source of tickets, there were still around a thousand fans without one of those precious scraps of paper. Patricia Smith, the FA's administration manager, immediately recognised a security problem: 'These fans made no plans in advance, but they were there and they thought it was their right to see the semi-final. It was hot, they were irritable and there would have been trouble if they hadn't got in; and, here we go again, there'd have been headlines about English hooliganism.' So, to ensure that one of the biggest days in its history was not spoiled, the FA bought 1,100 £33 tickets for £69 each – a take it or leave it price – from an agency in Turin. The tickets were then sold to the fans at face value. The price of peace: nearly £40,000.

Yet it was now apparent that England's supporters had been acceptably well behaved in their journey through Italy, not perfect but never a marauding army leaving havoc in its wake. The worst of them were deported, or hugely and expensively contained, while the decent majority made the best of things; and that was not easy. The Italian policing was oppressive, provocation was endless, campsites were grubby and transport after games was poor or non-existent. Yet during Italia '90 fewer than a hundred English fans were arrested. 'Overall,' said Leslie Walker, 'the English fans have behaved far better than some prophets of doom expected. They were sullen and resentful to begin with and felt the whole world was against them. We had to prepare for the worst. But, as the tournament developed, with England doing well and the sun shining, you could see them beginning to relax. We're relieved, pleased and grateful.' Colin Moynihan, having described the worst of England's fans as 'the effluent tendency' early in the tournament, was now talking about 'a new beginning'.

Bobby Robson, meanwhile, was fretting about the make-up of his side to face West Germany in the Stadium of the Alps in the north of Turin. He made one change in the end, Beardsley for an unfit Barnes, but with Butcher as the sweeper and Wright (with seven stitches in his forehead) and Walker (still troubled by his leg injury) as markers. Even on crutches they would have demanded to play. Robson told his players 'this is the most important match any of you have ever played in' – and, with Argentina beating Italy in a penalty shoot-out in the other semi-final in Naples the day before, Robson believed England's game with West Germany would decide the winner of the World Cup. Italy's defeat, which hit the host nation like a second fall of the Roman Empire, removed the tournament's most accomplished team. Argentina had four players suspended and Maradona was a sad, posturing shadow of his old self.

England and West Germany then gave the tournament its finest match. West Germany scored in the 61st minute, a deflection by Parker sending a free kick from Andreas Brehme looping over the head of Shilton, and Lineker equalised in the 80th minute, beautifully in control, after Parker had centred from the right. But the balance of the game was so fine, its rhythm and pattern so engaging, and its passion so honest that anything might have happened. England started best, removing the last traces of criticism from their shoulders like someone brushing off a bit of dandruff, but West Germany had a strong spell either side of half time, before Gascoigne, Waddle and Lineker made dangerous strikes. Robson played an ace, Steven for Butcher, fresh legs on the right, a man less in defence. Beardsley made some incisive runs and Gascoigne spoofed audaciously. But Shilton, too, was in splendid form and he needed to be because West Germany, directed by Lothar Matthaus, their captain and inspiration and one of the stars of the tournament, forced authentic chances for Jurgen Klinsmann, Olaf Thon and then Klinsmann again.

Another 30 minutes became necessary and, as the England fans sang 'Rule Britannia', Robson reminded his players they had already won two games in extra time. Waddle hit the inside of a German post, Thomas Berthold hit the outside of an English post – and Gascoigne shed a tear. He was booked for a mistimed tackle on Berthold, his second caution of the tournament, and as it dawned on him that he would not be playing in the final, come what may, the tears rolled down his face. A few million mums reached for their hankies at home … and a star was born. But neither tears nor sweat produced another goal. A marvellous game was going to be decided from the penalty spot. Expediency ruled.

It was England's first penalty shoot-out, but confidence was high: they had practised and planned for the ordeal. Lineker, Beardsley and Platt tucked theirs away but so did Brehme, Matthaus and Riedle for West Germany. Now it was the turn of Pearce, a man to count on, a free-kick expert and the hardest shot in the team. His contact was good and his direction straight, but as Bodo Illgner, the German keeper, dived left the ball struck one of his legs and spun wide. West Germany led 4–3 and then Waddle, his task closing in on him, ballooned his kick towards heaven. There was no help from that direction. England were out.

There were consoling arms, more tears and brave words – and even a slap or two for FIFA and their shoot-outs. But that was the way it was, and Germany's aim had been surer and their nerve steadier. Elation at reaching the last four was tempered by guilt that somehow they had let everyone down by not making the final; but later that night, back at Asti, Bobby Robson touched just the right note when he told them, simply, that everyone was immensely proud of them.

England then went down to Bari, on the heel of Italy, to play the host nation for third place, 'the alternative final' as it was called, an attractive and profitable time-filler which Italy won 2–1 with the help of a late penalty – what else? It was Robson's 95th and last game as England's manager and Shilton's 125th and last game as England's goalkeeper.

Robson and Lineker still had one little duty left in Italy. They were at the final in the Olympic Stadium to receive on England's behalf the Fair Play Award for committing fewer fouls (one every 6·79 minutes) and receiving fewer cautions (six out of 174) than any other country. The price they had to pay for staying on was a VIP's view of an appalling final in which West Germany made the best of a bad job by beating Argentina, who were awful, by a penalty. Again, what else?

The irony was that a World Cup which was short of goals and grace but long on controversy and cynicism had been viewed in England as one of the very best. The whole country was gripped by the same strange fever which afflicts some cities and towns before a big FA Cup tie. Enough people to fill Wembley Stadium were at Luton to welcome England home. The English game had won back its spurs – a message not lost on the Parliamentary Under-Secretary of State with responsibility for sport at the Department of the Environment. Moynihan recommended that England's clubs be allowed back into European competition; and UEFA gave their nod on 10 July 1990.

Robson left for Holland, a pleasant and forbearing man who cared passionately about his job and his sport and who, in his eight years as England's manager, did right by them both. He survived shameful invective, dispiriting failure and the cloudiest, most fragile years in the history of English football; but he will be remembered as the man who took England to the quarter-finals of the World Cup in Mexico and the semi-finals in Italy. He departed with dignity . . . and grey hair.

Interestingly, in view of Robson's suspenseful relationship with the media, he was succeeded by the son of a journalist and a man who worked for *The Times* and ITV during Italia '90. A man, too, who never played First Division or international football and who, as a manager, had never won a major trophy. But, when the FA chose Graham Taylor as England's sixth full-time manager, there was united applause from the game as a whole, its professionals, observers and followers. Taylor's route to the top of his profession was a little off the game's main arterial roads, but it was paved with achievement. Alf Ramsey somehow overlooked him as a player as he laboured with Grimsby and Lincoln during the 1960s, but as a club manager he made the best of everything. At the age of 28, as the youngest manager in the League, he led Lincoln to the Fourth Division championship; he lifted Watford from the Fourth Division to a runners-up place in Division One and an FA Cup final in six remarkable years; and then, as manager of Aston Villa, he won them promotion to the First Division, where they hounded Liverpool for the championship in the season before his country beckoned. He also served a higher apprenticeship as the manager of England's Youth, 'B', and Under-21 teams.

As a manager he pursued success singlemindedly, but he also looked beyond the price per pound of muscle and talent. Watford, in his time there, became an integral part of the community rather than just an extension of it. As a coach he was persuasive and innovative but also a pragmatist who did not set his sights above the level of his players' ability. Discipline mattered and so did character: he set standards. Taylor earned respect on all accounts.

Taylor was one of three possibles for the England job pencilled down by a special committee once Bobby Robson had decided to join PSV Eindhoven. The others were Howard Kendall of Manchester City (later to rejoin Everton) and Joe Royle of Second Division Oldham Athletic. Royle, a former England player, had just had a splendid season in the League, FA Cup and League Cup, and Kendall was a League and European winner with valuable experience in Spain. The selection committee consisted of Bert Millichip, Dick Wragg, Peter Swales of Manchester City (who succeeded Dick Wragg as chairman of the FA International Committee), Arthur McMullen, Bill Fox of Blackburn Rovers (the president of the Football League) and Graham Kelly. Millichip quickly identified Taylor as his firm choice and was away on UEFA business when McMullen, Swales, Fox and Kelly interviewed the Aston Villa manager – after which they, too, decided Taylor was their man. Kendall, in any case, had made it clear that his ambitions were at club level; and Royle was earmarked as a possible man for the future.

Taylor still had a year of his contract to run, and Douglas Ellis, the chairman of Aston Villa, made it clear that he expected compensation (more than twice what the FA had in mind) for the release of his manager. Ellis was in Italy for the World Cup, but Millichip decided not to allow the issue to overshadow or interfere with England's challenge. 'Nothing will happen,' he said, 'until after England are out.' Taylor would not be drawn on the subject. Millichip and Taylor did meet in Rome, but it was not until a few days after the final, at the Association's annual meeting at Blackpool, that the FA chairman met Ellis and settled the matter. Taylor, aged 45, was armed with a four-year contract and, instead of leading Aston Villa into the UEFA Cup, he prepared to shape England for another tilt at the European Championship.

Taylor recruited Lawrie McMenemy, the former Southampton and Sunderland manager, a big and knowing man and a good friend, as his assistant – but first Taylor faced the press who would also play a big part in his future. Taylor, neat, friendly and articulate, met them in the council chamber at Lancaster Gate, with a portrait of the Queen and the shield of the Football Association behind him. 'It's been a hard decade: the game's been hammered,' he said. 'But it's looking different now. England's success in the World Cup has been good for everyone, players, fans, you and me. It's something to build on. I would like to feel that in the next decade we might just start to love the game, take care of it and appreciate it a little bit more.'

FA Cup

Year	Date	Winners		Runners-up		Venue	Attendance	Referee	Entries
1985	18 May	Manchester United	1	Everton	0*	Wembley	100,000	P Willis	494
1986	10 May	Liverpool	3	Everton	1	Wembley	98,000	A Robinson	496
1987	16 May	Coventry	3	Tottenham Hotspur	2*	Wembley	98,000	N Midgley	504
1988	14 May	Wimbledon	1	Liverpool	0	Wembley	98,203	B Hill	516
1989	20 May	Liverpool	3	Everton	2*	Wembley	82,500	J Worrall	525
1990	12 May	Manchester United	3	Crystal Palace	3*	Wembley	80,000	A Gunn	541
Replay	17 May	Manchester United	1	Crystal Palace	0	Wembley	80,000	A Gunn	
1991	18 May	Tottenham Hotspur	2	Nottingham Forest	1	Wembley	80,000	R Milford	563
1992	9 May	Liverpool	2	Sunderland	0	Wembley	77,251	P Don	558
1992	15 May	Arsenal	1	Sheffield Wednesday	1*	Wembley	79,347	K Barratt	561
Replay	20 May	Arsenal	2	Sheffield Wednesday	1*	Wembley	62,267	K Barratt	

England's managers
(Complete records)

		P	W	D	L	% wins
Walter Winterbottom	1946–62	137	78	32	27	0·56
Alf Ramsey	1962–74	113	68	28	17	0·60
Joe Mercer	1974	7	3	3	1	0·42
Don Revie	1974–77	29	14	8	7	0·48
Ron Greenwood	1977–82	55	33	12	10	0·60
Bobby Robson	1982–90	95	47	29	19	0·49

①

②

① Graham Taylor (left), England's sixth full-time manager, with Lawrie McMenemy, his right-hand man, outside Lancaster Gate, July 1990. The Football Association paid Aston Villa £225,000 compensation for Taylor, who still had a year of his Villa Park contract to run when he succeeded Bobby Robson. It was the first time the FA had been called upon to pay a 'transfer fee' of this kind.

② The *Daily Express* on the challenge facing Graham Taylor as manager of England, 17 October 1990. The blithe spirits are (left to right): Ron Greenwood, Don Revie, Sir Alf Ramsey and Bobby Robson.

①

②

③

WOKING EVERTON

④

③ Kenny Dalglish watching Liverpool being beaten 3–0 by Arsenal at Highbury, 2 December 1990 – 11 weeks before he suddenly resigned. Liverpool were League champions for the 18th time and Dalglish was Manager of the Year for the third time in five seasons but, as season 1990/1 moved towards its climax, he surprised English football by announcing: 'I have been putting myself under too much pressure in the desire to be successful. Dalglish, an intensely private person and a family man with four children, was ten days short of his 40th birthday when he resigned. Ronnie Moran, Liverpool's senior coach (sitting on the right of the Highbury dugout, shouting), took over as caretaker manager until 16 April when there was another major surprise. Graeme Souness, the highly successful manager-director of Glasgow Rangers and a distinguished Liverpool old boy, returned to Anfield. Souness, a wing half of subtlety and resolution and a popular captain, played for Liverpool for nearly seven seasons (1978–84) and then had a spell with Sampdoria in Italy before joining Rangers. Three days after Souness's return to Anfield, UEFA welcomed Liverpool back into European competition – six years after the Heysel disaster. Dalglish returned to management with Blackburn in October 1991 and led them to fourth position in the new FA Premier League in 1992–93.

④ Only the FA Cup makes matches like this: Woking of the Vauxhall League Premier Division against Everton, four times winners of the trophy, 11 times finalists and League champions on nine occasions, 27 January 1991. The Surrey club beat West Bromwich Albion by 4–2 at the Hawthorns in the third round and, after conceding home advantage to Everton for practical reasons, lost 1–0 at Goodison Park. A crowd of nearly 35,000 gave Woking a standing ovation and Adie Cowler, their captain, said afterwards: 'We had 10,000 fans here, young lads were asking me for an autograph and old men wanted to shake my hand – who the hell am I?'

① Flight back into Europe. Ten thousand soaring balloons at Old Trafford help Manchester United celebrate the return of English clubs to European competition, 19 September 1990.

② United's return is crowned with success. Bryan Robson lifts the European Cup Winners Cup after their 2-1 victory over Barcelona in the final in Rotterdam, 15 May 1991. It was Manchester United's first European trophy for 23 years and the 23rd time an English club had won a European tournament.

① Holding hands. Brian Clough of Nottingham Forest, centre stage in his first FA Cup final, links up with Terry Venables of Tottenham Hotspur as they lead out their sides, 18 May 1991.

② Gary Mabbutt holds up the Cup to Royal applause after Spurs' 2–1 victory.

The Football Association Principals

Presidents

1863–67	A Pember
1867–74	E C Morley
1874–90	Major Sir Francis Marindin
1890–1923	Lord Kinnaird
1923–37	Sir Charles Clegg
1937–39	W Pickford
1939–55	The Earl of Athlone
1955–57	The Duke of Edinburgh
1957–63	The Duke of Gloucester
1963–71	The Earl of Harewood
1971–	The Duke of Kent

Chairmen

1938	A G Hines
1939–41	M Frowde
1941–55	Sir Amos Brook Hirst
1955–61	A Drewry
1961–63	A G Doggart
1963–66	J H W Mears
1967–76	Dr Sir Andrew Stephen
1976–81	Professor Sir Harold Thompson
1981–	Sir F A Millichip

Secretaries

1863–66	E C Morley
1866–68	R W Willis
1868–70	R G Graham
1870–95	C W Alcock (paid from 1887)
1895–1934	Sir Frederick Wall
1934–62	Sir Stanley Rous
1962–73	D Follows
1973–89	E A Croker
1989–	R H G Kelly (Chief Executive)

Homes of the FA

1863	Freemason's Tavern, Great Queen Street, London. Kennington Oval. Sportsman newspaper, Boy Court, Ludgate Hill, London EC. Cricket Press, 6 Pilgrim Street, Ludgate Hill, London EC.
1881	28 Paternoster Row, London EC. First regular headquarters. One paid clerk and one room reached by back staircase. Fifty yards from St Paul's Cathedral. A concrete office block now stands on the site.
1885	51 Holborn Viaduct, overlooking Farringdon Street, London EC. Two rooms, second floor. Rent £80 pa.
1892	61 Chancery Lane, London WC. Still one clerk. Rent £110 pa.
1902	104 High Holborn, London WC. FA secretary's staff doubled: two clerks.
1910	42 Russell Square, London WC1. Leased from British Museum. Said to be haunted.
1929	22 Lancaster Gate W2. Previously Eden Court Hotel.
1972	16 Lancaster Gate W2. Buildings exchanged with Association of British Launderers and Cleaners. '22' too small for FA (with staff of 50), '16' too big for ABLC.

England in World Cup finals

1950 (Brazil). Eliminated in first stage.

Opposition	Round	Result	Scorers	Venue
Chile	1st	Won 2–0	Mortensen, Mannion	Rio de Janeiro
United States	1st	Lost 0–1		Belo Horizonte
Spain	1st	Lost 0–1		Rio de Janeiro

1954 (Switzerland). Quarter-finals.

Opposition	Round	Result	Scorers	Venue
Belgium	1st	Drew 4–4	Broadis 2, Lofthouse 2	Basle
Switzerland	1st	Won 2–0	Wilshaw, Mullen	Berne
Uruguay	Quarter-final	Lost 2–4	Lofthouse, Finney	Basle

1958 (Sweden). Eliminated in first stage after play-off.

Opposition	Round	Result	Scorers	Venue
Soviet Union	1st	Drew 2–2	Kevan, Finney (pen)	Gothenburg
Brazil	1st	Drew 0–0		Gothenburg
Austria	1st	Drew 2–2	Haynes, Kevan	Boras
Soviet Union	Play-off	Lost 0–1		Gothenburg

1962 (Chile). Quarter-finals.

Opposition	Round	Result	Scorers	Venue
Hungary	1st	Lost 1–2	Flowers (pen)	Rancagua
Argentina	1st	Won 3–1	Flowers (pen), R Charlton, Greaves	Rancagua
Bulgaria	1st	Drew 0–0		Rancagua
Brazil	Quarter-final	Lost 1–3	Hitchens	Vina del Mar

1966 (England). Champions.

Opposition	Round	Result	Scorers	Venue
Uruguay	1st	Drew 0–0		Wembley
Mexico	1st	Won 2–0	R Charlton, Hunt	Wembley
France	1st	Won 2–0	Hunt 2	Wembley
Argentina	Quarter-final	Won 1–0	Hurst	Wembley
Portugal	Semi-final	Won 2–1	R Charlton 2	Wembley
West Germany	Final	Won 4–2	Hurst 3, Peters	Wembley

1970 (Mexico). Quarter-finals.

Opposition	Round	Result	Scorers	Venue
Rumania	1st	Won 1–0	Hurst	Guadalajara
Brazil	1st	Lost 0–1		Guadalajara
Czechoslovakia	1st	Won 1–0	Clarke (pen)	Guadalajara
West Germany	Quarter-final	Lost 2–3	Mullery, Peters	Leon

1982 (Spain). Eliminated in second stage.

Opposition	Round	Result	Scorers	Venue
France	1st	Won 3–1	Robson 2, Mariner	Bilbao
Czechoslovakia	1st	Won 2–0	T Francis, Barmos (og)	Bilbao
Kuwait	1st	Won 1–0	T Francis	Bilbao
West Germany	2nd	Drew 0–0		Madrid
Spain	2nd	Drew 0–0		Madrid

1986 (Mexico). Quarter-finals.

Opposition	Round	Result	Scorers	Venue
Portugal	1st	Lost 0–1		Monterrey
Morocco	1st	Drew 0–0		Monterrey
Poland	1st	Won 3–0	Lineker 3	Monterrey
Paraguay	2nd	Won 3–0	Lineker 2, Beardsley	Mexico City
Argentina	Quarter-final	Lost 1–2	Lineker	Mexico City

1990 (Italy). Semi-finals.

Opposition	Round	Result	Scorers	Venue
Republic of Ireland	1st	Drew 1–1	Lineker	Cagliari
Holland	1st	Drew 0–0		Cagliari
Egypt	1st	Won 1–0	Wright	Cagliari
Belgium	2nd	Won 1–0	Platt	Bologna
Cameroon	Quarter-final	Won 3–2	Lineker 2 (both pens), Platt	Naples
West Germany	Semi-final	Drew 1–1	Lineker	Turin
West Germany won penalty shoot-out by 4–3				
Italy	Third place play-off	Lost 1–2	Platt	Bari

English Club Honours

	League Championship	FA Cup	League Cup	European Cup	European Cup-Winners' Cup	Fairs Cup/ UEFA Cup
Arsenal	1931, 1933, 1934, 1935, 1938, 1948, 1953, 1971, 1989, 1991	1930, 1936, 1950, 1971, 1979, 1993	1987, 1993			1970
Aston Villa	1894, 1896, 1897, 1899, 1900, 1910, 1981	1877, 1895, 1897, 1905, 1913, 1920, 1957	1961, 1975, 1977	1982		
Barnsley		1912				
Birmingham City			1963			
Blackburn Olympic		1883				
Blackburn Rovers	1912, 1914	1884, 1885, 1886, 1890, 1891, 1928				
Blackpool		1953				
Bolton Wanderers		1923, 1926, 1929, 1958				
Bradford City		1911				
Burnley	1921, 1960	1914				
Bury		1900, 1903				
Cardiff City		1927				
Charlton Athletic		1947				
Chelsea	1955	1970	1965		1971	
Clapham Rovers		1880				
Coventry City		1987				
Derby County	1972, 1975	1946				
Everton	1891, 1915, 1928, 1932, 1939, 1963, 1970, 1985, 1987	1906, 1933, 1966, 1984			1985	
Huddersfield Town	1924, 1925, 1926	1922				
Ipswich Town	1962	1978				1981
Leeds United	1969, 1974, 1992	1972	1968			1968, 1971
Leicester City			1964			
Liverpool	1901, 1906, 1922, 1923, 1947, 1964, 1966, 1973, 1976, 1977, 1979, 1980, 1982, 1983, 1984, 1986, 1988, 1990	1965, 1974, 1986, 1989, 1992	1981, 1982, 1983, 1984	1977, 1978, 1981, 1984		1973, 1976
Luton Town			1988			
Manchester City	1937, 1968	1904, 1934, 1956, 1969	1970, 1976		1970	
Manchester United	1908, 1911, 1952, 1956, 1957, 1965, 1967, 1993	1909, 1948, 1963, 1977, 1983, 1985, 1990	1992	1968	1991	

	League Championship	FA Cup	League Cup	European Cup	European Cup-Winners' Cup	Fairs Cup/ UEFA Cup
Newcastle United	1905, 1907, 1909, 1927	1910, 1924, 1932, 1951, 1952, 1955				1969
Norwich City			1962, 1985			
Nottingham Forest	1978	1898, 1959	1978, 1979, 1989, 1990	1979, 1980		
Notts County		1894				
Old Carthusians		1881				
Old Etonians		1879, 1882				
Oxford United			1986			
Oxford University		1874				
Portsmouth	1949, 1950	1939				
Preston North End	1889, 1890	1889, 1938				
Queen's Park Rangers			1967			
Royal Engineers		1875				
Sheffield United	1898	1899, 1902, 1915, 1925				
Sheffield Wednesday	1903, 1904, 1929, 1930	1896, 1907, 1935	1991			
Southampton		1976				
Stoke City			1972			
Sunderland	1892, 1893, 1895, 1902, 1913, 1936	1937, 1973				
Swindon Town			1969			
Tottenham Hotspur	1951, 1961	1901, 1921, 1961, 1962, 1967, 1981, 1982, 1991	1971, 1973		1963	1972, 1984
Wanderers		1872, 1873, 1876, 1877, 1878				
West Bromwich Albion	1920	1888, 1892, 1931, 1954, 1968	1966			
West Ham United		1964, 1975, 1980			1965	
Wimbledon		1988				
Wolverhampton Wanderers	1954, 1958, 1959	1893, 1908, 1949, 1960	1974, 1980			

Graham Taylor, like so many of his successors, found the European Championship a maddeningly difficult obstacle. England were hounded by the Republic of Ireland along the road to the 1992 finals in Sweden; but, in a group completed by Poland and Turkey, England finished a point in front of Jack Charltons's team. England scored only seven goals in their six qualifying games, but the Irish drew four – including, all importantly, their home match with Poland.

England's record during the two years between Taylor's appointment and the start of the European finals was one of the best in the world. Only one of 21 games was lost and that was against Germany, the world champions, by 1–0 at Wembley in September 1991. There were times when England had to battle for results, even against opponents who might politely be described as modest, and there were times when Taylor's choice of player was acidly criticised. But his record spoke loudest of all.

The European Championship finals, however, proved again to be a long way beyond England's reach. Without the likes of Paul Gascoigne, John Barnes and Mark Wright, because of injury, they were locked up in goalless draws with Denmark (late replacements for war-torn Yugoslavia but carefree and deserving winners of the tournament) and France (regarded by some as favourites) before losing 2–1 to the host nation Sweden. England finished bottom of their group.

Taylor immediately discovered just how cruel one or two newspapers could be: it was a painful part of his education as England's manager. Nonetheless, in the Football Association's annual report for 1992, he assessed the tournament objectively. 'As manager, of course, I accept my share of responsibility,' he wrote. 'I selected the squad and decided on the format, balance and method of each team. I believed at the time that I made the right decisions for the right reasons.

'In the event, against three good sides, we managed two draws and were then narrowly beaten after leading at half-time. The difference between success and failure can be very small; but, in a nutshell, expectations were not matched by performances or results.

'It is the ambition of every England manager, for a tournament of this importance, to field his best players in top form and in perfect mental and physical tune. The reality is that several players are usually absent and that form and condition are undermined by the wear and tear of a long, hard season. This was certainly the case in Sweden where certain players did not do themselves justice. English football does not place the international game as high on its list of priorities as many nations do.'

This was one of the reasons which had already prompted the FA to look again at the concept of a separate league for the country's principal clubs – an idea which the 'Big Five' clubs, in pursuit of power and money, had nearly turned into a reality in the mid-'80s. The FA was better motivated. In April 1991, it produced a *Blueprint for the Future of Football* which was a clear indication of the way it felt the game at all levels should develop. And, as part of the plan, it proposed the setting up of an FA Premier League and confidently, if optimistically, predicted an annual income of more than £100 million – which appealed enormously to the clubs.

The FA's overall aims were higher playing standards, improved entertainment and a better deal (including free weekends before major internationals) for the England team. No-one was more aware of the need for progressive change, or the ramifications of the proposals, than Graham Kelly who had been Secretary of the Football League before becoming Chief Executive of the FA.

The Football League, not surprisingly, resisted with all the muscle at its disposal. It accused the FA of hijacking the cream of its clubs, of being elitist and divisive and of putting many small clubs at risk. Less than a year before, indeed, the League had proposed that English football should be governed by a Joint Board – consisting of five members from each side – which would 'provide direction and leadership for football which has undoubtedly been missing'.

Now, suddenly, the Football League was faced with losing its own head and it hastily directed the row towards the High Court. But it found no comfort there. Mr Justice Rose ruled that the FA was fully entitled to set up a Premier League 'for the good of the game' – and, he added, 'what is best for football can only be decided by those involved in it'.

The FA Council approved the most severe constitutional change in the history of English football in February 1992, and the 22 clubs of the First Division duly divorced themselves from the oldest league on earth. The Football League was left to re-organise itself into three divisions and, with Rick Parry, a chartered accountant, as its Chief Executive, the new FA Premier League soon negotiated the biggest television deal in British sport with Sky, the satellite channel, and the BBC. It was worth £304 million over five years.

The eye of television now focussed on the game harder than ever and, with a major game regularly shown 'live' on Sunday and Monday, the season lost some of its familiar shape. But, with promotion and relegation established between the Premier League and the Football League, gates continued to hold up well.

Alex Ferguson's Manchester United, with admirable style and sense of occasion, became the inaugural Premier League champions, their first title for 26 years. Arsenal, though, had an equally memorable season: they became the first club to win both the FA Cup and the League Cup in one season, beating Sheffield Wednesday in both finals, and helped to establish one or two curious milestones in the process.

The 1993 FA Cup final went to a replay and, on a wet Thursday evening, the kick-off was put back half-an-hour because an accident on the M1 motorway brought thousands of Wednesday fans to a long halt – the first time a Wembley kick-off had been delayed since the famous 'white horse' final, the first at Wembley, 70 years before. And because Wednesday did not sell all their allocation of tickets, the crowd of 62,267 was the smallest for an FA Cup final in the stadium.

It was also, very nearly, the first final to be decided by a penalty shoot-out, but a header by defender Andy Linighan in the last seconds of extra-time gave Arsenal their celebrated Cup 'double' – and made George Graham the first man to gain League Championship, FA Cup and League Cup winners' medals as both player and manager. There is no real end to any volume of history.

John Beresford of Portsmouth is wide of the mark and Liverpool win their FA Cup semi-final replay against the Second Division club in a penalty shoot-out (3–1) at Villa Park, April 1992. Liverpool's goalkeeper Bruce Grobbelaar (left) just sits and contemplates. The match had finished 0–0 after extra-time and was the first semi-final to be decided by a shoot-out – a device intro-duced reluctantly by the FA after a police decision that there should be a minimum of nine days between a Cup tie and a replay. This meant there would be major problems of organisation if a tie went to more than one replay. Scun-thorpe, Colchester, Newcastle and Manchester United all lost a penalty shoot-out during the 1991–2 season.

The unhappy last step of a long and distinguished international career. Gary Lineker, England's captain, leaves the pitch after being substituted in the 63rd minute of England's game with Sweden (1–2) in Stockholm during the European Championship finals, June, 1992. It was his 80th cap and he finished with 48 goals, one short of Bobby Charlton's record. Lineker, then 31, was never booked in his career, was awarded the OBE in 1992 and was twice voted Footballer of the Year (1986 and 1992).

FA's last obstacle is removed by clubs

Premier League gets under way from next season

By PETER BALL

THE Football Association Premier League will start next season. At yesterday's Football League extraordinary general meeting, the clubs voted to move regulation 11, the last obstacle preventing the first division clubs from breaking

"The hard work starts now," Rick Parry, the FA consultant and chairman of the first division clubs, said yesterday. "It is a momentous day for football," David Dein, the Arsenal vice-chairman

SOCCER COMMENTARY

By Colin Gibson

A brave new world or a false dawn?

ON Saturday, the 104th, and probably the final, year of the Football League begins. The contrast with last season could not be more startling. Accompanied by Luciano

FA show greater commitment to the formation of the Premier League that they have so far encouraged. Although the reality of this league may be somewhat different to Graham

① 'A whole new ball game' promised Sky Sports after agreeing, together with the BBC, to pay £304 million over five years for the right to televise the new FA Premier League. Limbs and light add a new dimension to Arsenal's Monday night game with Manchester City at Highbury, September 1992.

② David Platt scores the first of his four goals for England in their 6–0 victory over San Marino, new international opponents, in a World Cup qualifying game at Wembley, February 1993. Platt also missed a penalty – and five goals would have equalled England's individual record for an international match.

①

① Prisoners of hope. Fans at the FA Cup semi-final between Sheffield Wednesday and Sheffield United (2–1) at Wembley, April 1993. Arsenal and Tottenham, (1–0) met in the other semi-final and, for the second time in three years at this stage, were allocated the major North London stadium. The two Sheffield clubs asked for the same privilege, and the FA quickly agreed. Arsenal and Sheffield Wednesday reached the finals of both the FA Cup and League Cup; and as the FA Cup final went to a replay it meant the two clubs played at Wembley four times in six weeks.

② Ian Wright of Arsenal scored in both FA Cup final matches at Wembley, and also scored in every round except the semi-final.

②

① A city celebrates, May 1993. Steve Bruce (left) and Bryan Robson share the new FA Premier League trophy on the front page of a special edition of the *Manchester Evening News* to celebrate Manchester United's first championship for 26 years. Alex Ferguson, with Aberdeen and then United, thus became the first manager to win the League Championship, Cup, League Cup and European Cup Winners' Cup, both in Scotland and England.

② The Manchester United squad after the presentation of the FA Premier League trophy. Back row (left to right): Paul Parker, Mike Phelan, Peter Schmeichel, Lee Sharpe, Eric Cantona, Lee Martin, Les Sealey, Darren Ferguson, Dion Dublin, Clayton Blackmore, Alex Ferguson, Brian Kidd. Front row: Mark Hughes, Brian McClair, Steve Bruce, Gary Pallister, Bryan Robson, Dennis Irwin, Andrei Kanchelskis, Ryan Giggs, Paul Ince.

①

②

THE FOOTBALL ASSOCIATION

BY GRAHAM KELLY

In its simplest sense the Football Association is just a gathering of clubs and associations. More exactly, it is the governing body of England's national game and is responsible for its growth, health, image, organisation and discipline.

The Association sends international sides to all corners of the earth and it also safeguards the interests of the small, smaller and smallest. It is at one and the same time the leader and servant of English football – which is now a recreation, an entertainment and a business.

Some 42,000 clubs, with 2,250,000 players of all ages, are affiliated to the Football Association; and it sanctions, altogether, around 2,000 leagues and even more cup competitions. The Association organises, directly, six different knockout tournaments: the FA Challenge Cup (the oldest and best loved of them all), Trophy, Vase, Youth Challenge, County Youth and Sunday. Around 50 international matches are played every year at seven different levels: full, 'B', Under-21, semi-professional, Under-18, Under-17 and Under-16. The Association's comprehensive coaching system reaches into every corner of the country. Its turnover is upwards of £15 million a year.

The Association presents the interests of the game to the Government and Parliament. It represents England on the Councils of UEFA, the governing body in Europe, and FIFA, the world authority. It holds a privileged position as one of the eight members of the International Football Association Board, the law-makers of world football.

The Association is run at national and regional level by representatives from every plateau of the game, paid and unpaid, including the County Associations, schools, universities and the services. Its 'parliament' is a Council of nearly one hundred of these representatives.

Visit 16 Lancaster Gate, the West London home of the Association, on any day of the week and it is almost certain there will be a meeting in progress of one committee or another, organising tournaments or representative games, sanctioning leagues, examining rules, making arrangements for travel abroad, monitoring finances, hearing disciplinary cases, refining the coaching system, planning new publications and any number of other things.

There is a full-time staff of more than 50 at Lancaster Gate to service these committees and implement their decisions. My job, as Chief Executive of the Football Association, is to make sure all the cogs in this big wheel are running smoothly, and to generate ideas for making the game better in every respect, better played, better refereed, better supported by the fans and commerce and, of course, better in terms of crowd safety and control. The Association, as I write, has introduced a radical 'Blueprint' for the future of the game which includes the inauguration of an FA Premier League for the most successful clubs in the country. We believe it to be the way forward – but, without the gift of foresight, it is a way which must belong to a future history.

The Football Association's work is never-ending and its actions and decisions are always under close scrutiny by the media. And rightly so. The Association is charged with the care of the very best of team games.

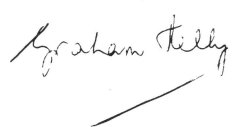

POSTSCRIPT

BY SIR BERT MILLICHIP

Nothing in football can be taken for granted. The 1980s proved this, sometimes tragically, and I am sure the years leading up to the start of the 21st century will prove it again. I am not alone, however, in believing there is a new determination within the game to learn from the past, a new spirit and a new sense of purpose.

Future historians may well see the lessons of the disasters at Heysel, Bradford and Hillsborough and our success in the 1990 World Cup finals as the start of an important and perhaps outstanding era for our national game. The Football Association has never been afraid of radical change when it is for the good of the game as a whole. The formation of the FA Premier League is evidence of this; but we must also remember that tradition is part of football's structure and appeal.

Professional football is now more intense and more demanding for all concerned and this is reflected by the increasing weight of my own duties as Chairman of the Football Association and as a member of UEFA's Executive and Organising Committees and of FIFA's Organising Committee. It is now a full-time job involving meetings almost every day of the week.

Football has always had its problems, of course, but hooliganism has undoubtedly been the biggest. My ambition when I became Chairman was to promote the game of football, but I have had to spend much of my time defending it. Not a single day has passed without some aspect of the hooligan problem crossing my mind. But the climate is changing and one of the reasons is the Government's belated acceptance that this mindless violence is a social disorder which must be tackled by the law. I wish only that the Government had listened to the Football Association 15 years earlier. I hear people say that politics should be kept out of sport, and I understand what they mean, but the job of a Government is to improve life for everyone – and sport does not and cannot stand alone.

I was delighted when England were awarded the 'Fair Play' trophy after the World Cup in Italy. The Football Association has always stressed that the behaviour of its international players must set an example to the rest of the world and the trophy was a reward for that discipline. Our playing technique can still be improved and, when it matches our discipline, our will to win and our stamina, we will be more than a match for any other nation. The Association is making technique a high priority all the way down to the grass roots.

There will always be differences of opinion within our game, some of them heated, and issues such as refereeing, discipline, finance, television and the ambitions and health of the Football League will regularly rise to the surface. But it is the duty of the Football Association to foster and enhance football at all its levels with independence, fairness, integrity and courage. It has shouldered this trust for nearly 130 years and will continue to do so during the next century.

Bert Millichip

Bert Millichip presents a photo album to Peter Shilton to mark the England goalkeeper's record 120th cap before England's game with Holland in Cagliari during the 1990 World Cup finals.

INDEX

PICTURE CREDITS

The publishers would like to thank the following for permission to reproduce copyright material:

Action Images 126, 178b, 179t, 192b, 229, 293; Allsport/Dave Cannon 242b; Associated Press 107t, 127t; Associated Sports Photography 204t, 230; Neville Chadwick 174t; Colorsport 129l, 192t, 294–5, 296, 297t & b, 298t & b, 299b; Daily Express 283b; Hulton Picture Co 26t, 57t & b, 70, 71tl & bl, 72b, 73l, 74b, 75, 76b, 86, 87t, 88t & bl, 89t & b, 105b, 128t & b, 144–5, 158br, 193b; The Independent 244b; Harry Langton 9b; Mark Leech 215b, 284b; Liverpool Sunday Echo 252; Paul Macnamara 51tl, 72t; Harry Ormesher 180; Press Association 161b, 174b, 176t, 194b, 204b, 216t, 217b, 243; Peter Robinson iii, 206b, 241l, 266t, 269t; Dave Shopland Sports Photography 268, 269b; Sport & General 179b; Sunday Times 253; Syndication International ix, 159t & c, 160t & b, 177, 181b, 267t & b, 283t, 285t; Bob Thomas Sports Photography vi, 10t & br, 12t, 24l & r, 25c, 26b, 36t, 37r, 38b, 39, 40b, 52l, 56t, 70 inset, 71tr, 73r, 85t & bl, 104b, 109b, 214–15, 216b, 217t, 228t & b, 242t, 244t, 254t & bl, 266b, 286t & b, 295; Chris Tofalos 284t; Topham Picture Source 181t; United Press International 175.

While every effort has been made to trace the owners of photographs used, this has sometimes proved impossible and copyright owners are invited to contact the publishers.